MARINER'S
WEATHER

By the same author

Mariner's Notebook
Mariner's Celestial Navigation
Sea Marine Atlas: Southern California, *Revised Edition*

MARINER'S

WEATHER

By William P. Crawford

W. W. NORTON & COMPANY, INC., NEW YORK

PHOTO CREDITS: The following U.S. government agencies provided photographs used in this book: Defense Mapping Agency Hydrographic/Topographic Center (DMAHTC), Environmental Data Service (EDS), National Aeronautics and Space Administration (NASA), National Oceanic and Atmospheric Administration (NOAA), National Weather Service (NWS), Satellite Data Service (SDC), Synchronous Meteorological Satellite (SMS), United States Coast Guard (USCG), and United States Navy (USN).

Library of Congress Cataloging in Publication Data

Crawford, William P
    Mariner's weather.

    Bibliography: p.
    Includes index.
    1. Meteorology, Maritime. I. Title.
QC994.C72 1978   551.6   78–12738
ISBN 0–393–03221–3

1 2 3 4 5 6 7 8 9 0

CONTENTS

PREFACE

We all approach weather with a spirit of resignation. It just happens and, for the present at least, there seems little we can do about it. Yet as mariners we are subject to its every caprice. Awareness of the forces at work within the atmosphere is a large part of seamanship. The aim here is to achieve a balance between the intricacies of science and the inexactness imposed by the nature of shipboard operation. No more nor less is sought than what might be of practical value.

This book reflects the influence of many years spent in class discussion with veteran mariners. So persuasive was this that when a choice was forced between scientific detail and nautical reality, the path of onboard relevance was always followed.

Each chapter pursues a topic or two and is then followed by a quiz to check comprehension. The tenor leans at times toward humor, and that is somewhat planned. No reader should be expected to attend, page after page, to weighty matters without diversity. And, anyway, prizing whimsey might well be the distinguishing trait of our kind. Discussion of an applied science has aspects which defeat any effort toward mirth. I welcomed the bits of trivia in the writing. Perhaps you will gain the same benefit as you read.

As a prelude, one facet of this study requires special mention. The metric system is upon us and must be served. In doing so here, an effort was made not to intrude on the basic purpose of understanding. Most of us still grasp images in terms of the older system. To struggle with difficult concepts in new measurements could deter comprehension. So you will find a double standard used. Side by side with one value will often be its counterpart in the other pattern. Mention of generalities might not warrant being hobbled by conversion, so it does not always appear. And as you read, you might find the two-fold presentation cumbersome. If so, just overlook the parentheses with the equivalent value inside. But should you bear with the double treatment you might receive an unexpected dividend. By subliminal perception matters metric can become more real when in company with more familiar measures.

Following progressively from beginning to end is probably the best procedure, for this text is one person's view of sequence as well as content. Since we all live in the ocean of air, we start with some degree of familiarity. Merging those impressions into a pattern of workable knowledge is part of the task. After the book was finished, I realized how vulnerable the meteorologist is. When weather fulfills prediction, his skill is slighted by the telltale pangs of "a football knee." When, though, a forecast goes astray, his flaw is all too evident.

This is a book by a mariner for mariners. It is my hope that you find its content of special value for that reason.

WILLIAM P. CRAWFORD

San Carlos, California
October 1978

MARINER'S WEATHER

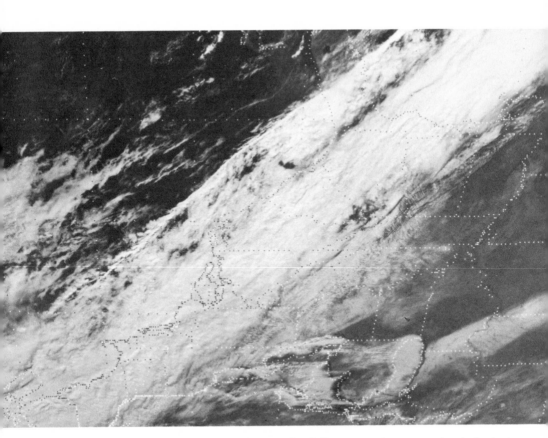

Figure 1. Satellite view of rope cloud line separating warm tropical air to southeast from cold air to the north. (*NOAA*)

Chapter 1

THE ATMOSPHERE

"Creatures of the deep" is hardly a usual description of us who dwell on the earth's surface. Yet we do live on the floor of a vast ocean, the atmosphere. Although a sea of gas it is no less fluid than any of the fabled seven. It has wave patterns, is alternately clear and murky, and is subject to the flow and counterflow of current. It even has a sort of tide. What we call weather is nothing more than movement and change in the bottom layer of that enormous ocean. And the key to understanding weather is the realization that, in fact, the atmosphere *is* a sea towering hundreds of miles above us.

Busy humans, though, often seem indifferent to that true character. Preoccupation with what happens on the surface confines awareness to a casual glance enroute to a heat register. The mariner is allowed no such nonchalance. He must sense the fluid character of the air just as surely as he senses the liquid sea heaving beneath him. For his vessel floats on top of one sea and at the bottom of another, subject to their buffets and interplay.

We seek first to recognize the atmosphere for what it is, and then to review how its movement and change are caused and can be anticipated. The skills of a professional meteorologist are beyond the reach of some of us. But that doesn't mean our forecasts need be based on the whim of a groundhog. Our aim is a rational grasp of the nature of the atmosphere in the simplest terms possible.

Before we get underway, a few cautions should be voiced. This study is like a jigsaw puzzle. Fact *A* fits with Fact *B* and both might well presume that Fact *C* is in position. We must first set out the pieces and recognize their basic natures. Then, when things are neatly labeled and identified, we can start putting them together. In the process we are bound to skirt by eddies and snags. At times the discussion might seem too complicated; at others, it might appear as not technically complete. What we seek, though, is a reasonable understanding. When the conversation has nettles of scientific principles, accept it as necessary for the aim. When it darts past a point or two, conclude that the point or two are not really necessary to our job. The science of meteorology is an emerging field. The subject is so far-flung that by no means is all of it yet understood. An international pool of knowledge and research is part of a current effort to find what weather really is all about. Yet key answers are still elusive. For us to poke heedlessly into uncharted waters would invite chucking the whole study for a TV forecast. We'll leave neat distinctions to be worked out by computer and satellite. Instead, our focus will be on accepted principles applied to a depth adequate to our task.

First off, let's investigate what it means to say that the atmosphere is a gas. As such, it is a vapor mixture of several elements in varying proportions. It is not important that in some layers it is more than three-fourths nitrogen and slightly more than one-fifth oxygen. Of even less value is the fact that it is laced with smidgens of argon, neon, and krypton, plus a dash of xenon for flavor. We have no interest here in the chemical formula for air.

Added to the compound, whatever its makeup, are dust particles, salt particles, and water vapor. So the atmosphere consists of a group of elements mixed to form a gas, with an independent gas—water vapor—added in varying strength. Suspended in the result are microscopic solid particles of dust and salt. And it all sheaths the earth's surface like a pod a thousand miles thick. This halo of air has a weight; in fact, it has an enormous weight —nearly six quadrillion tons. And the pull of the earth's gravity holds it snugly to the surface.

Layers of the atmosphere have been labeled according to height and characteristics. From the surface up, the arrangement is in this order:

Troposphere, from the surface to an average of roughly 7 miles (13 kilometers) high. It varies from about 10 miles (18.5 km) high over the Equator to a shallower 5 miles (9.3 km) over the poles. The *tropo-* part of its name comes from a Greek word describing turning or change. Either meaning is apt for us. The air in this belt is close enough to the earth to be influenced by its turning; and that region sees most of the atmospheric changes we call weather.

Tropopause, a thin transitional layer separating the troposphere from the next layer outward, the

Stratosphere, ending about 20 miles (37 km) above the earth. Its *strato-* has roots in words suggesting "uniformity" and "spread out." Within the region, sometimes called *isothermal*, atmospheric temperature remains quite constant. It is topped by the

Stratopause, another transitional layer leading to the

Chemosphere. This 26-mile (48-km) belt is a region of pronounced photochemical activity and ends in the

Chemopause, a thin separation between it and the

Ionosphere, over 200 miles (370 km) thick. Here, atomic particles can get electrically charged up and play all sorts of games with radio transmission. It blends at its top into the

Ionopause. Above this thin slice is the

Mesosphere, more than 370 miles (685 km) thick and reaching to an altitude exceeding 600 miles (1111 km) above the earth. Next comes the

Mesopause, still another transitional layer, leading to the

Exosphere, the outermost layer of our atmospheric skin. Beyond it is space.

So our atmospheric gas is stacked in a towering pile and arranged in six layers with five pauses between. Sometimes meterology disregards the divisions referring to chemistry and ions to simplify the pattern as *troposphere, stratosphere, mesosphere,* and *thermosphere.* By that definition, the lowest region, troposphere, is one of decreasing temperature with altitude, the stratosphere has uniform temperatures, the mesosphere is a region where temperature drops again, and the thermosphere, beginning at some 50 miles (92.5 km) out, describes a region where temperature increases dramatically from about —28°F (—33°C) to beyond +4000°F (+2204°C). Fortunately for us, sphere-tagging is not important. When, though, it does come up in conversation there can be some confusion. It is obvious that different labels are used at different times for different purposes. Figures 2 and 3 compare the two systems.

Imagine an airshaft which is one inch square and a thousand miles or so high. In it is a vertical slice of the entire atmosphere, no matter how labeled. The air in that shaft has a weight. It isn't six quadrillion tons, but it is measurable. And it has been found to be 14.7 pounds. Put another way, the weight bearing down on the sea level surface of the earth is 14.7 pounds for each square inch of area. This is called pressure in pounds per square inch or *psi*. So the atmospheric pressure at sea level is 14.7 psi. Metricwise, we would speak of it in grams per square centimeter and equal to

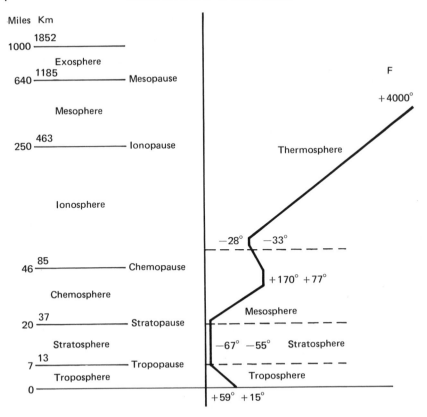

Figure 2.   Profile of the entire atmosphere.

Figure 3.   Weatherman's view of
the lower third of the atmosphere.
(Adapted from a diagram by U.S.
Navy Weather Research Facility)

1033.2 g/cm². But however described, what about pressure higher up in
the shaft? It must be less, for there is then less air piled on top. This brings
us to a basic principle:

> **1. Atmospheric pressure decreases with increase in altitude.**

And from it we learn a trait to distinguish air at altitude from that at the
surface. Although it might have the same chemical proportions, it doesn't
weigh as much. Air pressure at 18,000 feet (5486 meters), for example, is
only half as much as at the earth's surface. And on the outskirts of the
troposphere, at 36,000 feet (10,973 meters), it is down to less than 3.7
psi (that is the same as 260 g/cm²).

Another fact now becomes apparent. Air is not uniformly packed into that shaft, for over the first 3 miles (5.6 km) of altitude its weight is cut in half. The mixture becomes rarer as altitude increases, with the result that three-fourths of the atmospheric gas is compressed into the first 7 miles or 13 kilometers of height. This means that three-fourths of the air is in the troposphere. Since weather is movement and change of the atmosphere, it follows that most weather must occur within its lowest layer. In turn, it means that high-flying aircraft operating in the stratosphere fly above most of the atmosphere and its disturbing influences. Since, though, surface vessels, even on Lake Titicaca high in the Andes, are all well within the troposphere, it is to that layer that we will direct our attention.

We will focus on the bottom 7 miles of the sea of atmospheric gas, with an occasional reference to influences developing at somewhat higher altitudes. Our targets are the causes of movement and change within that block of air. We can safely leave the analyses of all the other spheres and pauses to students of chemos, ionos, or mesos, with the top of the pile reserved to the exo-buff. The first aim of our search is movement of air, or what we usually call *wind*. Then we will sally forth in pursuit of atmospheric changes, which primarily involve what we call *precipitation*. So, tally ho! we're off for some baying at winds and air currents.

Water seeps to the bottom of a can of gasoline and whipped cream will float on top of Irish coffee. In similar fashion, a gas will flow from one level to another because of differences in weight. It is easy to accept why the cream floats on the coffee, for they are distinct materials. But air has uniform composition throughout the troposphere. One layer is not so overrich in argon that it sinks below another holding an overdose of the lighter nitrogen. The reason for the weight difference is not so clearly in chemical makeup.

The personality of air can be profiled in another way: by temperature and pressure. As a gas warms it wants to expand and take up more space. If it is in a closed container, then the pressure will increase. But if the container has no lid, the gas will boil upward and its weight on the bottom will decrease. On the other hand, when a gas cools it tends to contract into a smaller volume. More room is left on top for additional gas to rest, and the weight will increase. The container for the atmosphere has a bottom. We live on it, for it is the earth's surface. But it has no top. So warmed air can bubble upward, decreasing surface pressure. And it can then flow sideways on top of contracted colder air to increase the pressure in an adjacent stack. We come now to another useful guide to the atmosphere: one block, identical to its neighbor in chemical makeup, can differ in its pressure or weight at the surface because of a difference in temperature. Set out as a principle, it says:

> **2. At the surface, cold air and high pressure go together; warm air and low pressure go together.**

Temperature and pressure are all-important keys to atmospheric differences, and we must zoom in for a closer look. As we do, though, keep in mind that in meteorology "warm" doesn't have to mean more than body temperature and "cold" need not suggest frozen toes. The terms are used in a relative sense. Warm is warmer than air around it; cold is colder than its neighbors. The same is true for pressure. High pressure will not require a decompression chamber and low is not approaching a vacuum. High is higher than a low surrounding; low is lower than a high next door.

The atmosphere is certainly subjected to heat. Looming outside the exosphere is the enormous furnace of the sun. Its heat floods down toward the earth in the form of shortwave solar rays. It is the basic source of heat for the atmosphere; and the process of transfer is called *insolation*. Not all of this energy succeeds in striking the earth. In fact, almost half of it bounces back into space from our shroud of gas. The balance, though, is efficiently used by the earth as a source of heat.

Simple logic would seem to dictate that the closer one is to a furnace, the higher will be the temperature. From that point of view the outer reaches of the atmosphere must be hotter than those regions close to the earth's surface, for they are closer to the sun. By coincidence (but only by such), Figure 3 shows that for the thermosphere. An ancient Greek named Daedalus was reputed to have demonstrated such logic to his personal sorrow. As legend has it, in order to flee an angry king, he devised harness-like wings and secured them to his son, Icarus, and to himself. Daedalus made the trip intact, but not the boy. At first all went well for the young pilot as he soared gracefully upward. But suddenly the wings fell off and Icarus plummeted to his death. His father had fastened the wings to the harness with wax. As the boy rose higher and higher toward the sun, the wax melted. The legendary cause of the tragedy was given as violation of the principle that the closer one comes to a furnace, the higher the temperature. This makes a touching story, but it might hint at faulty meteorology. At least that is true if we presume poor Icarus stayed within the troposphere. Above the first 7 miles, as shown by Figure 3, air temperature zigzags through the spheres and pauses. But within the troposphere it *decreases* with altitude. So, Daedalus, perhaps, was not so negligent a parent after all.

In scientific terms what we are discussing are the direct and indirect causes of atmospheric heat. The short wavelength of solar heat rays allows little heating of air as sunlight floods down toward the surface. The earth, though, accepts the heat and warms up. It then becomes a radiator and reflects long-wave heat rays back up into the air. Substances such as water vapor in the air absorb the energy from those rays and warm up. Logic now can try again: the closer one is to a radiator, the warmer he feels. This time logic prevails. Air close to the earth's surface is warmer than that at altitude. This brings us to another basic principle:

> **3. Within the troposphere, atmospheric temperature decreases with increase in altitude.**

The heating effect of the sun is not very uniform. It depends on the angle of approach and on the nature of the earth's radiating surface. Figure 4 illustrates the angle idea, with some exaggeration for emphasis. There we see a shaft of sunlight flooding the earth's Equator at Region *A* and another shaft striking Region *B* at a much higher latitude. Each shaft has the same energy, but the effect on the earth will be different. The influence at *A* is concentrated on a smaller area than at *B*, so the heating effect is greater. And the result is obvious: *A* gets warmer. In turn, an air mass hovering over *A* will receive more reflected heat.

Surface cover also plays its part. The earth is the water planet, for more than 70% of its skin is made up of ocean. And a characteristic of water is a relative reluctance to change temperature. The metal skin of an empty kettle warms up very quickly. On the other hand, place water inside and the temperature change is longer in the making. We can reasonably expect that water on the earth's surface will change its temperature more slowly than will the surrounding land. Often, as in the case of the North Atlantic's Gulf Stream, it will even redistribute heat by flowing from one region on the earth to another.

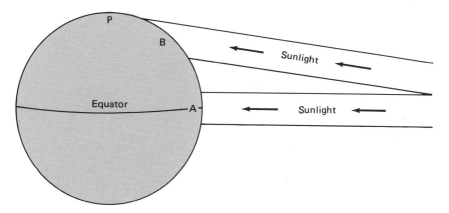

Figure 4. At high latitudes solar rays are less concentrated than near the Equator.

One thing is obvious. Our planet by no means radiates heat in a uniform fashion. Picture an old-fashioned fin-type steam radiator. Most of its vanes are the usual iron painted aluminum in color. But this old-timer differs from others of its type, for three of the vanes are unique. One is a wooden fin painted brown, another is a green plastic cube, and the third is a gray-white sheet of asbestos. Those unique vanes would radiate heat in different fashions because of color, material, and shape. Well, the earth, to an extent, is that offbeat radiator. Most of its surface is flat water; but other areas are as varied as green rain forests, sandy deserts, and rock-strewn mountain ranges. Add a swatch or two of shake roofs and freeways to find a mottled scramble of differing materials, hues, and shapes. Atmosphere resting on each "vane" of Radiator Earth must to some extent be conditioned by the nature of the surface cover beneath.

So we must expect a hodgepodge of temperature patterns varying by latitude and by the form of the earth's skin. Such contrasts will produce pressure contrasts from one region to another. And the ultimate result is a pattern of air masses differing in personality. Meteorologists use a system of abbreviations to suggest such differences. To begin with, they define an *air mass* as a distinctive part of the atmosphere within which common characteristics prevail over a reasonably large area (see Figure 5). And they key the abbreviations to the source. Four basic letters are used to spotlight the latitude of origin:

E, for Equatorial, refers to the area between the Trade Winds;

T, for Tropical, describes the Trade Wind belt and lower temperate regions;

P, for Polar, is a surprise; it does not refer, as one would expect, to the

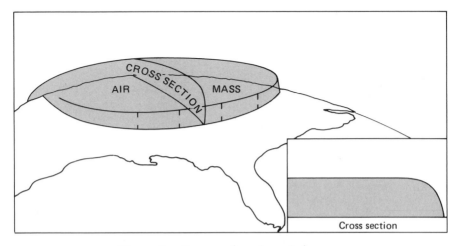

Figure 5.   Cross-section view of air mass.

north and south caps of the earth, but instead it speaks of the higher temperate latitudes.

A, for Arctic, takes care of the "top-of-the-earth" areas, both north and south.

Tropical (*T*) and polar (*P*) air masses are also referred to as *m* (for *maritime*) when they form over water surfaces, and as *c* (for *continental*) when the surface of the source is a land mass. Also, *w* can be added (for *warm*) when the air mass is warmer than the underlying surface, or *k* (for *cold*; *c* has already been appropriated for continental) when the air is colder than the surface cover of its source.

Put together, the system produces a quick means to describe blocks of the atmosphere. Here are two examples of how it all works:

1. *m T w* refers to an air mass which has been parked over a tropical ocean and is warmer than the surface. One would expect that, because of evaporation, it would have a high content of water vapor.
2. *c P k* speaks of one which has been over a land mass in the high temperate region and is colder than its surface. It could be expected to be drier than a contrasting *m* pile.

Mastery of these labels is not at all essential. Competent weather prediction should not be based on recollection of codes and symbols. But to recognize the purpose of such a pattern is entirely worthwhile. For we want to underscore the fact that the atmosphere is not a standardized and featureless blob of gas girdling the earth. Rather, it is made of chunks differing, if not chemically, then by such measures as temperature, pressure, and water content. We are one step closer to perception of the atmosphere as a true ocean subject to fluid motion of its segments.

For those of us casual in observation, Mother Nature could have been more explicit. She could, for example, have colored the air masses to give us a visual contrast. Red could serve for warm blocks and blue might show us cold. It is not good form to interfere with Mother Nature, so we're not about to spill pots of dye from a jet liner. Instead, later on we'll investigate the meteorologist's scheme of depicting contrasting air by contour lines tagged with numbers.

But to gain a more vivid picture of that ocean resting on our shoulders, we can risk at least a covert mending of Mother Nature's oversight. As you reconsider this first chapter, look around the atmosphere as if through red and blue lenses. The air will not be so invisible, at least to the mind's eye. A daytime breeze blowing up the side of a nearby hill is caused by warmed air rising from the valley. We now see it as a mass of red air flowing upward. At night the wind reverses as cooled air settles from the mountaintop down into the valley. To our eyes it is a current of blue. In

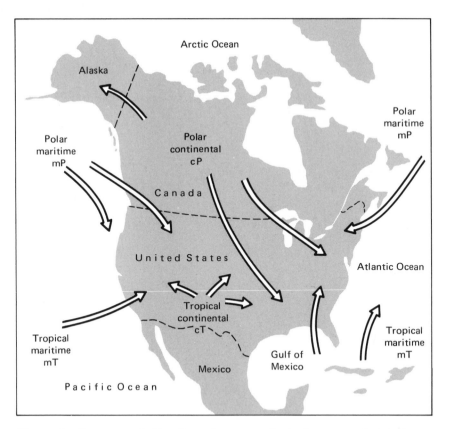

Figure 6. Sources and direction of movement of air masses that influence North American weather.

the afternoon, cool (blue) sea air flows toward the land to seep under the rising warm (red) air on the shore. This is an onshore sea breeze. In early morning the land air has cooled more than that over the adjacent water. The colors now reverse, and blue land air moves out to sea as an offshore land breeze.

On a grander scale we can picture a mass of red-tinted air towering over a tropical ocean, with a pile of blue-shaded air shrouding an adjacent continent. Much of the story of weather involves what happens when such red and blue blocks come together. The result is not going to be a purple mixture. Instead, the piles stay more or less separate. We "see" currents of blue or red flowing up, down, and sideways in an effort to get over or under a neighbor. Blue air, being heavier, nudges under a low-pressure block. Red, lighter air flows over the top of a blue pile. The motion is really fluid, just as much as in a can filled with water and gasoline.

Such an image as we have fashioned might not always hold together with scientific nicety. But a profitable trade-off is to exchange precision for a basic concept. Why not, for a while, think in colors? After such an exercise the true character of the atmosphere should be more recognizable. And that was our aim in these introductory pages.

QUESTIONS

Time to judge progress. The equipment needed? A pair of glasses with one red lens (the left, of course, by Rules of the Road mandate), and the other blue. The locale? At or near the bottom of the troposphere—except for readers in Kashmir. By dispensation they may perch on a Himalayan crag while trying the quiz. Ready, set, go!

1. The troposphere is
   a. higher over the Equator than over the poles.
   b. higher over the poles than over the Equator.
   c. about the same height everyplace on earth.
   d. about 27 miles high.

2. At sea level, atmospheric pressure is about
   a. 4.7 psi (330.3 g/cm²).
   b. 7.4 psi (520.1 g/cm²).
   c. 14.7 psi (1033.2 g/cm²).
   d. 17.4 psi (1223.0 g/cm²).

3. Atmospheric pressure within the troposphere
   a. increases with an increase in altitude.
   b. decreases with a decrease in altitude.
   c. decreases with an increase in altitude.

4. Transfer of heat from the sun to the earth is called
   a. isolation.
   b. insulation.
   c. insolation.
   d. consolation.

5. Cold air at the surface tends to have _____ pressure than warm air.
   a. higher
   b. lower
   c. the same

6. Within the troposphere, atmospheric temperature normally
   a. increases with an increase in altitude.
   b. decreases with a decrease in altitude.
   c. decreases with an increase in altitude.

7. An air mass has been resting over a tropical ocean. The air temperature is

less than that of the water surface beneath. The air mass would be described as

a. m T w.
b. m T k.
c. c T w.
d. c T k.

8. In early morning, air tends to move from land toward the sea
   a. because the land air is colder than the ocean air.
   b. because the land surface is colder than the ocean surface.
   c. both of the above.
   d. none of the above.

9. The atmospheric layer separating the troposphere from the stratosphere is called the
   a. mesopause.
   b. ionopause.
   c. stratopause.
   d. tropopause.

10. Generally speaking, air at 10,000 feet (18,520 km), compared to air at sea level, would be
    a. colder and of lower pressure.
    b. warmer and of higher pressure.
    c. colder and of higher pressure.
    d. warmer and of lower pressure.

ANSWERS

Report Card time. Here is the scoring procedure. Allow 10 points for each correct response and tote up the result this way:

        100, Ceiling Unlimited
         90, Scattered Clouds
         80, Partly Cloudy
         70, Threatening Skies
    under 70, Carl Sandburg was right: "The fog comes on little cat feet."

1. a   6. c
2. c   7. b
3. c   8. c
4. c   9. d
5. a   10. a

Chapter 2

WINDS

Before we resume discussion of interaction between air masses, we had better make a minor change in approach. The colored glasses are now to be stowed away. We don't want Mother Nature so irked by brash censure that she visits us with an Ice Age. So from here on, reds and blues remain hidden from her view. Instead, we'll use "low" to describe a red block and "high" to describe a blue.

Figure 7 depicts a simplified view of the troposphere pressure belts surrounding the earth. Straddling the Equator is a low-pressure zone produced in the concentrated glare of the sun. Immediately north and south are bands of air with relatively higher pressure. At the polar caps are two more highs. And sandwiched between are two more lows.

The earth we see here, though, is quite unusual. First off, we specify it as totally covered with water. At least then we have a uniform radiator and can for the moment disregard modification in heat values caused by changes in surface cover. The second unreal specification is that the earth is stopped. To begin with we don't want to encounter the changes caused by the earth's spinning.

Were there, then, such an unorthodox world we would expect wind patterns as shown in Figure 8. Equatorial warm air (E) would rise and begin to flow poleward at altitude. Air of higher pressure on either side (H_n, a northern high and H_s, a southern one) would flow toward the Equa-

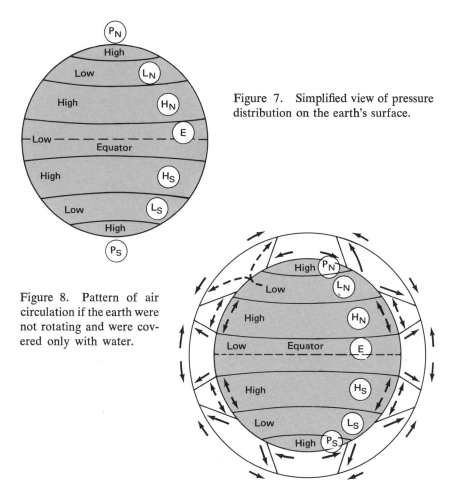

Figure 7. Simplified view of pressure distribution on the earth's surface.

Figure 8. Pattern of air circulation if the earth were not rotating and were covered only with water.

tor to fill in gaps. A chimney-like convection current would develop in the equatorial region. Warm air would rise and so exert less pressure on the surface. High up, air would be moving poleward; near the surface it would be flowing toward the Equator.

The cold high-pressure blocks at top and bottom would be denser than adjoining air masses L_n and L_s. So movement would be from the poles toward the Equator in those regions. In turn, the lows at L_n and L_s would, because of pressure differences, tend to be invaded by high-pressure air from H_n and H_s. The result is movement into those two low areas from both north and south, that is, from the adjacent high-pressure regions. So we now see that at each of the three Lows (E, L_n, and L_s) air would flow outward at the top and inward at the bottom. Figure 9 illustrates what such flow over our unreal earth would produce in the lower regions of the tropo-

Figure 9. Basic principle that "High
Blows to Low" applied.

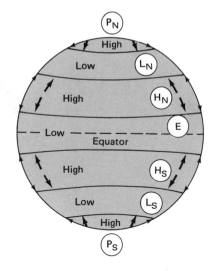

sphere. Wind arrows point north and south from highs to lows. This brings
us to another basic principle:

> **4. High blows to low near the surface.**

Of course we know Figure 9 is nonsense. There are not just two wind directions on earth—north and south. Another factor must be considered.
Beforehand, though, let's pin down this matter of describing wind direction.

The pattern is backward. Wind, apparently, is not interested in where it
goes; rather, it speaks of where it *comes from*. So a north wind really flows
southward, and a south wind goes northward. This system is unique to wind
and to wind-driven waves. Throughout most of navigation to state direction
is to describe the compass mark *toward* which something moves. A course
of 090° surely means going east; a current set of 180° says the water flows
south. But a wind of 180° means the exact opposite.

The upshot is a somewhat clumsy practice; but is so deeply imbedded
in usage that little hope of change exists. Why the system exists is not important; but we can risk some coffee time speculation. The scene is Italy,
centuries ago. It could just as well have been Addis Ababa or Angkor Wat,
but we'll make it Italy. A brisk wind is pouring over a plain. Some observant
person notices it is coming *from* the mountains. So from then on in his
community such a wind is termed a mountain wind. At another time the
breeze flows from lands across the Adriatic. It is labeled a Greek wind. The
pattern is set to name airflow by its source. Later on some mariner placed
a compass rose over the scheme and we were in for it. The alpine mountain

wind of Italy became a north wind; the one from Greece became an east wind. The suggestion makes sense even if it might be lacking in historical accuracy. What matters, though, is that we have somehow inherited an indelible routine. But let's begin by emphasizing the direction of flow as the key. Let's start by concentrating on which way the wind blows *toward*. In that manner we'll more readily preserve the image of fluid motion. Then, when the picture is clear, we can rejoin the custom by reverting to the backward method.

However viewed, Figure 9 is still nonsense. North (flowing south) and south (flowing north) are not the only winds on earth. What brings us closer to reality is the application of an intriguing influence called the *coriolis effect*. And to see what results, we must now place our fictional Earth in motion. Figure 10 shows a space view from above the North Pole. In rotating from west to east the earth is spinning counterclockwise. In Figure 11 the view is from space above the South Pole. Now the earth's spin from west to east appears as clockwise.

Point *E* in each sketch is a location on the Equator; Point *M* in each is at a latitude of 60°. In one day each *E* will rotate once with the earth. So, of course, will each *M*. But the *E*s have a longer trip to make. The Equator is 21,600 nautical miles (40,000 km) around. The *E*s travel that far in 24 hours, so they are moving at 900 knots (1667 km/hr). At a latitude of 60°, though, the earth's girth is only 10,800 miles (20,000 km) around. The *M* points travel only that far in the same 24 hours. They are loping along at a mere 450 knots (833 km/hr). Obviously, the earth's speed is not constant from Equator to pole. It diminishes from a 900-mph maximum at the Equator to 0 mph at the poles. (This would suggest that if one wants to travel in fast company he should frequent the tropics, for high latitudes

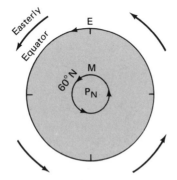

Figure 10. Earth's rotation as viewed from above the North Pole.

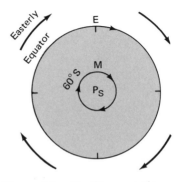

Figure 11. Earth's rotation as viewed from above the South Pole.

are peopled by slowpokes.) In any case, the rate at which that speed decreases is not constant. Influenced by a trigonometry tidbit called the cosine, the change is less near the Equator than as one approaches a pole. For example, the difference in speed between the Equator and a latitude of 5° is a scant 3½ mph (6.5 km/hr); but the difference between that at 80° and at 85° latitude is almost 77 mph (143 km/hr). For those who collect little-known facts scarcely worth knowing, here is the formula to determine the earth's speed at any latitude:

900 mph (1667 km/hr) × the cosine of the latitude = the speed

But it is much more important to understand what happens to an object which itself is in motion over the spinning surface of the earth. It cannot avoid the influence of the earth's motion beneath. And the influence can become more pronounced with a change in location. Figures 12 and 13 show two phonograph discs. The pictures are very similar to the earth views from beyond the poles shown in Figures 10 and 11. Suppose that in Figure 12 or 13 you were to start drawing a chalkline from the center straight out to the edge as the disc was spinning beneath. The result would

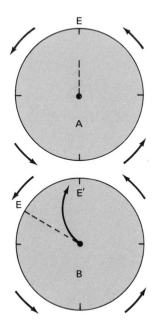

Figure 12.   Coriolis effect as viewed from above the North Pole.

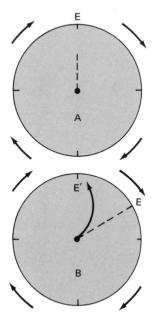

Figure 13.   Coriolis effect as viewed from above the South Pole.

be a curved line. In Figure 12 the line curves to the right of its aim; in Figure 13 it curves to the left. Even though the chalk was heading toward *E* it would end up at *E'*. The reason? While the chalk was enroute, *E* would be rotating out of line. This Coriolis business sometimes seems like sleight-of-hand. It is termed an *apparent* effect. The chalklines really are heading for *E* in Figures 12 and 13; they just looked curved, says Coriolis.

Anything in motion over the spinning earth is going to act like that chalk-line; it will appear to change direction. How much and in what way depends on location. But to some extent, from insignificant to a lot, the influence is there. Stated as a basic principle, called Ferrell's Law, this says:

---

5. Because of the Coriolis effect, anything in motion over the earth appears to change direction
a. to the right in the northern hemisphere; and
b. to the left in the southern hemisphere.

We don't often perceive this in daily life. Resting on a park bench we see an eastbound passing car move only relative to us. We disregard the fact that two motions are actually involved. We, the bench, and the car are all moving eastward with the earth. Place the park on the Equator and we are all spinning along at a very swift clip. Relative to each other, though, there is no hint of that movement. Instead, we think we're stopped and the car is moving, not at 955 mph (1769 km/hr), but only at 55 mph (102 km/hr).

In most earthbound relationships Coriolis is not critical. But on some occasions its influence is very important. When test missiles are fired from Florida's Cape Canaveral toward the middle of the South Atlantic Ocean, where is the missile aimed? Not at the mid-South Atlantic. Were that done, the ocean would rotate eastward while the missile was enroute and the bulge of Brazil might be in jeopardy. Instead, the aim would be closer to the West African coastline. Then, while the missile wings southerly, the world's eastward turn would provide open ocean for splashdown. The high-flying object would be less subject to the earth's spin than the surface beneath, so allowance must be made. Air moving over the earth's cover is in somewhat the same condition. It might not be as free from some earth influence as the missile, but it certainly won't be as controlled as the park bench and the automobile. A Coriolis effect will be evident.

Coriolis conversation can be addicting, for it suggests an interesting and overlooked facet of our everyday existence. To remain uninformed, though, is really no impediment to a normal lifestyle—until a study of weather is undertaken. Then this teasing concept becomes important. One of its commonplace effects is quite valuable to an understanding of many weather principles: which brings up "The Case of the Draining Washbowl."

We all have noticed what happens when the drainplug is pulled in a basin filled with water. Flow begins toward the hole suddenly created at the center; but that motion is not in a direct line. Instead, water will spiral around the drain in a circular fashion. Described in the most general of general terms, with all other factors ignored, the pattern in the northern hemisphere is a curve to the right of straight-in; the pattern in the southern hemisphere is a curve to the left. Only on the Equator will it seek to move straight toward the drain. Figures 14 and 15 show the idea. Notice that the pattern is counterclockwise in Figure 14's northern hemisphere view and is clockwise in the view for the southern. Should you try an experiment, don't lose faith if the swirl is not as predicted. Blame it on water pressure or on the shape of the bowl. Usually, though, the cycle will be as expected.

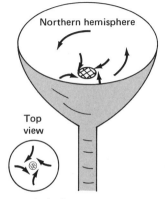

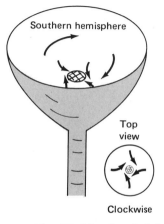

Figure 14. Washbowls draining north of the Equator.

Figure 15. Washbowls draining south of the Equator.

A study of washbasins is not so irrelevant to our discussion. As soon as the plug is pulled there is a low-pressure area at the drain in the center. Regions of high water pressure are all around. High moves toward low; that accounts for the flow toward the center. Direction changes right or left; that is due to Coriolis. If we were speaking not of washbasins but of dissimilar air masses, the action would be much the same. The center of a tropical cyclone is, like the basin drain, a core of very low pressure surrounded by high. And the rotation within a tropical cyclone around its central eye is very similar to that in the bowl of water. More of this as we go along. For now, though, we'll set the record player aside on top of the washbasin and rejoin our track.

A restatement of Basic Principles 4 and 5 is worthwhile, for they are the most important rules applicable to surface winds:

> **4. High blows to low; and**
> **5. turns right in the northern hemisphere;**
> **turns left in the southern hemisphere.**

Fortunately, only a small fraction of wind patterns develop into washbowl cycles around deep low-pressure holes in the atmosphere. Still, though, Principles 4 and 5 apply throughout. Time now to connect all this to the circulation pattern we were building around our unreal earth.

In Figure 16 we see the general system again, with new wind arrows dictated by Coriolis. Air blows from high to low according to form. Then it is diverted to the right of its line of motion in the northern hemisphere and to the left in the southern. To note this change it is important to sight first toward the arrowhead on each dotted line. This shows the high-to-low direction *toward* which the flow will tend to move. Then compare the direction of the solid arrow shaft. The change is clearly to the right when north of the Equator and to the left when south. The result when we revert to customary terms is this. Instead of just north-south winds we now have them *from* the northeast and southeast, *from* the east and west.

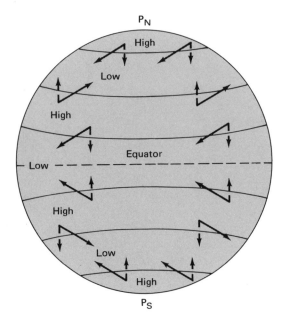

Figure 16. General atmospheric circulation over ocean areas.

Reality is being restored. We've set our earth spinning and have the key to ocean wind patterns. Remember, though, our special earth is still all covered with water; we are not yet back to normal. But for ocean areas—and they comprise more than 70% of the earth cover—the general pattern is set. Land masses will distort the picture, as we'll see in our encounter with topographical or local winds. But the fundamental motions are now in focus: high to low with a right or left turn. Figure 17 adds some familiar labels, outgrowths of the world's trading history.

Approaching the equatorial low are the Northeast and Southeast trade winds. Reliable and strong, they pushed Columbus to the New World and Captain Bligh's longboat filled with castaways from Polynesia to the islands of Southeast Asia. The northeast trades are high-to-low winds with a right turn. They divert from a southerly flow to one going southwest. They *come from* the northeast. The southeast trades follow the southern hemisphere rules to blow high-to-low with a left turn. They flow northwesterly and *come from* the southeast.

Blowing poleward from the middle highs are the prevailing westerlies. They are turned sharply to right and left to approach from the westward. These winds pushed ships laden with Australian wool across the bottom of the Pacific to Cape Horn and treasure-filled Manila galleons from the Philippines to Acapulco. At Cape Horn the westbound sailor would meet these rugged blows bow-on as he struggled to round the corner.

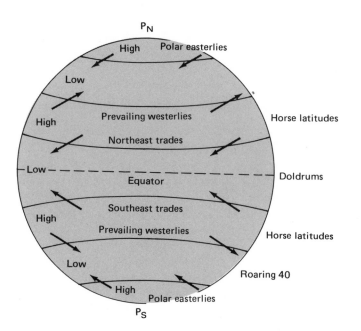

Figure 17. Significant wind regions of the earth.

From the earth's caps the high-pressure arctic air moves down and is turned right and left by Coriolis. The results are the high-latitude or polar easterlies of each hemisphere. They play an enormous role in the development of mid-latitude winter weather.

We've taken liberties with customary wind direction to build our pattern. For in applying Principles 4 and 5 we've been looking *toward* the direction of flow to apply our right and left turns. Once the image is implanted, we can face astern to describe direction in normal terms. But the device is very much worthwhile. Principles 4 and 5 will come up again. When they do, accept that to apply them we become logical and look ahead. Conforming to customary parlance comes after we see the picture.

Notice also on Figure 17 the mention of the areas of doldrums, horse latitudes, and the roaring 40s. They cry out for comment. To do so, lets consider one more analogy. Look on highs as hills of closely packed air and lows as valleys formed by less dense atmosphere. Air flows from such hills to such valleys just as water in a stream will flow down the riverbed. This is another way of saying that high blows to low.

But hills can have flat tops or plateaus, and valleys can have floors. On the top of such a flat hill no swift-moving stream would be found. The slant of the bed would not be sufficient to make water gush down. The stream would inch along until it found the side of the hill; then it would tumble into the valley. But on the level valley floor it would again resume its sluggish flow.

With that analogy in mind, we gain a simple explanation for two of the labels on Figure 17. The *doldrums* is a belt of uniformly low pressure within the equatorial zone. It is the floor of a valley. There, little wind blows, ships lay becalmed, and seamen fret. The *horse latitudes* are flat plateaus on the summits of highs. There, also, the air-pressure difference is not enough to cause any but light, variable winds. Both doldrums and horse latitudes bring calms or fitful, weak winds.

One version of how the horse latitudes were named is worthy of mention. During the Spanish conquest of the New World, says the tale, cavalrymen being transported across the Atlantic with their mounts could be confronted by a painful dilemma. While the ships lay becalmed in these plateaus of high pressure and scant rain, the horses were drinking precious water. Sometimes progress was so slow that further water for the horses meant not enough to sustain the men. So on occasion the grieving Conquistadors would force their animals to walk the plank.

What about the *roaring 40s*? This is a term applied to prevailing westerly winds in the southern hemisphere between about latitudes 40°S and 55°S. There the winds from the west are very strong and very constant, for no land masses intervene to break their force. This brings us to another

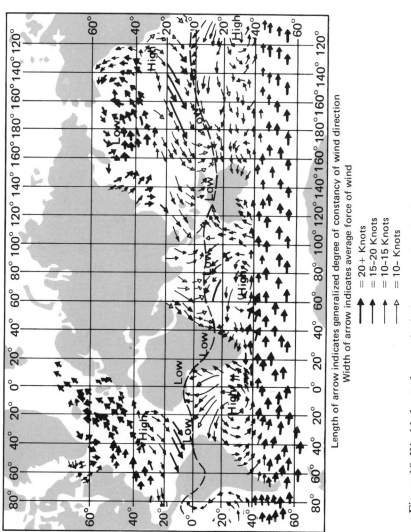

Length of arrow indicates generalized degree of constancy of wind direction
Width of arrow indicates average force of wind

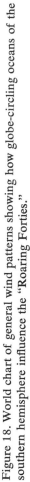

   = 20+ Knots
   = 15–20 Knots
   = 10–15 Knots
   = 10– Knots

Figure 18. World chart of general wind patterns showing how globe-circling oceans of the southern hemisphere influence the "Roaring Forties."

term, *fetch*. When wind blows over water without interruption by land masses it has little reason to change. The farther it blows over water, the more constant it tends to remain. And fetch means nothing more than that: the distance over open water that a wind blows without a change in direction. The term is restricted to conversation about ocean waves and really says that as fetch increases, waves get higher. But the idea of fetch, coupled with a glance at a world chart, can suggest why the roaring 40s roar.

At the high southern latitudes of 40° to 55° the fetch is almost 360° around the world. Already the zone is south of Africa and Australia. The only intruding land is New Zealand's South Island, Tasmania, and the spiny tail of South America. By contrast, the same latitudes in the northern hemisphere contain three large continents. So, south of the Equator the prevailing westerly belt is a region of whistling winds of 25 knots or better.

We've done it! The general wind system on earth has been dissected, tagged, and reassembled. We'll meet more about wind, of course. But the fundamentals are behind us. We've all but restored our special earth to normalcy. And we've now reached a snug and welcome haven to drop anchor. So, down falls the hook and we'll swing idly for a while in still waters to reconsider this chapter.

QUESTIONS

Hidden in the Cave of Winds waits the stern quizmaster, ready to measure progress. Don't expect, though, to meet him face to face. From ancient habit he looks only over his shoulder to see where he's been. Perhaps it is more fitting to approach his presence walking backward. So, about face! One, two, one, two . . .

1. Low pressure is to be expected in the
   a. equatorial area.
   b. Arctic area.
   c. Antarctic area.
   d. all of the above.

2. Near the earth's surface, air
   a. moves from high to low.
   b. is diverted toward the right in both northern and southern hemispheres.
   c. both of the above.
   d. none of the above.

3. Due to the Coriolis effect, rotation around a low-pressure core is
   a. counterclockwise in the northern hemisphere.
   b. clockwise in the southern hemisphere.
   c. both of the above.
   d. none of the above.

4. The "roaring 40s" is the name given westerly winds found in
   a. the northern hemisphere.
   b. the southern hemisphere.
   c. both hemispheres.

5. The horse latitudes are regions of
   a. brisk prevailing winds.
   b. light airs and calms.
   c. none of the above.

6. The northeast trades
   a. are south of the northern hemisphere horse latitudes.
   b. blow toward the southwest.
   c. both of the above
   d. none of the above

7. Point *A* is at a latitude of 50° North, Point *B* is at 60° North, and Point *C* is at 70° North.
   a. *A* travels eastward with the earth's surface faster than either *B* or *C*.
   b. The difference in speed between *A* and *B* is less than that between *B* and *C*.
   c. both of the above.
   d. none of the above.

8. In regions near the poles, the winds are generally described as
   a. westerly.
   b. easterly.
   c. northerly.
   d. southerly.

9. Associated with a low-pressure region
   a. are the horse latitudes.
   b. are the doldrums.
   c. both of the above.
   d. none of the above.

10. The distance over open water that a wind blows without a change in direction is called
    a. wretch.
    b. ketch.
    c. zetch.
    d. fetch.

ANSWERS

To score the results it is not necessary that you hold the answer page up to a mirror. There is a limit to topsy-turviness, even with the wind. As usual, allow 10 points for each correct response. Then, to check status, use this scale:

> 100, Clipper Ship
> 90, Lumber Schooner
> 80, Spanish Caravelle
> 70, Spanish Caravelle minus a few horses
> under 70, Deep, deep in the doldrums

1. a   6. c
2. a   7. c
3. c   8. b
4. b   9. b
5. b   10. d

Chapter 3

MORE ON WINDS

On the last leg of our passage we met the analogy of air masses to pressure hills and valleys. Few such images fit glove-tight, and this is no exception. For it suggests that the summit of the atmosphere, like a pipe organ, is a jumble of columns uneven in height. That is not the case. Unevenness, though, does exist in weight. In one block of air the gas is more compacted than in another. What we mean by a hill is a denser column and not a taller one.

That justifies the meteorologist's extension of the hill-and-valley theme to a weather map. On it he depicts pressure differences by contour lines. And they very closely resemble the contour lines used by a cartographer to show real hills and valleys on Earth. In meteorology these lines are called *isobars*. They connect locations with equal (that's what *iso-* means) atmospheric pressure (that's what *-bar* suggests). The result is a pattern giving a synopsis of pressure distribution at a given time. So a meteorologist calls it a *synoptic weather chart*.

In order to gain this view he needs the cooperation of many observing stations. Ships at sea, satellites, land-based units—they all supply him with essential data taken at the same time. When his aim is an analysis of pressure he selects the barometer reading from each report. The next step is to plot the positions of the stations. Then he draws an isobar through those reporting the same pressure. The outcome is a contour map. It might not be valid for long, since the atmosphere is fluid and its formations undergo constant change. But for the moment it will display pressure distribution over an area. Figure 19 shows one with a low center. Figure 20 has one centered on a high.

These are plan views, looking down. Were we to tip them sideways we would have the profile pictures of Figures 21 and 22. These more clearly show the hill-and-valley concept. Also evident in Figure 21 is the wash-bowl analogy. But such vertical atmospheric slices are not at all useful to depict patterns over a large area. Each slice would only show a cross section along a given line; and a great number would be needed to display the design for a total air mass. On weather maps the down view alone is practical. We'll delve more into this later on. Here the aim is introduction to the scheme so we can better identify general types.

The patterns need not be concentric as shown in Figures 19 and 20. In fact, they are rarely so. The perfect-circle approach suggests a symmetrical deep hole or conical hill. Most of the time the isobars form odd figures of very different shape. Figure 23 is a sketch of a more customary pattern. Low cores appear northeast and northwest of a high area. As contours of land, the view would show a plateau grading off into a canyon to the north-west and a deep gulch to the northeast. Viewed as air masses, they suggest a well-filled block of air flanked by slacker piles on either side.

Names have been given to the two basic forms. That with a low core is called *cyclonic*; that with a high center is *anticyclonic*. To a meteorologist a cyclone is not solely the roof-raising monster of our Midwest states. It is a pressure system centered on a low core.

Basic Principles 4 and 5 now reappear from Chapter 2. Several times we've emphasized that high blows to low near the surface and makes a right turn in the northern hemisphere and a left turn in the southern. Figures 24 and 25 apply those principles to northern hemisphere cyclones and anticyclones. Figures 26 and 27 put them to work in the southern hemisphere.

Look at the northern hemisphere view of a low shown in Figure 24. The high-to-low flow starts air moving toward the center. Then it is slanted to the right. At each of the four points shown, wind direction is different. Point *1* has it as from northeast; *2* shows it as southeast. For *3* it is south-west; at *4* the wind is northwest. And the general view is of a counterclock-wise swirl. In Figure 25's northern hemisphere high, the flow emerges as a clockwise cycle. And the wind directions change regularly around the compass.

South of the Equator, as shown in Figure 26, the low core produces a clockwise pattern. In Figure 27 the high core brings a counterclockwise one. Enough for us now to recognize that wind flow is either in or out, with a twist.

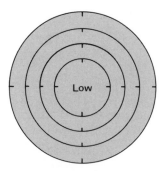

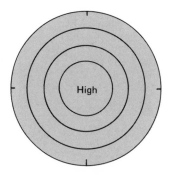

Figure 19. Plan view of a simplified low-pressure area.

Figure 20. Plan view of a simplified high-pressure area.

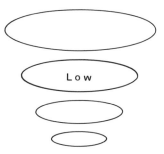

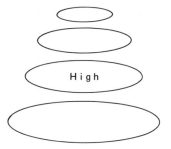

Figure 21. A simple low in profile.

Figure 22. A simple high in profile.

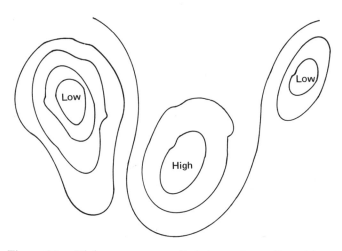

Figure 23. High pressure prevails between two adjacent lows.

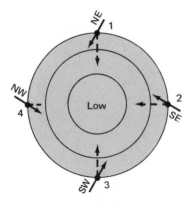

Figure 24. Circulation around a
northern hemisphere low.

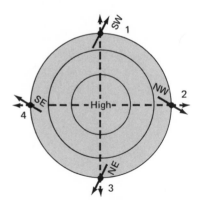

Figure 25. Circulation around a
northern hemisphere high.

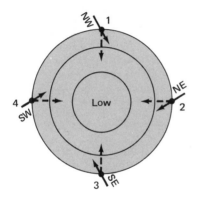

Figure 26. Circulation around a
southern hemisphere low.

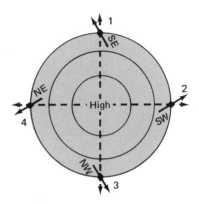

Figure 27. Circulation around a
southern hemisphere high.

The clock comparison is often emphasized; yet that approach can be a
real burden on the memory. To say "counterclockwise around a northern
low and clockwise around a northern high; clockwise around a southern
low and counterclockwise around a southern high" is to have too many
clocks. Short-circuit the memory banks and the whole picture is askew.
Moreover, the image is not so realistic. To a satellite's camera eye the
swirls *do* follow the clocks. Figure 28 is a photograph of cloud patterns
around a deep northern low, and the spirals *are* counterclockwise. Try,
though, to tell that to an observer at Point *1* in Figure 24. For him, the
wind is not kinking his hair into counterclockwise curls. He has a northeast wind, and no one can tell him otherwise.

Figure 28. Satellite view of low-pressure system (in this case, 1976's Hurricane Belle) off the eastern United States. (*NOAA*)

What never strays off course is the application of Basic Principles 4 and 5. Used at each of the four cardinal compass points in a pattern, they first reveal individual wind directions. Then the curve of the clock can easily be identified. Let's try all this with an example. An observer is in the northern hemisphere and learns that a severe low-pressure core is 100 miles (185 km) to the east. He is to determine the compass quadrant of his wind. He is also to identify the general circulation as clockwise or counterclockwise.

First of all he could draw a bull's-eye, as in Figure 29. Its center is marked as low. Then he marks off the major compass directions of north, south, east, and west. Next, he places himself to the westward. How far by any scale is not important, for he is only after generalities. So he places himself at *A*. Now he applies his true friends, Principles 4 and 5: high-to-low and a right turn. The result? Wind from the northwest quadrant. As for

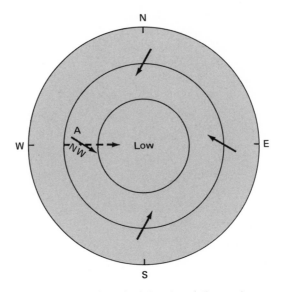

Figure 29.   Basic principles 4 and 5 reveal counterclockwise circulation around a northern hemisphere low.

general circulation, he could repeat the steps at each of the other compass
points. A counterclockwise pattern is now obvious.

Oversimplified? Very much so. Many factors can intrude to mask this
direct approach. But the fundamentals always apply. And just as in any
endeavor, the root principles must be kept in mind. Otherwise knowledge
will be just a veneer of dissociated odds and ends without cohesion.

Let's look again at Figure 29. We see the airflow heading toward the
center and turning right. Good questions now are: How much of a turn
is involved? What factors influence that change in direction? The answers
are reasonable, but they require some close attention.

As we've already seen, the right and left business develops because of
Coriolis. A surface observer spins eastward with the earth. The air, bound
from high toward low, is not so firmly connected to the earth that it must
go along. Like the missile being tested, it is in motion over the surface
but not fully affected by surface rotation. At a high altitude there is little
reason for it to feel much earth influence at all. Lower down, though, surface friction will drag the air somewhat along with the spin.

Vector diagrams can be drawn to show what all this brings; but vectors
are sometimes sticky bogs of horrors to throw us off course. Sufficient

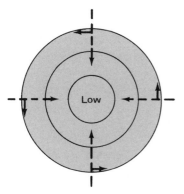

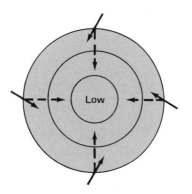

Figure 30. High-altitude winds tend to follow isobars.

Figure 31. Air at low levels tends to cross isobars.

to our task, perhaps, is our acceptance that Coriolis, tempered by frictional drag, will vary the turn from a reasonable one to hard right or hard left. Figure 30 shows a 90° turn. Instead of blowing across the isobars toward the center, air is moving almost parallel to them. This would be the idea at a high altitude.

At low levels an air column is dragged along by the earth and tends to follow a more directly high-to-low track. The turn is less, as shown in Figure 31. No wonder, then, that a person basking under a tree can note air moving in two directions. Falling leaves will move one way in the low-level currents, while high clouds head in a different direction.

Here is a recap of all this. Air at altitudes less than 2000 feet (610 m) tends to move more or less from high to low. At higher altitudes it flows more nearly along the isobars; its change in direction can be a full 90°.

One further influence gets into the act: *centrifugal force.* An object placed in circular motion around a point tends to be pushed away from the center. It wants to fly away like a fugitive (*-fugal*) from the center (*centri-*). Our air, once it begins to turn right or left, encounters this force. The result? It will turn more away from the center; and the faster it moves, the more centrifugal force it will meet. This is very apparent in the awesome tropical cyclone. Air might start heading toward the low core, but Coriolis makes it turn. The centrifugal influence on wind blowing at such furious speeds finishes the job. The air is turned out so much that it flows not into the center, but around it. An eye of dead air is formed as the centerpiece of all that power. It is the stagnant vortex of a gigantic washbowl of air.

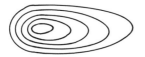

Figure 32.   Plan view of Gibralter-
like high-pressure air mass.

Figure 33.   That Gibralter high in
profile.

Even in less vicious storms the net result of all these influences is pronounced. Over land the greater frictional drag of the earth keeps the flow aimed more at the center; yet the turning influence can exceed 30°. Over water the drag is not half as effective in overcoming Coriolis. There the air can be deflected from its aim to flow at a greater angle from straight across the isobars.

The spacing between isobars tells its own story. Again the similarity to contour lines on the earth is striking. Should a map show topography as seen in Figure 32, the profile view would be somewhat like that in Figure 33—Gibralter. A steep cliff is on one side and a slope on the other. When contour lines bunch together, a rapid change in height is indicated; when they spread farther apart, the grade is more gradual.

Isobaric patterns follow the same rule. Should they be a tight spiral, pressure differences occur over a short distance. The result would be a sudden change and a strong wind flow. Figure 34 shows that. But when spacing is more open, the pressure change is less pronounced relative to distance along the surface. There, as in Figure 35, wind would be of less strength. Another label approaches: *pressure gradient*. It is the relation of pressure change to distance. When the change is large over a short distance, as in Figure 34, wind is strong. When the change occurs over a greater distance, as in Figure 35, the wind is weaker.

Figure 34.   Closely spaced isobars
mean strong winds.

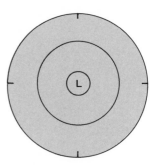

Figure 35.   Wide spacing tells of
weak winds.

A few exercises are in order to check that the routine of wind selection is under control. Here are three situations. The first observer is in the northern hemisphere. He learns that hovering over the ocean a few hundred miles to the westward is a large high-pressure air mass. What wind direction might he expect?

Figure 36 shows high-to-low with a right turn. The result could be wind from the northwest quadrant. And since the isobaric patterns are tightly drawn, a steep pressure gradient is indicated. The wind could be expected to be quite strong.

Our second observer is in the southern hemisphere. He learns of a low to the south of his position. Figure 37 tells his expected wind pattern. High-to-low and a left turn indicates, again, northwest winds. This time his position in the isobaric spacing suggests that wind force might not be great, for the pressure gradient appears weak.

For our third example we find the observer in the northern hemisphere. Weather reports advise a severe low is to the northwestward. What might he expect? Figure 38 joins with Principles 4 and 5 to do it again: high to low with a right turn. He could encounter a southerly wind, but not, says pressure gradient, of severe force.

No more examples should be necessary, for the basic principles are by now abundantly evident. Something else, though, needs attention. To continue describing pressure patterns as high or low is like speaking of a

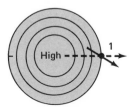

Figure 36. Northwest wind when east of a northern hemisphere high.

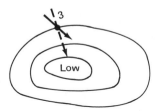

Figure 37. Northwest wind when north of a southern hemisphere low.

Figure 38. The wind is from the south near this northern hemisphere low.

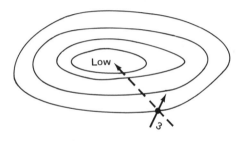

stick as long or short. Eventually the time comes to use some type of measurement; and for us the time is now. A later chapter on instruments will pick through data on shipboard weather tools. We'll leave for then a close view of how they work. Meanwhile, though, we need a preview of at least the systems of measuring pressure. Here is the general scheme.

Normal air pressure, we've seen, exerts 14.7 pounds of weight on each square inch of sea level surface (that equals 1033.2 g/cm²). But meteor-ologists don't use either a psi or a g/cm² measure. Instead, three alternative systems are met. Air pressure bearing down on an open dish of mercury will force the liquid metal up a vacuum tube to a measurable height. In essence we've just described the principle of a *mercury barometer*. A slender glass pipe is closed at one end and filled with mercury. Then it is capsized into an open cup containing more mercury. Some of the liquid will begin to flow down out of the tube into the cup. But resisting will be the pressure of the atmosphere pushing down on the mercury already in the cup. At one point the weight of mercury left standing in the tube will be exactly balanced by atmospheric pressure. Figure 39 is an illustration.

If the cross-sectional area of the tube were one square inch, then the weight of metal in the tube would be 14.7 pounds at sea level. If the area were 1 cm² the metal would weigh 1033.2 grams or 1.03 kg. But neither is a statement of how the pressure is read. The height of the mercury column is determined and then the atmospheric pressure is described as being equivalent to that value. Should air pressure increase, then metal would be forced farther up the tube and the column would be higher. When air pressure lessens the column falls a bit.

All we need now is a pattern to measure the height of the mercury column. Using the *foot-pound-second* system, we would break out a ruler calibrated in inches. The standard height at sea level is taken as *29.92*

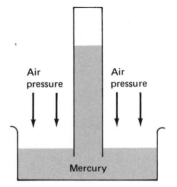

Figure 39.   Principle of a mercury barometer.

inches of mercury. The metric system would show *760.0 mm*. Meteorologists seem to have thrown up their hands at the rumpus over rulers, for they usually employ another way to describe pressure. Their unit, like the millimeter, is part of the metric system. But instead of measuring length it tells what force would be necessary to support mercury at such a height. They begin with a *bar*, which amounts to one million tiny pressure units called *dynes* on each square centimeter. Then they select a basic unit called the *millibar* to describe 1000 dynes per square centimeter. The original idea was to have one bar or 1000 millibars equal the atmospheric pressure at sea level; but by the time finer measurements were allowed for, the standard reading at zero elevation emerged as *1013.25 mb*. We'll meet more of this in Chapter 11's treatment of instruments.

For now, though, influenced by an international spirit of détente, we can define standard atmospheric pressure at sea level as 14.7 psi or 1.03 kg per cm^2, or as 29.92 inches of mercury or 760.0 mm of mercury, or as 1013.25 mb. The extremes of pressure which have been measured might be interesting to note. Perhaps the highest was in Siberia, at 32.01 inches, 813.1 mm, or 1083.8 mb. That is nearly 15.7 psi. Mentioned as one of the very lowest was that reported in the eye of a supertyphoon near Okinawa. It is said to have been 25.28 inches, 642.05 mm, or 856 mb. That was a vein-popping 12.4 psi.

Absent such eerie extremes and the storm systems keeping them company, the overall pressure range, worldwide, more or less straddles the standard 1013 mb by about 20 mb on either side. There is, though, a noteworthy *diurnal* (daily) pattern of pressure change. Because of a mysterious influence called *solar* or *thermal tide*, air pressure seems to reach daily peaks at 10 A.M. and 10 P.M. with lows at 4 A.M. and 4 P.M. This variation is pronounced in tropical and subtropical regions. At higher latitudes it seems masked by other influences.

Where do we now stand in our study? Well, the atmosphere is made up of air piled in masses with distinct characteristics of temperature and pressure. The temperature is related directly to the earth as a radiator and indirectly to the sun as a furnace. Temperature causes pressure differences. They, in turn, separate air masses into regions of high and low. The high-pressure piles move toward low areas and are diverted to right or left by Coriolis. Centrifugal force puts in its oar to magnify the course changes.

We can view this atmospheric ocean as a varied gas-scape of hills and valleys. And the meteorologist charts the patterns by contour lines called *isobars*. When pressure extends outward on the long axis of an elliptical high to form a ridge of high pressure, he calls it a *ridge*. Figure 40 shows one. Should a low core be of the same shape, then its long axis would develop a *U*- or a *V*-shaped valley. He terms that a *trough*, as shown in

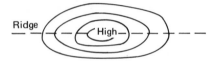

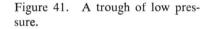

Figure 40.   A ridge of high pressure.

Figure 41.   A trough of low pressure.

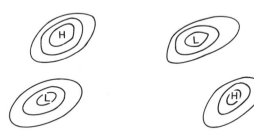

Figure 42.   An atmospheric col.

Figure 41. Added to the fund of crossword-puzzle ammunition can be a *col*. It is the sort of neck which develops in the central area between two highs on either side flanked by lows on the other two sides. Figure 42 has it.

None of these formations is static. Each is part of the fluid atmosphere; and, with it, will develop, move, merge, and dissipate. "Will-of-the-wisp" is certainly an apt phrase. And all of this mutation causes wind. The meteorologist, indeed, has a delicate task. He is looked to for reliable predictions, but his facts undergo constant change. If nothing else, a study of weather generates much empathy between citizen and science.

We've now reviewed in considerable detail the basics of general air circulation. What remains is to pursue some definable local circumstances which can modify the patterns. We're ready for topographical or local winds. Here we take the last step to restore to reality the fictional earth which was our model during last chapter's discussion.

As we saw then, the variety of land shape, material, and cover can modify temparture patterns. And from those changes pressure differences are bound to follow. At the outset, though, we must recognize that the diversity of modification is immense. Earth cover appears in numerous combinations. And the influences on resulting airflow are just as manifold. Alterations can be nearly constant or they can be seasonal. With reference to a limited area, such as one near a large industrial complex, they can even depend on the daily work schedule of a manufacturing plant.

For us to attempt a catalogue of all such factors, region by region, is folly. Far better on that score are a few hours spent reading *Coast Pilot* or *Sailing Directions* for an area. In condensed form the vagaries of local winds and weather will be found there. Equally worthwhile are visits to an office of National Weather Service. And don't overlook pierhead chats. Harbor pilots, tugboatmen, marine operators—they all have valuable information and a welcome eagerness to share it. A mother lode of local knowledge on winds can be uncovered at a nearby airport. This is particularly true if an experienced glider pilot is willing to be debriefed. He is condor-like in his feel for every nuance of air current in his region of operation.

What we can do, though, is to focus on the principles which underlie such topographical features. Then a quick study of surrounding terrain will key the influences one might expect to follow. Incidentally, a survey of the names given to local winds is like reading a roster of ships. It is immediately revealed how fruitful and apt is such a source to choose the name for a vessel. *Monsoon, Sirocco, Chubasco, Shamal*—they and many more appear. Controversy even raises its head on occasion. One school of thought insists that the name for a Southern California wind should be *Santana*; another just as forcefully maintains the name is *Santa Ana*. That *Coast Pilot* subscribes to the latter view is really not significant to our consideration. For we will outflank all such terminology as best we can. It is important, of course, to know the regional name given any disturbance of consequence. But of more importance is recognizing that, regardless of name, a particular conformation coupled with a prevailing condition will likely make a special kind of result.

The departure point for this discussion is the diurnal or daily wind reversal noted in coastal regions. During daylight hours the heat of the sun beating down on a coastal land mass will cause the ground to absorb more heat than adjacent water. By early or midafternoon, air over the land will be warmer, and so of lower pressure, than that over the sea. Basic Principle 4 now goes to work: high blows to low. The result is an *onshore* or *sea breeze*. Figure 43 depicts the motion.

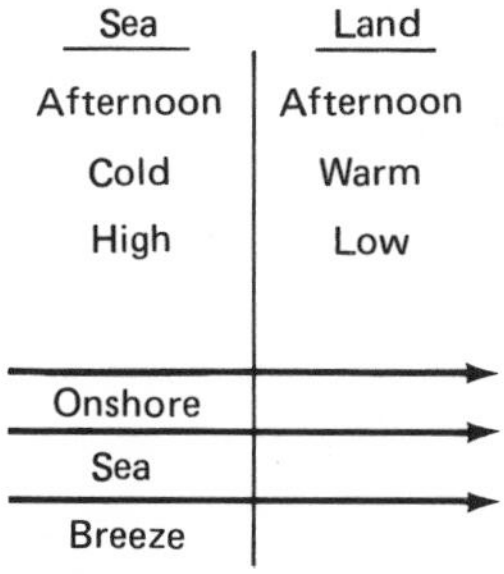

Sea	Land
Afternoon	Afternoon
Cold	Warm
High	Low

Onshore
Sea
Breeze
→

Sea	Land
Early morning	Early morning
Warm	Cold
Low	High

Offshore
Land
Breeze
←

Figure 43. From sea to land in the afternoon.

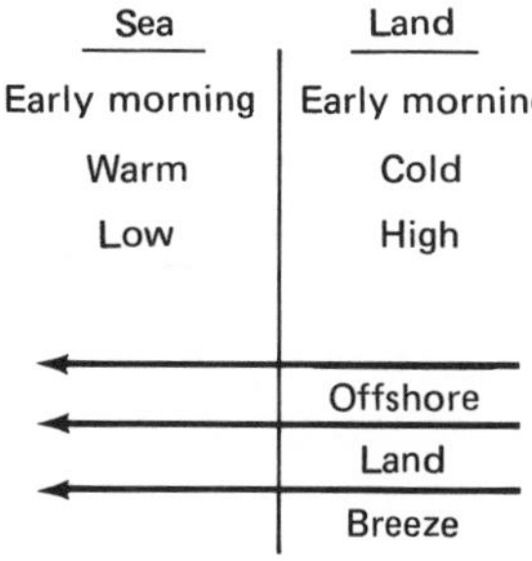

Figure 44. From land to sea in the morning.

But after sundown the land begins to radiate its heat. By early morning the situation is reversed. Now the land is colder than waters offshore. In turn, the air over the land is of higher pressure than that nearby. So the wind pattern reverses: high blows to low, of course; but now the flow is from land to sea. This is the *offshore* or *land breeze*. And Figure 44 shows the idea.

These patterns are most pronounced in the tropics, for there the contrast in land temperature between 3 P.M. and 3 A.M. is accentuated. But in many latitudes this daily transformation is quite evident.

In Asiatic regions the same principle develops to olympian proportions. For the *monsoon* is really no more in essence than an onshore-offshore pattern. We'll blithely bypass such critical trivia as the provincial conditions in Vietnam and Southeast Asia. There, local topography causes further changes in the patterns. But the basic idea of the monsoon is really much the same as any nearby land- and sea-breeze reversal.

Figures 45 and 46 sketch the subcontinent of India with the Indian Ocean to the south and the lofty Himalaya Mountains to the north. During the northern hemisphere's summer months the sun cycles regularly on its course to shed the focus of its heat on the land mass of India. By contrast, the Indian Ocean to the south is less beneath its rays. Day after day it adds more heat to India than it does to the adjacent ocean. By the time August comes the surface of India is warm; and the air mass sitting overhead is also warm and of low pressure. The Indian Ocean then is colder and its air mass is of higher pressure. Basic Principle 4 again: high blows to low. The result is the southwest monsoon, bringing moist air and floods to the continent.

Six months later, in February, the sun is tracing its daily path over the southern hemisphere. Now the ocean is warm compared to India. Over the land is high pressure and the wind reverses. This causes the northeast monsoon, sucking cold and dry air from the mountains and land. So the monsoon, at least on a general basis, can be reduced to an annual onshore-offshore wind.

Both the daily and annual sea / land wind reversals result because land abuts on water. The influence of shape and formation is next to be considered. At sea, contrasting water temperatures will certainly affect weather, but shape is of no influence since sea surfaces are at the same level.

Land, though, comes in a wide assortment of contours, and distinct patterns will have their way with wind. A mountain range can shunt air to a high altitude. It might even act as a dam, with air piling up against its side. A mountain pass can serve as a pipe through which air flows swiftly past the barrier. A deep canyon emptying to the shore along a rugged coastline sometimes spells trouble for the mariner. Wind at gale force

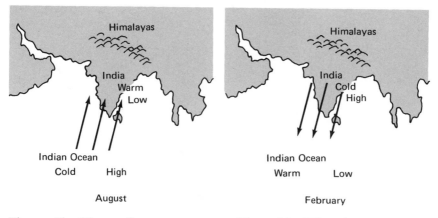

Figure 45. The southwest monsoon of summer.

Figure 46. Wintertime's dry northeast monsoon.

might spill through the break to cause a very dangerous local condition. A for instance? On the 20-mile coast south of Southern California's Point Conception. Even structures on earth cause diversity in wind flow. Aviators are well aware of the eddies and swirls to be expected near a large hangar at an airport.

As a general rule it is expected that a wind will follow the lines of least resistance, particularly if the wind is light. It will move along flat areas and avoid high banks and shores. Of course, given more force, or a temperature change or some other influence, the wind might overrun an obstruction. It is almost impossible to itemize the result for every time, place, and circumstance. But some of the more definable conditions have been analyzed and tagged. One such is the outcome when air encounters a mountain barrier.

Air will tend to flow up one side and down the other. That statement seems likely to become the week's most obvious remark. Even so, names have been given to the two flows. Warm air rising up the side of a hill causes an *anabatic* wind. The meaning of the label tells it all: a motion upward. As that air rises to higher altitudes it will cool. When cold air settles down the side of a mountain it is a *katabatic* wind. *Kata-*, like *cata-* in the more familiar *cataract*, means motion downward. Water falls down in a waterfall, and air flows down in a katabatic wind. Figures 47 and 48 illustrate these two concepts.

Downward winds have been further divided into *foehns* and *fall winds*. The foehn term is of Germanic origin and its pronunciation requires a knowing tongue. Rather than like Ma Bell's tele*phone*, it is closer to the

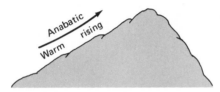

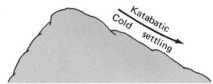

Figure 47. An upslope wind.   Figure 48. A downslope wind.

barnyard *hen*. However pronounced, though, the foehn is a classic type of local wind.

When air moving sideways encounters a mountain range it flows upward toward the top. As it does so it is cooled and dumps much of its moisture on the windward side. By the time it reaches the peaks it can be very dry. Then begins the descent. On the way down it warms and arrives at the bottom on the lee side as a dry wind, warmer than the surroundings. It arrives as a foehn. And its definition, then, could be a warm, dry wind with a downward component.

One such is the Rocky Mountain Chinook. Occurring in late winter, it can produce an early thaw, with snow melting into every rivulet and stream. *Bowditch* applies the foehn label to another such, of more importance to mariners—the Santa Ana (or is it really Santana?) of Southern California. A winter wind, says *Coast Pilot*, it descends with little or no barometric warning on the coastal plains from the northeast and carries unseasonably warm, parchy air through the Santa Ana canyon to the shore. Emerging near the boating center of Newport Beach, it pushes over coastal waters to a distance of about 50 miles. In prevailing weather the easterly shores of California's coastal islands are comfortable. During a Santa Ana they become lee shores, bringing problems. Also to be noted is the interaction of two local conditions when this wind is on the prowl. In early morning it can be reinforced by the offshore or land breeze, while in the afternoon it is weakened by the sea breeze.

The *fall wind* is quite a different thing. When air encounters a barrier and ascends to hurdle it, the result is cooling. That flow leaves the top and descends the other side as a cold wind. It, like the foehn, is warmed on the way down; but it reaches the bottom on the other side still colder than the neighborhood. It is a cold wind blowing down an incline. An example is the sudden gale in Mexico's Gulf of Tehuantepec. This Tehuantepecer starts in the Gulf of Mexico as a strong wind from the northeast quadrant. It piles up on the eastern slopes of Mexico's tall mountains and begins a climb toward the summits. In the southern neck of Mexico it finds its way through the mountain range. The result is a sudden breakthrough of cold air which gushes down over the Pacific coastline near Salina Cruz.

It is characteristic of these winds that there is no significant advance warning by a barometer. Both the foehn and the fall wind are, in effect, releases of dammed-up air which abruptly invade a particular region. They are not the same in principle, but do share some common traits. That might explain an occasional mixup in terminology. The conflict, though, should be of little importance to the practical mariner. Toward the end of the next chapter we'll find mention of a basis for distinction between them, but to know whether one was capsized by a fall wind or a foehn might well just be material for a logbook entry. Both blow vigorously and with little warning. At least, though, we can generate tolerance for those who dispute a particular definition. The old sailor's saying of "Different ship, different long splice" is sometimes appropriate to weather lore.

Residents of an area subject to these winds often seem to be "walking barometers." Their senses detect that the formula for the local blow is being concocted. A stranger to such a region is well served to seek local counsel and to keep track of weather developments on the other side of the mountains.

Fall winds are not restricted to the Gulf of Tehuantepec. Other examples are the Aleutian *williwaw*, the *bora* of the Adriatic, and the Argentine *pampero*. *Bowditch* also applies the name to the *mistral* of the western Mediterranean. Added to the list might be the *papagayo* of Central America's west coast. Even the *norther* gusting southward from Texas into the Gulf of Mexico is involved, for it has significant influence on the development of the Tehuantepec blow. Now, though, we are fast approaching that roster of ship names. It could be serviceable in completing a crossword puzzle to know the identification of the *shamal* as a northeast wind of the Persian Gulf, of Gibralter's strong easterly as a *levanter*, of the *simoon* as a desert wind. It might be noteworthy when cruising in Alaskan waters that in Juneau a williwaw is termed a *taku*. The Hawaiian mariner should be aware of *kona* weather, and those passing along California's northern coast might find value in the knowledge of Crescent City's nighttime *kickback*.

Each pattern, though, will usually come to rest in a recognizable niche. It might have spilled over a mountain to punish whatever is in its path, or it might have been forced up a normally lee slope because of changing pressures or temperatures. At the heart of the disturbance, though, will be a significant change in the conformation of the earth's surface cover. We come back full circle to our starting point on local winds. It is not feasible to index them all. Rather, the application of some informed common sense to observations of topography, to details gleaned from official references, and to conversations with those versed in local knowledge will produce far better comprehension of what one might expect to encounter.

Up ahead is a snug cove, free of pesky land contours which might cause some fitful wind. Time for us to slip gratefully under the lee of its headland and savor a lull from the rigors of our study of weather.

QUESTIONS

A col is being chased pell-mell over the horizon by a kona-clad taku riding a two-humped simoon. The only hope of rescue is for you to make a respectable score in this quiz. To arms! Sound the battle cry and stream the banners! *Allons, enfants de la . . .*

1. The form of pressure pattern shown would be
   a. anticyclonic.
   b. cyclonic.

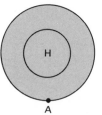

2. The wind direction at Point *A* in the northern hemisphere would be from the _____ quadrant.
   a. northeast
   b. southeast
   c. northwest
   d. southwest

3. Referring to the two pressure patterns shown, and assuming that isobars in each represent the same values, the winds would be stronger at
   a. A.
   b. B.

2 Miles

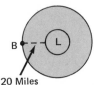

20 Miles

4. Atmospheric pressure of 30.50 inches is
   a. normal.
   b. lower than normal.
   c. greater than normal.

5. A daily pattern of pressure changes is
   a. for pressure to be lower at at 4 A.M. than at 10 A.M.
   b. more pronounced in tropical regions.
   c. both of the above.
   d. none of the above.

6. In early morning the wind is expected to blow from
   a. land toward the sea.
   b. sea toward the land.

7. Early in the year the monsoon of India blows, in general, from
   a. southwest toward northeast.
   b. northeast toward southwest.

8. Winds of Mexico's Gulf of Tehuantepec
   a. are called fall winds.
   b. have a downward component.
   c. both of the above.
   d. none of the above.

9. Anabatic describes a wind
   a. flowing up a slope.
   b. flowing down a slope.

10. A downward wind blowing from land to sea would tend to be stronger
    a. in the afternoon.
    b. in the morning.

ANSWERS

We have met the enemy and they are . . . whose? Allow the usual 10 for each correct response and then score the war games this way:

    100, Sighted simoon, sank same
     90, Send us more takus
     80, That taku was tough!
     70, Names withheld until notification of next of kin
    under 70, Advance to the rear!

1. b   6. a
2. a   7. b
3. a   8. c
4. c   9. a
5. c   10. b

Chapter 4

HEAT AND ITS CONSEQUENCES

So far our voyage toward understanding weather has been free of shoals. But now for a while we must thread a treacherous passage littered with bad water. What we are about to undertake is the subject of atmospheric heat and the ways in which it influences the air around us.

Underlying the discussion is the physics of heat. The atmosphere has been described as a heat engine. Following that view, water could be termed its fuel and the oceans its fuel tanks. To a great extent much of weather is tied to their interaction. Earlier we spoke of the earth as a radiator which transfers some of the sun's incoming heat back into the atmosphere. A good starting point now is to review what heat is all about.

Heat is energy. *Energy*, in turn, is the capacity for doing work. We need not wallow long in this bewildering maze, but a few more comments are necessary. Nature manifests this energy in several ways, and heat is but one such. What it involves is motion of the molecules of a substance. When the degree of heat is high—that is, when we use the term "hot"—the motion is rapid. The molecular particles are highly agitated, careening off each other with wild abandon. A hot body needs more room to contain this melee, so its volume must expand. When the heat value is diminished, the molecular free-for-all calms down. A result is that the body's volume diminishes. This expansion and contraction can accompany changes in the appearance or state of the material. It will back and fill, with appropriate changes in heat, among solid, liquid, and gaseous states.

The measure of heat can be by a variety of yardsticks. The physicist may speak of *British Thermal Units* or *BTUs*. Then, again, he might employ the word *calorie*. This last term is so familiar that our reflex action is an intake of breath to separate the waistline from its girdle of elastic. No matter how measured, though, heat is the cornerstone of much of our physical world.

Temperature is not heat. Rather, it measures the degree of heat. And over the centuries science has evolved quite an array of temperature scales. Kelvin, Rankine, Reaumur, Fahrenheit, and Celsius were all physicists whose names survive as labels for such measures. We have little need to understand them all, for Fahrenheit and Celsius are in widest lay use. But at least we can profit by a quick glance.

Of the five mentioned, the last three speak in relative terms. Reaumur, Fahrenheit, and Celsius developed scales to indicate the degree of heat relative to that in water as it passes from ice through liquid to a vapor. *Reaumur* we can shuck off quickly. His research showed that the difference in heat between water at the freezing point and water at the boiling point was divisible by 80. So his measure says 0° is equivalent to the heat in a quantity of water at the freezing point and 80° equals that in the same amount at the boiling point. The arithmetic, though, is so unhandy to us laymen that we do well to place him and his measure back on the laboratory shelf.

Celsius applied the centum system to the problem. He whacked up the heat values between freezing and boiling water into 100 parts or degrees. So we know his measure as one that says 0° is the degree of heat in freezing water and 100° is that in boiling water. Several generations of Americans recognized that scale as the *Centigrade*. But not too long ago the international fraternity of scientists embarked on a program to standardize terminology as well as to honor outstanding fellows, so Celsius is the now name for the old Centigrade scale. A bit of history is barely worth note. It seems that Celsuis first had his degrees reversed. 100° was for freezing water and 0° for boiling. With that in mind, precise honor to Celsius would require us to spell his name backward and label the scale as "Suislec." No matter, for the scale is now transposed. Celsius is Centigrade, and Centigrade is Celsius.

Fahrenheit, a contemporary of Celsius, mixed snow and common salt to fashion his starting point. His 0° represents the degree of heat in a 50–50 mixture of each. By his reckoning, plain old water's freezing point is 32° and its boiling point is 212°. He came up with 180 graduations for the span Celsius covered with 100; and the relationship between the two measures is based on the ratio of 180 to 100, or 9/5, with adjustment for Fahrenheit's head start of 32 numbers.

But the problem with these three scales is that each is married to water as the standard for measurement. To say that a horse weighs ten times as much as the average man is not to tell the weight of the horse unless the weight of the man is also known. In the same way, to say that the degree of heat is 0°C only tells that it is the same heat as that in water at the freezing point. Many substances common in a laboratory freeze and boil at degrees of heat far below and far above such an arbitrary standard as water. So, science was in the market for a system of measure disconnected from a standard. It sought one by which 0° would mean no heat at all, with inert molecules lying fallow. There is heat present in frozen water at 0°C, for its molecules are still flitting around. Science wanted to start from *absolute zero*, the point of no heat whatsoever. And the measuring sticks starting from there are *absolute* scales.

An English physicist, William Thompson, is associated with one such scale. Its name is *Kelvin*, for Mr. Thompson was later honored by the Crown as Lord Kelvin. He, of course, needed some pattern to space degrees from absolute zero up the line, and he adopted the Celsius scheme. So, a Kelvin scale is a reading from absolute zero in Celsius units. On it, $-273.15°C$ equals $0°K$ and $+273.15°K$ equals $0°C$.

William Rankine was honored by his scientific peers when his name was applied to another absolute scale. This one is graduated in Fahrenheit units. By the *Rankine* measure, absolute zero is $-459.67°F$ and $0°F$ equals $+459.67°R$. Figure 49 compares all five measures, and suggests it is time for us to heed the advice of P. T. Barnum. We should seek out the egress, for our lay world has little contact with Rankine, Reaumur, or, for that matter, the scale of Lord Kelvin.

Even so, what looms on the horizon is the tardy appearance of the metric system. With it will come much greater currency for the Celsius (not Suislec!) scale. It behooves us to have at hand a quick means to convert our familiar Fahrenheit to Celsius. Many nautical books contain a conversion table. *American Practical Navigator (Bowditch)* has one such. By it, Celsius, Fahrenheit, and even Kelvin become compatible. You'll find it reprinted in the "Ready Reference" section of this book as Table 9.

Suppose, though, Bowditch fell overboard and our "Ready Reference" should self-destruct in sympathetic grief. And suppose, further, that it was necessary to relate some *F* reading to a *C*. What then? More than one hand calculator with scientific notation would fill the gap. Pressing *F* or *C* buttons could flash an equivalent. But, now, another suppose. What if the hand calculator should fetch up on deck with scrambled circuits? Now what? The answer would be a formula, and there are several varieties. The two basic ones are that $F = 9/5 \, C + 32$ and that $C = 5/9 \, (F - 32)$. The aerologist's recipe $F = 9/5 \, (C + 40) - 40$ and $C = 5/9 \, (F + 40) - 40$

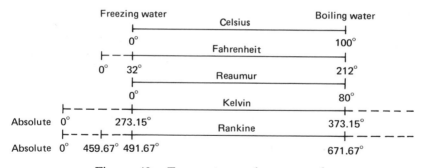

Figure. 49.   Temperature scales compared.

can also be useful. But whatever your approach when all these supposes might happen, test it first by converting 100°C to F. If the answer isn't 212°, it's high time for a change in formula.

Now a pointed question: How important is all this? More so than one would think! For the atmosphere *is* a heat engine, and its awesome power is better understood when one recognizes the nature of heat and of temperature. In and out from here on will be references to heat and to its degrees. Our diversion on this short aside was much worthwhile.

A few pages back we spoke of water freezing and boiling, and of its changes in state. Water, like substances in general, can exist as a gas, or it can condense into a liquid, or it can be a solid. Atmospheric water is no exception. When it is a gas we call it *water vapor*. In liquid form it is termed *water droplets, rain,* or *dew*. In solid form the tag is *ice, snow, hail, sleet,* or *frost*. The Rubicon separating its appearance as a solid from that as a liquid is called the *freezing point*. That setting apart its liquid and vapor states is termed the *vapor point*. The meteorologist applies specific terms to the processes involved, as shown in Figure 50. When water vapor becomes a liquid he terms the process *condensation*. The result is our rain or dew. When liquid switches to solid he terms it *freezing* and the outcome

Figure 50.   Processes of change in atmospheric state.

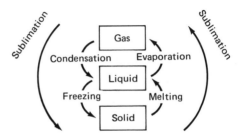

is hail, sleet, or ice. When the liquid graduates to a vapor he calls it *evaporation*, and when the solid upgrades to a liquid he calls it *melting*. Note, though, that water can leapfrog over liquid and pass from the gas to the solid state and from the solid to the gas. With nary a nod toward the realm of psychology, he calls that *sublimation*. We recognize the nonstop downshift from vapor to solid as frost or snow. Incidentally, let a meteorologist hear you describe frost as frozen dew and he is likely to show antisocial tendencies. Frost is not liquid water which has been frozen. It was never liquid at all.

Enough for that! More important to us is that all these processes are continually going on within the atmosphere. And each step involves enormous exchanges of heat. To warm a pound of solid water from 31°F to 32°F requires half a BTU. In metric terms that means half a calorie is needed to raise one gram of solid water from −1°C to 0°C. To transpose the same pound of solid water at 32°F to a puddle of liquid water at 32°F calls for the addition of a whopping 144 BTUs. Bringing the liquid puddle from 32°F to 33°F, and thereafter up the line toward evaporation, requires 1 BTU per pound. The metric measure is 1 calorie per gram per 1°C. Our focus, though, is more on the heat required to evaporate or to condense one pound or one gram. To flip a simmering pound of liquid water at 212°F to water vapor at the same temperature could involve more than 980 BTUs. In the metric system that is described as 540 calories to vaporize 1 gram of water at 100°C without a change in temperature. All day long, water is evaporating and condensing. And every time a pound of water, or even a gram, changes state there is an outsize exchange of heat, either by intake or release. The numbers are not important, but the principle is crucial. We live within a body of atmosphere constantly trading off huge amounts of energy.

Relatively speaking, there is not much water in the atmosphere. As water vapor it is an independent gas added to the ocean of air, and its maximum volume is seldom more than 4% of the total. But that little dab will more than do the job. Consider that dab tripping from gas to liquid to solid and back, with some sublimation thrown in for good measure, and you spotlight the gigantic forces of nature. No wonder the statement is made that water fuels the atmosphere's heat engine and that the ocean is the fuel dump. No wonder so many storms are ocean-spawned and fall to pieces when they run inland out of fuel.

Time to recap where we are. Water, in changing state and temperature, uses outlandish volumes of heat. This heat exchange so affects the atmosphere that it triggers colossal displays of energy which we recognize as atmospheric phenomena. The source of the heat, as we've seen, is the solar furnace. It has been noted already that little of this energy is transferred to the atmosphere on the inbound trip from the sun. Only by rebound from the earth does the atmosphere receive appreciable heat. Our next concern is how that energy is passed along to our ocean of air.

Figure 51 shows four means of heat transfer. *Insolation* we've already met in Chapter 1. By it, shortwave heat rays from the sun strike our atmospheric envelope. Barely half finds its way to the earth's surface. Our present attention is to the other three processes.

By *conduction* heat passes *through* a material. A painful example is burning an unwary finger on a hot skillet. The heat of the stove passes through the metal of the skillet to cause the outcry. Iron frying pans are highly conductive of heat, but air is not. In fact, air is a pretty good insulator. So the

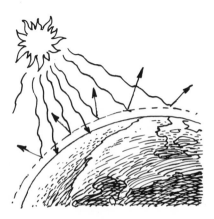

Insolation

Conduction

Convection

Radiation

Figure 51.   Methods of heat transfer.

sun's heat isn't readily passed along from the earth *through* the atmosphere by conduction. The process is at work, but only in the portion of the atmosphere touching the earth's surface. At that restricted level heat can pass between the surface and a film of air hovering above. But there the relay is likely to end. No further conduction of the heat "baton" through successive layers of air is to be expected.

Convection is another story. It deals with transfer by movement of the very substance heated. So, heat appears at the top of a kettle because water which was warmed at the bottom actually rose to the top. The atmosphere is, indeed, subject to such a transfer. Air heated by the earth does rise and carry with it heat to higher regions.

Radiation, the remaining process, is a standard means used by the earth to heat its atmosphere. Incoming sun rays are rebounded in longer wavelengths within the heat spectrum. The earth acts as a radiator and the air receives the benefit. It was mentioned a few chapters back that air closer to a radiator is warmer than that farther off. As Daedalus might have reasoned, temperature decreases with altitude.

What does all this suggest? An image of the atmosphere as a churning mass of air moving sideways as wind, vertically as convection currents, and trading off, from land and sea, water in one state or another. Our focus must narrow again.

The measure of water vapor in the air is called *humidity*, and there are several means of its expression. *Absolute humidity* speaks of the actual weight of water vapor in a measured *volume* of air. An example would be 5 grains or about 0.01 oz. per cubic foot. (A metric example is 11.5 grams per m³.) *Specific humidity* refers to actual weight of water vapor in a specified *weight* of air. An example would be 66 grains or 0.15 oz. per pound. (Metric would say 9.5 grams per kilogram.) Practical seafaring should have little contact with either of these measures. More a part of shipboard conversation is *relative humidity*. It is expressed as a percentage and is derived from this ratio:

$$\frac{\text{actual water vapor content in the air mass}}{\text{the capacity of that air mass to hold water vapor}}$$

In effect it is *water vapor present* divided by *water vapor capacity*.

The instrument used to make the measure is the *hygrometer* or, by more common description, the *wet- and dry-bulb thermometer*. Specifics on this device, as well as on thermometers in general, will be met in a chapter to come dealing with instruments. As a preliminary, though, we should discuss its general principle. Two thermometers are fitted side by side, with the bulb of one wrapped in a strip of muslin cloth. The end of the muslin is dipped in a vial of water. Wick-like, it soaks up water and wets the bulb. The two thermometers, then, are distinguished as the one with the wet bulb swaddled in muslin and the one with the dry bulb in direct contact with the atmsophere.

For water to evaporate it needs heat energy. To the extent that water evaporates from the wet bulb and its muslin into the atmosphere, it takes heat from the bulb. So there will be a difference in temperature readings between the two thermometers, and the amount of that difference is the key to the measure of relative humidity. In use, the dry bulb is read to learn prevailing atmospheric temperature. Then the wet bulb is read and the difference between them noted. When there has been a lot of evaporation, as in the case of dry air, the difference is great. When there has been little evaporation, as in the case of muggy air, the difference is small. When there has been no evaporation, as in the case of air filled to capacity with water vapor, there is no difference at all. Reference to special tables or graphs with the dry-bulb reading and the difference will then yield the percentage of relative humidity. In "Ready Reference" you will find Table 10 to do the job for Fahrenheit measures.

Note that there is a limit to the amount of water vapor a given air mass can hold. When that limit is reached the air is said to be *saturated*, and the relative humidity is 100%. The stage is set for a change in the state of atmospheric water. Switching from a vapor, it will seek to precipitate as a liquid or a solid. And the air mass is said to be at the *dew point*. Recasting this, we can say that the dew point is the temperature of saturation or of 100% relative humidity. Our "Ready Refence" has Table 11 as a guide to Fahrenheit dew points.

In order to trigger this precipitation or change in water state it is necessary that the air be saturated, that it have a relative humidity of about 100%, that it be at the dew point. But such a condition in itself is not the sole requirement. There must also be something for the water to precipitate *on*. When the air mass is in contact with a surface, such as the earth, then that surface supplies the base. The result would be condensation into dew if the temperature is above freezing. The outcome would be sublimation into frost if the temperature is below freezing.

What, though, if the air does not have a surface to act as a base? Then the atmosphere must fill the bill from its own components. It must contain microscopic particles, such as dust or salt. The water vapor puts them to work as nuclei or cores around which the change in state takes place. When the temperature is above freezing, tiny liquid water droplets will form. They then can collide with each other and grow into raindrops. When the temperature is below freezing the water may sublimate around the core in the lacy pattern of a snowflake. In any case, the two requirements of saturation and a base must be met.

The next question to answer is this: How does an air mass reach the saturation point? Simplicity would reply, "By receiving more water vapor." If it is only partly filled, then add more until its cup runneth over. Simplicity, though, is not always reality, as in this case. The usual means by which an air mass reaches saturation is by another route.

Cold air cannot hold as much water vapor as warm air can. As temperature decreases, the capacity to hold water vapor also decreases. Put another way, as temperature decreases, the relative humidity increases. It is by losing temperature that an air mass customarily becomes saturated. And now we are up to a critical nub of our review: In what manner and at what rate does the temperature of air change within the atmosphere? Here, if ever, is a sticky wicket requiring close attention. Decades of classroom experience discussing capsuled weather principles pinpoint this part of the study as most nettling. The normal mariner can live out his golden years without such punishment and, perhaps, never suffer the loss of enlightenment. But the principles have value. Even a porthole glance can assist in building a workable view of the hows and whys of everyday weather happenings such as clouds with all their fluff and streamers. We should undertake these next few pages expecting some bewilderment. What is absorbed will be helpful; what remains murky will by no means defeat our aim.

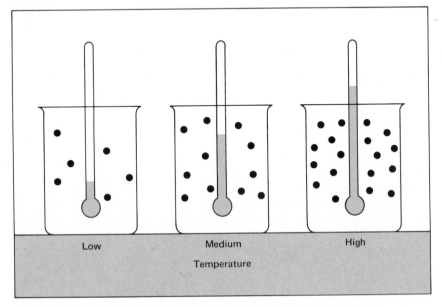

Figure 52.   Warm air holds more water vapor than cold air.

Let's first picture an air mass which is just resting on the earth and subject to no up, down, or sideways motion. Further, let's assume it is 5000 feet (1524 m) high. The temperature at the 1000-foot (305-m) level should be less than that at the surface, but more than that at the 2000-foot (610-m) level. We conclude this because temperature decreases with altitude. But by how much? There are several names for this rate of change: *vertical temperature gradient, existing lapse rate, vertical lapse rate,* and so forth. Whatever the name, the rate varies, and the causes of the decrease are also the reasons for its variations. As altitude increases, air is getting farther away from Radiator Earth. That is one obvious explanation for the drop in temperature. Also, though, whatever amount of water vapor there is in the air becomes less dense with expansion at lower pressures. That, coupled with the very process of expansion at levels where the pressure is less, produces even greater temperature drop. The same amount of water is not always present to become less dense; and, since pressure patterns are not constant, there is not always the same amount of expansion. The outcome is that what we'll hereafter call the *existing lapse rate* is not fixed.

Some authorities say it is a loss of 1°F for every 300 feet of altitude increase. This works out to 3.3°F per 1000 feet. Others describe it as 3.5°F for every 1000 feet. Those statements are averages only. Actual values fluctuate by composition and location of the air mass. They vary not only from place to place but even within the same pile of atmosphere from time to time. What prevails at the moment is what is important. And that temperature drop is the existing lapse rate from one altitude level to another within a particular air mass at a particular time. Since the seas will be running high for a while, we'll temporarily discontinue our double-standard practice of showing metric alongside the older units of measure. Existing *Bowditch* tables to which we might refer still speak of Fahrenheit; and, anyway, one adversary at a time is more than enough to encounter.

Figure 53 shows our air mass stacked 5000 feet high over a surface whose temperature is 70°F. We'll assume that the pile has the statistically average existing lapse rate; and to make the arithmetic easier, we'll take it as 3.5°F for every 1000 feet. The temperature drop could then be as marked in Figure 53.

But the atmosphere is by no means a uniform, tranquil mass. Within Figure 53's pile is a block of air which has been sitting over a hot, rocky base with a surface temperature of 80°F. That heated chunk in the center would tend to rise upward independently of, but still within, the total air mass, as shown in Figure 54. It leaves the surface at 80°F. What temperature change will it undergo?

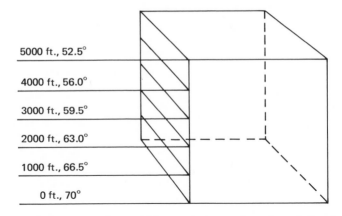

Figure 53. Temperature drop within an air mass when the existing lapse rate is 3.5°F per 1000 feet.

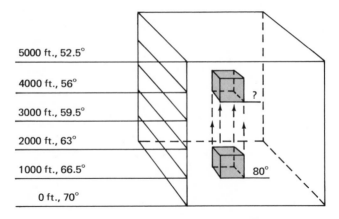

Figure 54. Warmer block of air rising within an air mass.

First off, we must remember that air is a poor conductor of heat. So, as the parcel rises, it will not tend to exchange heat with surrounding levels. It will not be cooled by air at the 1000-foot level or at the 2000-foot level. That doesn't mean it won't change temperature, for a new factor enters. As the chunk rises it reaches areas of lower pressure and so expands. That requires work and the expenditure of energy. The energy is found within the heat of the parcel. It will lose temperature because of expansion, and at a determined rate. For dry air this loss, called the _dry adiabatic lapse rate_, is pegged at 5.5°F for every 1000 feet. Figure 55 puts the show together for our example and indicates the comparison between the ascend-

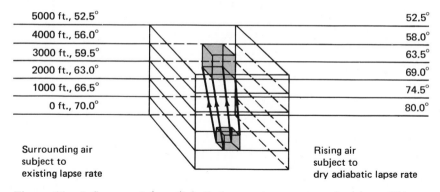

5000 ft., 52.5°		52.5°
4000 ft., 56.0°		58.0°
3000 ft., 59.5°		63.5°
2000 ft., 63.0°		69.0°
1000 ft., 66.5°		74.5°
0 ft., 70.0°		80.0°

Surrounding air   Rising air
subject to   subject to
existing lapse rate   dry adiabatic lapse rate

Figure 55. Influence of dry adiabatic lapse rate on warm air rising within an air mass.

ing block of air and its surrounding environment. The rising air would be warmer than its surroundings, level by level, until it reaches the 5000-foot mark. There the temperatures would equal.

What this means is just what you would expect. For as long as the rising block has a higher temperature than its level, it will continue to rise. But should it equal the prevailing temperature at a given height, then it will stop rising. Things are getting complicated, so we had better regroup our knowledge. Air temperature normally falls with altitude, and at a rate which can be measured with special equipment but which is by no means constant. This existing lapse rate averages 3.5° or so per 1000 feet and is due, among other influences, to increasing distance from Radiator Earth. But the temperature within a vertically moving air mass changes because of its change in volume. This is an *adiabatic* lapse: *a*- means "no" and *dia*- means "across." It disregards any influence of its environmental level and focuses only on the physics of heat lost or gained by expansion or contraction. It amounts to a decrease of 5.5°F for every 1000 feet of altitude increase and a gain of that much for every 1000 feet of decrease.

Now, stand by! Still another factor comes into play. This adiabatic rate was labeled as for *dry* air; and that restricts it to air which is not at the saturation point. It refers to air of 80% relative humidity, or 50% or 30% —but not 100%. Its air is not yet ready to flip the state of its water vapor. Should, though, that air be *moist* (that is, at the saturation point), and should a change of state take place, then another heat modification develops. During the process of condensation, air temperature *increases*. We experience that when warming air accompanies rain. So, rising air which is losing temperature by expansion will gain some back should it condense.

We can't say, then, that vertically moving air will always change temperature at the adiabatic rate of 5.5°F for every 1000 feet of altitude. That is only true if the air is dry. The offset of heat change by condensation on the way up or by evaporation on the way down will alter the rate. This brings us to the adiabatic lapse rate for moist air, another variable. The upshot seems to be that there can be a 5.5°F change per 1000 feet while the air is dry and minimized by a variable change when the air reaches the dew point. The consensus seem to average the net result as 3°F per thousand feet and label it as the *moist* or *pseudo-adiabatic lapse rate*. Don't despair! The worst might nearly be upon us, but it will soon be over. If we can master this adiabatic anarchy we will have cleared up a hefty part of the mystery.

Back now to our block of air within the 5000-foot pile standing patiently in Figure 55. That central parcel's dry-bulb reading at the surface would be the prevailing 80°F over the hot base. Suppose the wet-bulb reading by hygrometer was 66°F. The difference is 14° and we can put Tables 10 and 11 (in "Ready Reference") to work to learn some other facts. Table 10, entered with the dry reading of 80° and the difference of 14°, tells us that the relative humidity of the parcel at the surface is 47%. Enter Table 11 with the same 80° and 14° to find the dew point as 58°F. Should the temperature drop to that reading and should there be particles to act as nuclei, then water vapor would condense and a cloud of water droplets would form.

Refer again to Figure 55. The rising air would drop to 58°F at the 4000-foot level. There a cloud, visible evidence of the switch from water vapor to water liquid, could begin to show. What next, though? The rising air would now slow down its temperature drop, for it would be moist and change at a different lapse rate. We'll consider its moist or pseudo-adiabatic lapse rate to be 3.0°F for every 1000 feet. At the 5000-foot level it would not have dropped from 58° to 52.5°, as shown in Figure 55. That change presumed continuation of the dry adiabatic rate. Rather, it would have dropped only 3.0° from 58° to 55°. And when we compare 55° with what Figure 55 shows as 52.5° for the surrounding air at 5000 feet, we learn that the central parcel at that level remains warmer than its environment. It would continue to rise instead of stabilizing. Any cloud it might form would be vertically developed by the further updraft. We are now infringing on the next chapter, which discusses clouds and fogs; but at least a suggestion can be made. Combine temperature changes with dew points and changes in state to get at least a glimmer of some logic in all this welter. Just a few more pages and we can put into a port of refuge. This business of varying temperature lapses within an air mass all has to do with updrafts, downdrafts, clouds, fog, and even that troublesome demon, smog.

Time for our 5000-foot air mass to go off watch. Relieving him will be his more hulking mate, a 10,000-foot block of air, to act as model. In

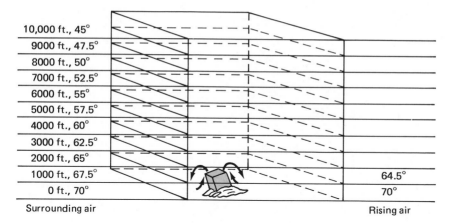

10,000 ft., 45°	
9000 ft., 47.5°	
8000 ft., 50°	
7000 ft., 52.5°	
6000 ft., 55°	
5000 ft., 57.5°	
4000 ft., 60°	
3000 ft., 62.5°	
2000 ft., 65°	
1000 ft., 67.5°	64.5°
0 ft., 70°	70°

Surrounding air   Rising air

Figure 56. Stable air mechanically lifted tends to return to its original position.

Figure 56 we see him influenced by an existing lapse rate of only 2.5°F for every 1000 feet. On the bottom he is warmed to 70° by Earth's surface. Then he cools off at the 2.5° rate to a temperature of 45°F at the 10,000 level. Within him a block of dry air encounters a sloping hill and begins to move upward. Such a nudge is called *mechanical lifting*. The surface temperature for all hands including the hill is 70°, so the parcel of air has no temperature reason to tend to rise. But reality dictates that within our 10,000-foot block, sufficient local vagaries exist to nudge that parcel over the hill. Immediately it will begin to lose temperature, and at the dry adiabatic rate of 5.5°F. With every inch of altitude it might gain it will become colder than its surroundings. For example, should it ever gain the 1000-foot level it will be at 64.5° compared to the surrounding 67.5°. Either the slant of the hill or some other external force must start the upward trend, for without such it has no reason to rise at all.

Such air would be termed *stable*. Any attempt to move it from its original position of equilibrium would be resisted. Equilibrium is the key. To begin with, that parcel is content to stay put. And when its inertia might be overcome by an upward push, it will want to return to the surface. The reason can be phrased this way: its adiabatic lapse rate of 5.5°F exceeds the existing lapse rate of 2.5°F. It will become colder, level for level, than its surroundings, and will seek to restore the original situation.

Figure 57 revisits what we've already seen in Figure 55. The existing lapse rate is a normal 3.5° and the dry adiabatic rate is its regular 5.5°. The chunk in the middle sits over hot rocks at 80° while the prevailing surface temperature around is 70°. That central parcel would begin to rise

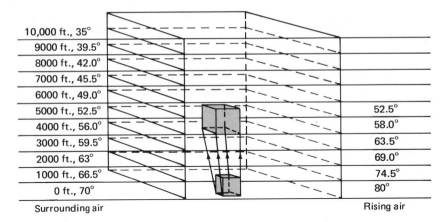

10,000 ft., 35°	
9000 ft., 39.5°	
8000 ft., 42.0°	
7000 ft., 45.5°	
6000 ft., 49.0°	
5000 ft., 52.5°	52.5°
4000 ft., 56.0°	58.0°
3000 ft., 59.5°	63.5°
2000 ft., 63°	69.0°
1000 ft., 66.5°	74.5°
0 ft., 70°	80°
Surrounding air	Rising air

Figure 57. Warm rising air will tend to come to rest when its temperature matches that of its surroundings.

because of its extra warmth. By the time it reaches 5000 feet the dry adiabatic rate would make its temperature equal that of the surroundings. So it would stop there and stay put. This is another case of *stability*. The displaced air rises to a new level of equilibrium and then comes to rest. And the reason is the same as before: the adiabatic rate of 5.5° exceeds the existing lapse rate of 3.5°.

Figure 58 suggests the story of Figure 56, but with a twist. This time the existing lapse rate is much more than normal. We'll peg it at 6°F for every 1000 feet. But the dry adiabatic rate of 5.5° still prevails. Our central block of air encounters the same hill met in Figure 56 and begins an upward trip. Even though at the surface it and the surroundings have the same temperature, mechanical lifting overcomes its resistance to change and makes it rise. In no way now can that ascending parcel be deterred. For so long as those rates persist, it will remain warmer than each surrounding level and will continue upward until a new lapse rate relationship develops. This is an example of *unstable* air, with warm rising and shouldering aside cold during its ascent. The reason? The adiabatic rate of 5.5° is less than the existing lapse rate of 6.0°.

Figure 59 shows a pesky and common relationship of lapse rates. So far we've paid little heed to such irritants as dew points, saturation, and the change in adiabatic rate because of condensation taking place while a chunk of air is vertically enroute. Figure 59 blows the whistle on such naïvete and brings us to task. We see there the same 10,000-foot air mass, still with a surface temperature of 70°F. The existing lapse rate this time

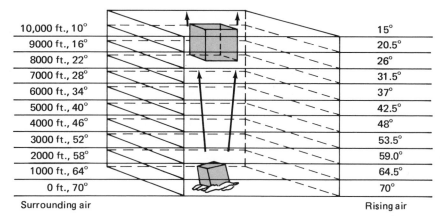

Surrounding air		Rising air
10,000 ft., 10°		15°
9000 ft., 16°		20.5°
8000 ft., 22°		26°
7000 ft., 28°		31.5°
6000 ft., 34°		37°
5000 ft., 40°		42.5°
4000 ft., 46°		48°
3000 ft., 52°		53.5°
2000 ft., 58°		59.0°
1000 ft., 64°		64.5°
0 ft., 70°		70°

Figure 58.   Unstable warm air rising will tend to continue its ascent.

Surrounding air		Rising air
10,000 ft., 30°		40°
9000 ft., 34°		43°
8000 ft., 38°		46°
7000 ft., 42°		49°
6000 ft., 46°		52°
5000 ft., 50°		55°
4000 ft., 54°		58°
3000 ft., 58°		63.5°
2000 ft., 62°		69.0°
1000 ft., 66°		74.5°
0 ft., 70°		80°

Figure 59.   Conditionally unstable air undergoes a change in lapse rate when the dew point is reached.

is 4° for every 1000 feet. At the top of that pile the air temperature is a chilling 30°F. Our central parcel sits over a heated surface and shows 80° at its base. So up it starts, cooling off at the standard dry rate of 5.5°. Somewhere between 6000 and 7000 feet it would equal its surroundings. The outcome will be stability at that level.

Now, though, we'll add some conditions. Our centerpiece leaves the surface with a relative humidity of 47% and with a dew point of 58°. When that parcel reaches 4000 feet it will be at the dew point and ready to change its water from vapor to liquid. At that level the ascending block is still warmer than its surroundings, for the prevailing temperature at 4000 feet, says Figure 59, is 54°. Now the upward-bound block will begin to cool off at a slower rate. The moist or pseudo-adiabatic rate is in vogue and we'll specify it as 3.0° for every 1000 feet. The parcel will continue to ascend because, level for level, it remains warmer than its environment. What has happened is that the existing lapse rate of 4° is *between* the adiabatic rates of 5.5° for dry and 3.0° for moist. The mass will be stable until saturation is reached; then, since the existing rate thereafter exceeds the moist adiabatic rate, the mass will become unstable. This is called *conditional instability,* for the mass will undergo a change in its state of equilibrium due to a change in its adiabatic rate.

Time, again, for a very pointed question or two: Why should the practical mariner be concerned with these niceties? Can he make any use of the information or, for that matter, can he even acquire such data as existing lapse rates thousands of feet above him? Well, now! Knowledge, says the seer, is never to be despised. Of course, the voice of an old farmer might be heard cautioning, "Stop milking when the pail is full!" There is a point of diminishing returns, and we see it close aboard. Even so, there is solid value to this discussion.

Normally the atmosphere tends toward instability, for temperature normally decreases with altitude. Low-level air wants to rise and air higher up wants to sink. The result is a sort of head-over-heels motion mixing up the air mass. But conditions of stability can develop. Should the low air be colder than that above, it would tend to stay at the surface. Chapter 6, dealing with fogs, will speak of such stability in more or less this way. In early morning, land cover is cold and air contacting it will also be cold. Should that low air be colder than layers higher up, there will be no head-over-heels action. Lowdown stays down and keeps with it whatever condensation might have occurred. We are now talking of a ground fog at dawn. We are also speaking of a *temperature inversion.* Instead of following the customary trend of decreasing with altitude, the temperature increases with altitude. Figure 60 gives the idea.

Sometimes that kind of abnormality can develop above the surface, as shown in Figure 61. The temperature might have been dropping up to a level of, say, 2000 feet; but then it begins to invert its tendency. For the next 2000 feet the temperature is rising. Thereafter, it resumes its normal decline. What could now occur is the fashioning of an atmospheric *lid.* Air below the 2000-foot level would be blocked from going up. It, and whatever pollutants it might contain, would stay trapped near the surface. Let topography lend a hand by ringing a population basin with mountains downwind and you might be smog-beset in Southern California.

Toward the end of Chapter 3 we were told that coming up would be some further mention of a foehn. What happens to air moved along by

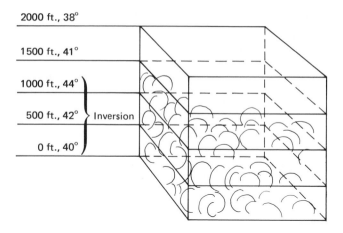

Figure 60.   A temperature inversion produces a low fog.

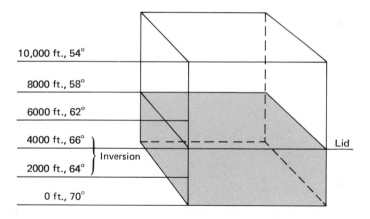

Figure 61.   A temperature inversion at altitude fashions an atmospheric lid.

this unique wind provides a striking example of the results of change from moist to dry adiabatic rates. Figure 62 pictures moist air ascending the side of a mountain barrier. The locale could be southern Europe with Mediterranean air flowing northward over the Alps, or it could be western North America when Pacific air moves eastward to climb the Rockies. In either case the outcome would be a foehn- or chinook-type wind. Figure 62 shows that when the air reaches the 4000-foot level on the windward side its temperature is 50°F and it is at the dew point. Condensation will begin and will continue as the air climbs upward. On that side, clouds will form and precipitation could occur. And when the air reaches the 10,000-foot

10,000 ft., 32°		10,000 ft., 32°
9000 ft., 35°		9000 ft., 37.5°
8000 ft., 38°		8000 ft., 43°
7000 ft., 41°		7000 ft., 48.5°
6000 ft., 44°		6000 ft., 54°
5000 ft., 47°		5000 ft., 59.5°
4000 ft., 50°		4000 ft., 65°

Figure 62.   Chinook winds occur when the lapse rate changes as air crosses a mountain barrier

top, it is wrung out of moisture. Note particularly that during the passage from the dew point level to the top, the air was cooling at the moist adiabatic rate of, say, 3°F for every 1000 feet. By the time the summit is crossed, the temperature is 32°.

Now, though, the air is dry, and starts its downward motion subject to the dry adiabatic lapse rate of 5.5°F for every 1000 feet. It will warm up at that rate and will arrive back at the 4000-foot level at a temperature of 65°F. The downward flow will be warm, dry, and cloud free. In crossing the mountains the air will have risen 15° in temperature and undergone a great decrease in relative humidity. There is not a lot of seafaring on the eastern slopes of the Rockies, nor, for that matter, on the north slopes of the Alps. But the example is still apt to point out the mechanics of what takes place in an air mass.

Understanding weather requires that we at least recognize what influences come into play. The suggestion is valid, of course, that the practical mariner is not usually supplied with details on temperature, pressures, humidities, and dew points on every story of the skyscraping air mass towering above. And without such details he is shorthanded in making predictions. Meteorologists invoke the aid of instrument's packages carried aloft by a host of air vehicles from balloons to rockets and aircraft. Surface bound, we must limit our observations to what seems to be happening or to what seems already to have taken place. But there lies our justification for fussing with adiabats and their ilk. In order to interpret what we see at altitude we must have some general idea of underlying factors.

Moreover, we are not so far removed from practicality. Some of this background can be put to work to measure cloud height. The procedure is not always applicable and the results are "more or less" in value. Even so, we owe ourselves an exercise. Here is the rationale. The dry adiabatic lapse rate of 5.5°F per 1000 feet tells us the temperature decrease within rising air. It is also said that the dew point of such air decreases at the rate of 1°F per 1000 feet. The result is a sort of stern chase by air temperature after dew point; they approach at the rate of 4.5° for each 1000 feet. From that relationship we gain a means for the surface observer to estimate the height of some cloud bases.

The steps are simple. The first procedure is to measure surface air temperature, both wet and dry, and to determine the surface dew point. Then the difference between dry air temperature and the dew point is divided by 4.5°. The result is the expected cloud base altitude in thousands of feet. Here is an example. On the surface the hygrometer readings are 80°F dry bulb and 68°F wet bulb. We are to estimate the altitude of the cloud base hovering overhead. Here are the steps:

1. The difference between dry-bulb and wet-bulb readings is 12°F. We enter Table 11 (found in "Ready Reference") with the dry-bulb reading of 80°F and the 12° difference to find that the surface dew point is 62°F.
2. Next, we determine the difference between the dry-bulb reading and the dew point. In this case it is 18°F.
3. The last step is to divide that 18° difference by 4.5°. The result is 4. We estimate cloud base to be at 4000 feet above the surface.

There are limitations to this approach. First off, it will only work when clouds are formed by convection currents. That restricts use to cumuliform clouds, or those formed by air being lifted. Second, the observer must be within the rising air mass. He can't measure dew point in one air mass and ask it to key cloud height within another. Don't expect this to work out for clouds viewed over the horizon a score of so miles away. Nonetheless, the simplicity of the procedure recommends that it be known.

It was previously advertised that we would shortly deal with clouds and fogs. There the distinctions between cumuliform and other forms of clouds will be further emphasized. When we encounter that study, keep in mind the dew point / air temperature relationship. That, coupled with the tussle we've had during this chapter, should make us better prepared to take the discussion in stride.

The old farmer is muttering again, for milk is spilling out of the pail. Time to take a well-earned break from matters meteorological.

QUESTIONS

Things are getting serious! This is not the time for us to set our quiz in the background of Reaumur chasing sublimating adiabats, or in any other light-hearted scene. Tight-lipped and taut-nerved, we face up to the reckoning.

1. When water vapor changes state to liquid, the process is called
   a. fusion.
   b. evaporation.
   c. condensation.
   d. sublimation.

2. Air is a _____ conductor of heat.
   a. good
   b. poor

3. _____ is most commonly measured on shipboard.
   a. Relative humidity
   b. Specific humidity
   c. Absolute humidity

4. As temperature increases, the relative humidity
   a. increases.
   b. decreases.

5. Cold air can hold _____ water vapor than warm air.
   a. less
   b. more

6. The dry adiabatic lapse rate
   a. is 5.5°F for every 1000 feet of altitude.
   b. is more than the moist or pseudo-adiabatic lapse rate.
   c. both of the above.
   d. none of the above.

7. Assuming that the surface temperature throughout all parts of an air mass is equal and that no condition of mechanical lifting is present, when the adiabatic lapse rate exceeds the existing lapse rate, air within the air mass will tend to
   a. rise.
   b. be stable.
   c. both of the above.
   d. none of the above.

8. When a parcel of air within an air mass is forced upward and its adiabatic lapse rate is less than the existing lapse rate, that parcel would be termed
   a. unstable.
   b. stable.

9. Conditional instability describes a condition when the existing lapse rate
   a. is more than both the dry and moist adiabatic lapse rates.
   b. is less than both the dry and moist adiabatic lapse rates.
   c. is between the dry and moist adiabatic lapse rates.

10. A temperature inversion exists when air temperature
    a. decreases with altitude.
    b. increases with altitude.

11. And, now . . . for extra credit! While cumulus clouds float overhead, you consult a hygrometer aboard and find that the dry bulb reads 70°F while the wet bulb reads 64°F. By referring to Tables 10 and 11 (found in "Ready Reference") you determine that
   a. the relative humidity is 72%.
   b. the base of the cumulus cloud formations is 2000 feet above the sea.
   c. both of the above.
   d. none of the above.

ANSWERS

Now is the time to encounter reality. The scoring pattern remains as 10 for each correct answer, and the personality is profiled this way:

   100, Tranquility
   90, Slight tremors
   80, Somewhat uptight
   70, Environment?
   under 70, Heredity!

Should you be successful with Question #11, then advance one level up in the ranking. If you are already at a tranquil 100, award yourself the rare Order of Euphoria with Cumuliform Cluster.

   1. c   6. c
   2. b   7. b
   3. a   8. a
   4. b   9. c
   5. a   10. b

11. c
Solution:

(1) Dry 70° —Wet 64° = 6° Dry-Wet difference
(2) Table 10, entered with Dry 70° and 6° difference = 72% relative humidity
(3) Table 11, entered with Dry 70° and 6° difference = 61° Dew Point
(4) Dry 70° —Dew Point 61° = 9° Dry-Dew Point difference.
(5) 9° ÷ 4.5° = 2
(6) Cloud base is at 2000 feet.

Chapter 5
CLOUDS

Clouds should be included on any roster of shipboard weather "instruments." And since instrumentation is often directly proportional to the size of the vessel, yachtsmen and other operators of small craft should place these natural aids high on the list. They don't relate a full weather story; in fact, all by themselves they tell little. But in the context of such factors as how they change and travel, the tale they tell can be considerable.

The cloud we see floating serenely in the atmosphere contains water, but by no means is all of it in the gaseous state. Water vapor is invisible. Only when it has made the switch to liquid or solid, as in a cloud, does it become apparent to our eyes. So a cloud is evidence that air has reached the dew point and that condensation, sublimation, or some other "-ation" is taking place. We had better attend to such matters as the "how" and "where" of this change.

When a cloud's water has switched to liquid or solid, its new state depends on the temperature. We can say that there are "wet" clouds holding water droplets when the temperature is above freezing; we can say there are "solid" clouds containing ice particles when the temperature is below freezing. Of course, should an aircraft fly into one there is no sensation such as plunging into a vat of water or ramming a bank of ice. The particles, whichever state, are widely diffused throughout the atmosphere of the cloud. They are bobbing around within its confines, buoyed up by air currents, rising, falling, colliding, and doing whatever else comes naturally. But, as water, they are either liquid droplets or tiny solids.

Let's introduce our survey with an inquiry into how this comes about. We already have in hand some of the essentials. When water vapor is reduced to its dew point and there are microscopic nits of matter present to serve as nuclei, then the vapor will precipitate on the nits as liquid or as solid. We've seen that a way for the dew point temperature to be reached is by lifting vapor-laden air to higher altitudes. So, the how could be answered simply by saying air is cooled as it is forced to higher altitudes. This is not a comprehensive answer, but will serve for a first glance. Now we can retrieve from the memory bank some principles seen in the last chapter and put them to work.

Stable air, we learned, is that which has an adiabatic lapse rate greater than the existing lapse rate. Should it be forced to rise it will cool faster than surrounding air. At some level it can reach the same temperature as its environment, find equilibrium, and come to rest. If the temperature at that level is also the dew point, its water vapor could there condense into a sheet. The cloud form would be spread out. It would be a *stratus* form. Figure 63 shows the result.

When unstable air is ascending, it tends to keep going up because its adiabatic lapse rate is less than the existing rate. It doesn't cool as fast as its environmental level. Even so, it could still drop to its dew point. When that is reached, the water vapor will begin to condense. But the air is still rising, so condensation will take place on the move. The cloud will be vertically developed or accumulated, and the result would be a *cumulus* form. Figure 64 shows what would happen.

Stable or unstable, the air has to begin an ascent. That can be triggered in several ways. In one case, local heating can raise its temperature to one greater than its surface environment and initiate an upward current. Another time, topography can do the job. An upslope of land might nudge the mass skyward and start the process. We'll see later that a block of colder air at a weather front can act as a similar wedge to begin the upward motion.

There is a fourth means we've not yet encountered. This brings us to convergence and divergence. When airflows seems to be converging into one area, the result will not be a crowded surface mass of air at the intersection. Instead, the converging air will create an updraft. There would be upward motion due to *convergence*. The other side of that coin shows air diverging from a central area. All that air streaming out from the center will not produce a surface vacuum, of course. Instead, it will leave room for air at altitude to descend into the intersection. Such a *divergence* would

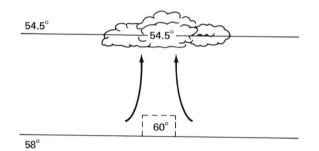

Figure 63.   Dew point and surrounding air temperature coincide to produce sheet-like clouds.

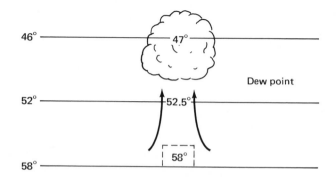

Figure 64.   Unstable air condenses while still rising
to form vertically developed clouds.

cause a downdraft. Figure 65 illustrates the idea. It is pretty obvious, then,
that the convergence of air flow toward a surface point is another way air
can be lifted aloft to start the cooling process.

The general principles of how air can cool are not too difficult to grasp.
Now for a quick look at where this cooling might take place. The sky
has been divided into blocks or zones according to altitude; and with laud-
able directness they have been labeled as *low, middle,* and *high.* Not so
troublefree is the assignment of heights to the dividing lines between the
zones. One school of thought aims to define the lines of demarcation by
averaging the heights at which a cloud's lower structure or base seems to
form. By that thinking, low extends from near the surface to about 6500
feet, middle stretches from there to about 20,000 feet, and high reaches
from that level up. Another school inserts the influence of latitude; accord-
ingly, low is left alone as a zone ending at 6500 feet, but middle and high
are subject to adjustment. In equatorial regions, middle is then said to

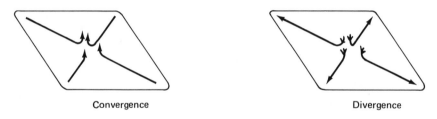

Convergence   Divergence

Figure 65. Surface air converging inward causes an updraft; divergence outward at the surface produces a downdraft.

reach to 25,000 feet and high to begin at 20,000 feet. Having sewn the seeds of puzzlement, that view goes further to point out that in areas near the poles, middle might reach only to 13,000 feet and high can start at 10,000 feet or even lower. Still another precinct will set the limits as 8000 feet for the division between low and middle, but hold onto 20,000 feet as the threshold from middle to high. Yet to be counted are the votes from the metric party.

All this can be mind-boggling to the observer on the average craft. There are, surely, valid reasons for the distinctions; but he is bound to ponder how essential they might be to his purpose. Without pilot balloons, ceilometer, or high-flying homing pigeon, he cannot judge cloud heights with such nicety. And anyway, cloud nomenclature involves appearance as well as any guesstimate of altitude. What we'll do to lessen the anguish is accept as fact that cloud heights can vary by region and then make artful use of the word "about." Figure 66 pegs the divisions as first defined. *Low* is shown as from near the surface to about 6500 feet, *middle* is from about 6500 feet to about 20,000 feet, and *high* is above a level of about 20,000 feet.

Simplicity would now suggest that we put the picture together in the manner seen in Figure 67. There we have classified clouds as formed either horizontally or vertically and in the three zones by altitude. Note the maverick, the cloud which doesn't respect any one altitude region, but rises through two or even three. It is a cloud with great vertical development.

A few paragraphs back, mention was made of cloud appearance. In 1803 a Mr. Luke Howard introduced such as a basis of distinction. Whether he had a well-trained pigeon to bring back high-level data has found no mention in history; but, certainly, in those early years he was not equipped with today's array of instruments. So, perhaps his approach has survived because it still applies to the situation of us modern lay weather watchers. In any case, he based a pattern on what he saw as the three primary forms of clouds. The classification he proposed was this: *cirrus*, for fiber-like

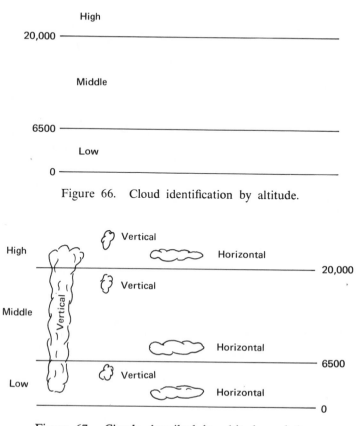

Figure 66.   Cloud identification by altitude.

Figure 67.   Clouds described by altitude and form.

strands extending in any direction: *cumulus*, for flat-based heaps extending upward; *stratus*, for horizontal sheets widely spread out.

Over the intervening decades Howard's basic approach has been shaped and extended to obscure his original idea somewhat. In fact, it would seem that on occasion present-day usage is barely connected to what was first suggested. Yet, our reaction should be: no matter. Possibly we all know someone called Johnson whose father's name was not John. Let's just accept that clouds are classed by appearance as well as altitude, and have a go at breaking the code of labels. Thereafter will come the really important aspects of cloud watching—recognition and portent.

Cloud nomenclature frequently involves a compound name. The forward half tells one story and the after half another. Marshalled here are the bow and stern sections of the more significant combinations, with a few complete hull forms thrown in for good measure. As you look them over,

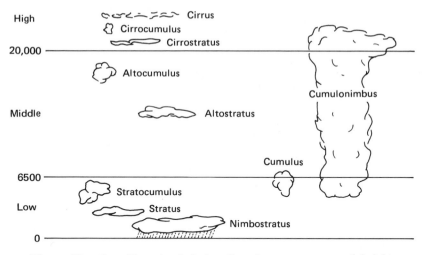

Figure 68. Prevailing cloud designations by appearance and height.

refer to Figure 68. It places the combinations in the presently accepted mode by altitude.

alto- really suggests *high,* and is sometimes described as referring to a thin cloud that appears above its normal level. As a prefix, though, it is used to identify a cloud in the *middle* zone of the sky.

cirro- comes from *curl.* If appearance were the only criterion, this would fit nicely as a description of Howard's feathery clouds. But when used as a prefix it identifies a cloud in the *high*-altitude zone.

cirrus, a compete name, refers to a specific cloud form. It is very high, is composed of ice particles, and appears as delicate curls, feathers, or tufts of white sprinkled miles above the earth.

cumulo- or *-cumulus* can appear forward or aft in a compound name. They both emerge from Latin roots meaning *heap* or *mass.* Howard might now be nodding agreement, for that was probably what he had in mind. And today either one of them still suggests a vertically developed pile.

cumulus all by itself speaks of a particular cloud type, with a dome rising from a flat base.

fracto- and *-fractus* present no problem. They should refer to a broken-up or fragmented cloud structure, and that they do.

nimbo- and *-nimbus* have to do with clouds from which rain is either very likely or already falling.

strato- is another prefix. Its derivation is from a Latin word meaning *spread out.* But as a prefix it speaks of a cloud in the *low* part of the sky.

-stratus as the trailing part of a compound name not only is derived from

spread out, but also means that. It labels a cloud as sheet-like or layered.

Stratus is a complete name without a fo'c'sle head or poop. It speaks of a low-level sheet which covers a great part of the sky.

What emerges in Figure 68 seems to be a pattern combining the two approaches of appearance and altitude. In the high department are found *cirrocumulus* and *cirrostratus* clouds. The "cirro-" identifies them as high. The second half of each name describes the appearance. Cirrocumulus is high and vertically developed; cirrostratus is high and horizontally developed. Also in the high region is the *cirrus* type, showing its wisps and curls.

The *middle* zone has *altocumulus* and *altostratus*. "Alto-" places them in the middle region; "-cumulus" and "-stratus" speak of their development.

In the *low* portion of the sky are found *stratocumulus* and *stratus*. For the first one, "strato-" indicates the altitude zone and "-cumulus" tells of development. Consistency might suggest that the same pattern be used for the second to produce the name stratostratus. But that is double-talk, with one too many strats. Its name is shortened to just stratus to describe both height and appearance. There's another cloud in this zone: *nimbostratus*. Our previous discussion would rightly suggest that this is a low, shapeless layer and a rainmaker.

Not respecting any altitude level are two other classes. *Cumulus* doesn't earn a "cirro-," "alto-," or "strato-" to peg its height. Without reference to zones, the term covers a vertically developed mass rising from a horizontal base. As for *cumulonimbus*, it is a towering mountain caused by great vertical development and standing ready to dump all kinds of water from its massive body.

This review shows a more or less plebian approach to the clouds. But discretion would again dictate a trade-off of precise definition for clear understanding of the general idea. The Latin scholars have gone much farther to create a formidable array of modifying barnacles to shade the meaning of a basic term. Examples are *castellated* to describe a turreted cumulo- type, *floccus* to speak of wool tufts, *lenticular* to suggest a sort of double-convex-lens appearance, *incus* to label the horn of a thundercloud's anvil, and *mammato-* for the bag-like protuberances hanging down from the underside of severe thunderclouds. Substituted for this last term could well be femme fatale. Mammato-cumulus are the fascinating but frightening structures from which vicious tornadoes are often spawned.

But more important than a recital of the entire litany of cloud formations is recognition of cloud structures. That, coupled with an understanding of what weather conditions might keep them company, is a much more worthwhile goal. We shouldn't expect, though, any magical pellet of wisdom to supply that knowledge. Clouds are as disparate as people, and almost just as difficult to pigeonhole. Arrays of "representative" forms will not tell the story nearly as well as interpretation of actual observations in the light of basic principles.

Next comes a series of cloud photographs accompanied by comment on manner of formation and associated weather. We should view them as "for instances" only. Absent the context of such "here and now" factors as values of pressure, temperature, and humidity, no certain prediction of clear skies or rain can be made on these alone. Even so, they are a start. Let's take them on, one by one, and learn what they try to tell.

LOW CLOUDS (UNDER 6500 FEET)

Figure 69 is a classic low-level sheet. Rising air has reached the dew point at a uniform level and spread out its condensation into a thick, fog-like layer composed of water droplets. Viewed from underneath it appears dark; from above it is white. No violent weather patterns are suggested. The air is stable and not subject to much buffet or churn. Poor visibility and drizzle, though, can be expected. And if the form is nimbostratus, then heavy rain or snow is falling. To observe nimbostratus is already to be in the presence of conditions which cause precipitation. This cloud form, we'll learn shortly, often appears when a warm front has been passing through. To learn from observers to the westward that nimbostratus is pelting them with rain is forewarning that your turn is close at hand.

Figure 69. Stratus thickening to nimbostratus. (*NOAA*)

Figure 70.   Wind-ripped sheet clouds become fractostratus. (*NOAA*)

Figure 70 shows what happens when strong winds break the stratus up into ragged swatches of *scud*. When that form tags along with nimbostratus the forecast is really a now-cast: bad weather with wind and precipitation is in progress.

Figure 71 shows stratocumulus formed by air condensing while still being lifted, and piling up above a more-or-less level base. The effect is quite evident near the horizon. The water state is liquid, for the temperature beneath 6500 feet would usually be above freezing. The weather indications are overcast sky with either rain to come or already felt.

Figure 72 displays stratocumulus as the end product of cumulus (Cu) masses spreading over the sky. The prospect would be for clear nights and fair weather unless the scattered tufts should merge into a sheet of rain-producing nimbostratus (Ns). The soft, gray rolls of this stratocumulus are wind-driven in the direction of their short dimension and can vary in altitude within the low range.

MIDDLE CLOUDS (6500 TO 20,000 FEET)

The thin, semitransparent veil seen in Figure 73 is made up of water droplets with, possibly, ice particles at high levels. The sun and moon

Figure 71. Stratocumulus threatening rain. (*NOAA*)

Figure 72. Fair weather stratocumulus. (*NOAA*)

Figure 73. Watery sky of altostratus. (*National Center for Atmospheric Research*)

Figure 74. Altostratus thickening for rain.

would appear as if seen through ground glass, but without halos. This formation suggests air wedged upward by encounter with an underlying air mass and condensing at the line dividing them. Weathermen consider altostratus as the least ambiguous cloud form. Its guileless evidence is that warm air, flowing over a wedge of cold, is condensing into a sheet of overcast. The prognosis is for continuous rain or snow. A few chapters on we will be discussing weather fronts. Altostratus is a most credible witness to the onset of a warm front and its murky weather.

In Figure 74 the thickened altostratus (As) is lowering into dark gray nimbostratus (Ns). Forming on the underside would be *virga*, the whiskers of rain. The water state is probably liquid, and the whiskers should soon sprout into a full beard of rain or, perhaps, snow. Sometimes the liquid fallout doesn't survive the trip to the ground, but reevaporates into the atmosphere. Then the cloud cover wears a misty stubble on its underside.

Turreted altocumulus (Ac) appears in Figure 75. The scattered cloud tufts, formed by air ascending while being cooled through the dew point, are white or gray but not numerous enough to cause definite shadows. The water state would be liquid, with ice particles possible at high levels. This is a fair-weather formation. Should, though, the pattern thicken and lower, then some thundery weather with showers might result.

Figure 76 shows a more widespread cloud cover of altocumulus (Ac). A fairly regular wave pattern separated by some clear spaces should be apparent. If this pattern parades ahead of cumulus clouds, then the anticipation would be stronger that short-term thunderstorms are imminent.

The two pictures in Figures 77 and 78 show altocumulus in strengthening concentrations and building toward definite promise of stormy skies. In Figure 77 the altocumulus is in an advancing layer or two of irregular thickness. In Figure 78 the clouds reach out from the horizon to spread and thicken over the sky.

The photographs in Figures 75–78 indicate that altocumulus clouds appear in varying subforms to signal varying weather. What can be expected depends on what company these clouds keep. Parallel rolls or bands might forewarn of an invading warm front. When in the vanguard and on the flanks of altostratus layers they warn of rain. A line of castle-like altocumulus rising from a uniform base tells of impending change to chaotic, thundery weather.

More mutations of the species altocumulus are seen in Figures 79–81, and it doesn't take the practiced eye of a Luke Howard to recognize that dirty weather is nearby. A chaotic sky foretells that confused patterns of air currents are at work aloft. Mixed-up lapse rates and dew point levels are setting the stage for wet, thundery weather.

Figure 75.   Altocumulus in turrets and tufts. (*National Center for Atmospheric Research*)

Figure 76.   A sky full of altocumulus. (*USN*)

Figure 77. Altocumulus advancing to cover the sky. (*NOAA*)

Figure 78. Thickening bands of altocumulus. (*NOAA*)

Figure 79. Altocumulus at different levels. (*NOAA*)

Figure 80. Altocumulus massing for wet weather. (*NOAA*)

Figure 81.   Layers of altocumulus produce a chaotic sky. (*NOAA*)

Figure 81 shows a combination of altocumulus (Ac) and altostratus (As) in one or two layers. The jumbled air has reached its dew point, not only at a near-uniform level, but also while on the rise. All three photographs warn of a change to even more chaotic skies.

HIGH CLOUDS (ABOVE 20,000 FEET)

In the formations of Figures 82 and 83 the water state would be expected to be ice particles. The white, feathery curls of Figure 82 indicate fair weather. Figure 83 shows the result when strong winds string out the curls into strand-like *mare's tails*. Should either of these forms thicken and lower, then a weather front bringing precipitation could be coming.

Figure 84 pictures the brush-like cirrus in company with the milky-white sky of cirrostratus. Rain may be only a day or so off if thickening and lowering should continue. The Ancient Mariner would recognize in Figure 85 the cirrostratus which prompted him to say, "Last night the moon had a golden ring." He spoke of the halo often formed when moon or sun appears diffused by the thin veil. His next remark, "Tonight no moon we see," tells of low rain clouds following to block out the sky.

Figure 85 shows the pebbly view of cirrocumulus (Cc) clouds, suggesting some vertical motion as the air passes the dew point. Sometimes the underside looks like fish scales and turns gray as it thickens. This is *mackerel sky*, an indication that wet, stormy weather is on the way. Whether cirrocumulus is a harbinger of good or bad to come seems to depend on

Figure 82.   Fibrous cirrus suggests fair weather. (*NOAA*)

Figure 83.   Wind shreds cirrus into mare's tails. (*NOAA*)

Figure 84.   Cirrus streamers in advance of cirrostratus. (*NOAA*)

Figure 85.   Sun halo caused by cirrostratus veil. (*NOAA*)

Figure 86.   Mackerel sky from cirrocumulus clouds. (*NOAA*)

geography. The expectation is said to be good weather for observers in Britain and on the northeast and west coasts of the United States. But bad weather is in store for some Mediterranean observers, they say. It should also be noted that these clouds are infrequently seen. Perhaps it is enough for us to accept them as giving not-too-significant testimony in any case.

Figures 87 and 88 show cloud forms not limited by description as low, middle, or high. Figure 87 shows "woolpack" patchy clumps of cumulus (Cu). They are usually based in the low level under 6500 feet, but can begin at higher altitudes. Their water is usually in droplet form, and the portent is fair weather. But the story can be varied by extent and time of vertical development. The fair-weather type of Figure 87 has no great vertical development, for the air is not subject to violent updrafts and downdrafts. Should these clouds form early in the day, there is evidence of moist air which could pile higher as the day progresses. Then might come some afternoon thunderstorms. If, though, formation is not until later in the day, the air is drier, the clouds are fewer, and the chance of

Figure 87.   Floating tufts of cumulus in a friendly sky. (*NOAA*)

Figure 88.   Cumulus domes and towers. (*NOAA*)

thunderstorms is less. In any case, development over land is usually in the daytime. At sea and in coastal regions the process just as usually occurs at night.

In Figure 88 the cumulus pattern is more massive. The suggestion here is turbulent and bumpy air, but still fair weather. Should the clouds merge with altocumulus, then some bad weather can be expected.

The two pictures of Figures 89 and 90 show the towering giants of the cloud families. They can extend upward literally for miles from a low base to a high top. The water state would be droplets topped by ice particles. Cumulonimbus (Cb) make no effort to disguise how they are formed. Sudden drafts of air moving upward for many thousands of feet give them great vertical development. The "-nimbus" end of the name tells of likely rain.

The forces at work within a full-blown cumulonimbus (Cb) are powerful and quite intricate. We should accept that no purpose is served by tarrying to analyze what whims of nature fashion such majesty; but we can generalize. Air within these mountains moves vertically at elevator speeds. Water droplets are flung upward to freeze, then dropped suddenly to pick up more liquid. Like an onion on a yo-yo string, a hailstone grows with layer after layer of water. With all the updrafts and downdrafts, fearful electrical charges are built and stored. Then a lightning bolt jumps like a spark from one pole to another. And the sudden heating of the air nearby causes an explosive clap of thunder. This cloud form is also called the *thunderhead*, with an anvil-shaped tower. We've already met the name for the horn of that anvil, incus; and it points in the same direction as the wind flow.

The weather which can accompany cumulonimbus is no surprise: rain, snow, hail, lightning, and thunder. It is said that at any instant the earth is pummelled by about 1800 thunderstorms and is struck by lightning 100 times a second. It is said by optimists that lightning never strikes twice in the same place. It is comforting to recognize that the earth has an enormous surface and that thunderstorms are usually in motion. Even so, one shouldn't gamble on the optimist's prediction.

Lightning gains a variety of names, yet the phenomenon always involves the dual personality of high electrical current and dangerous heat. The most commonly seen form is *streak* lightning. It is the line or lines of light between cloud and surface. *Forked* lightning more precisely outlines the actual path of conduction between them. *Sheet* lightning is usually a formless flash seen over a large area to evidence discharges between clouds. *Heat* lightning is probably one of the other forms seen at a great distance reflecting over the horizon. *Ribbon* lightning appears as parallel strokes when high winds group the streaks into a pattern. *Beaded* lightning is, in effect, an interrupted

Figure 89.   Cumulonimbus, giant of the cloud family. (*NOAA*)

Figure 90.   Rain torrents form base of cumulonimbus. (*USN*)

Figure 91. Lightning strikes the sea with depth-charge force. (*USN*)

stroke. *Ball* lightning seems to be careening spheres of light which hiss and sizzle as they roll or dart or hang eerily in the air. And sometimes the lightning bolt will cause a terrifying whistle.

Deeply embedded in the lore of seafaring is *St. Elmo's fire.* Ghostly luminous fingers of light can issue from mast, yardarm, or even the hand of a startled navigator. Termed *corposants* because they seem the embodiment of supernatural power, such brush discharges of electricity are kin to lightning, for both involve a potential difference between surface and air. But the intensity of the discharge is far less than the peaks of current achieved by true lightning bolts. During thundery weather the ghostly show can appear when static electricity leaps from shipboard objects to the sky. Sometimes corposants are said to be accompanied by loud claps and an acrid smell, as if from gunfire. It is justified here to emphasize that, in truth, there is such a thing as St. Elmo's fire. It is not an old salt's fiction. Rather, it is another evidence of the transfer of electricity between air and surface —even though seldom in sufficient amounts to cause any more than understandable awe.

Dorothy of the *The Wizard of Oz* would have no difficulty recognizing mammatocumulus, the cloud form of Figure 92. Like the Wicked Witch of the West, it spreads evil across the sky. *Tornados* can dart from it. And they are probably the most dangerous weather forms to be met. No one yet, it seems, has verified the frightful speed within a tornado's whirling core. The reason? No instrument has stood up under its blast. Estimates

Figure 92. Threatening bags of pendulous mammatocumulus. (*NOAA*)

Figure 93.   Tornado scatters debris along a Midwestern road. (*USN*)

Figure 94. Waterspout pierces the sea close aboard. (*USN*)

of more than 400 miles per hour have been reported before the instruments joined Dorothy on the other side of the rainbow. The seagoing twin of a tornado is called a *waterspout*. Its destruction is not so well advertised. One reason given is that its power is less. By another view its effects are less pronounced because houses, farmgirls, and puppy dogs are not so often in its path. Whether tornado or waterspout, though, the result is a terrifying atmospheric monster.

The photographs we've seen span cloud forms from fleecy to fearful. Should they also suggest a license for indolence, then our mission has been accomplished. Time spent reclining on a grassy knoll while watching the parade of clouds is an excellent idea. Luke Howard must have done so, and his name has survived for nearly two centuries! Now is our opportunity to follow his lead. Go ashore and find that grassy knoll. Then, spend a while watching the progress of clouds across the sky. Speculate on why they are sheet-like or piled in heaps. The ocean of our atmosphere will be

Figure 95. Not flying saucers, but rare cloud formations over Marseilles, France. (*USN*)

churning right before your eyes. Lapse rates, dew points, updrafts, and stability will be newfound measures of poetic beauty. Should a glowering cumulonimbus start its approach, then flee from that knoll with dignity but great dispatch. St. Elmo has not been known to shield the unwary from the danger of thunderbolts. With that caution in mind, then, it is time for the landing party to bear away. Time to accumulate a cirrus here and a stratus there while we ponder the content of this chapter.

QUESTIONS

A high, white cloud approaches over the western horizon. On it rests a shadowy figure, his head haloed by a veil of cirrostratus. In tow astern is a string of all sorts of clouds, ready to pass in review. Who is that figure? Mr. Luke Howard, of course. He wants you to observe his cloud parade and then to answer these questions.

1. A mass of stable air is forced to ascend.
   a. It will cool faster than surrounding air.
   b. Clouds formed within it would tend to be of the stratus type.
   c. both of the above.
   d. none of the above.

2. A mass of unstable air is ascending.
   a. It will cool more slowly than surrounding air.
   b. Clouds formed within it would tend to be of the cumulus type.
   c. both of the above.
   d. none of the above.

3. _____ would be considered a low cloud.
   a. Stratocumulus
   b. Stratus
   c. Both of the above
   d. None of the above

4. High clouds are usually composed of
   a. ice particles.
   b. water droplets.
   c. either of the above.
   d. neither of the above.

5. When strong winds shred stratus clouds, the result is called
   a. mare's tails.
   b. scud.
   c. mackeral sky.
   d. none of the above.

6. _____ are considered fair-weather clouds when not accompanied by thickening.
   a. Cirrus
   b. Altocumulus
   c. Both of the above
   d. None of the above

7. Mackerel sky is a name applied to
   a. altostratus.
   b. cirrostratus.
   c. altocumulus.
   d. cirrocumulus.

8. The moon would appear with a halo when seen through
   a. altostratus.
   b. cirrostratus.
   c. either of the above.
   d. none of the above.

9. Cumulonimbus clouds are associated with
   a. thunder.
   b. lightning.
   c. hail.
   d. all of the above.

10. A castellated cloud form would likely be
    a. of the stratus type.
    b. of the cumulus type.
    c. neither of the above.

ANSWERS

Mr. 'Howard is writing busily on a slate! To learn what is his reckoning of your progress, allow 10 for each correct answer. Then find your level this way:

> 100, Carefree, feathery cirrus
> 90, Cirro-, but with some thickening
> 80, Alto-, yet still fair weather
> 70, Strato-, and threatening
> under 70, Chaotic sky!

1. c	6. c
2. c	7. d
3. c	8. b
4. a	9. d
5. b	10. b

Chapter 6

FOGS

For every mariner who has not met a typhoon there is another who has never endured a Hatteras gale. But nearly all have encountered fog. Could a poll be taken of sailors since the Odyssey, fog would probably rank as weather's most irksome show. A storm's fury can be frightening, but at least adrenalin surges with the fright. The blind solitude of groping through fog brings no such excitement. Even the radar age has not relieved the strain. Some nearby objects may be overlooked, for electronic eyes are not all-seeing. When detected, their actual courses and speeds must be determined if avoidance is to be assured. And not everyone has radar. Fog can still be blindman's bluff, with some modern players tempted to cheat because they see shadows outlines of who's on the playing field.

We've already discussed the atmospheric mechanics which cause fog. When an air mass reaches the dew point and particles are present to serve as nuclei, then its water changes from the vapor state to become visible. That, we learned, is how a cloud is formed. And fog can be defined as a cloud based at or very near the ground. A 50-foot altitude is sometimes termed as the dividing line. When the mass reaches up from that level it is termed a cloud; when it bottoms out at a lower height it is a fog.

To set the record straight, we should first discuss what fog is *not*. It isn't another name for *haze*. Fog is comprised of condensed moisture while haze has fine particles of salt, dust, or smoke with little or no water vapor.

Smog is a mixture of smoke and fog, so it has an element of both. Should we ever tire of the term smog, perhaps we could substitute "faze" or "hog." *Mist* is another thing fog isn't, for as a very fine rain it is a step above a soggy fog. We can describe fog, then, as a cloud but not as haze, smog, mist, or even such spinoffs as faze, hog, or fist. All of them block visibility when they appear in the line of sight, and some of them distort shape and color more than others. By far, though, the most prevalent is fog. Moreover, it is the most likely to bother a mariner.

Since fog is a cloud, its formation shares with clouds the requirements of three essentials: hygroscopic particles to serve as nuclei, water, and a cooling process. It is in the last factor that fog and clouds seem to differ. Cloud formation is tied to air cooling because it rises and expands. By contrast, most fogs receive the necessary cooling by contact with a changing subsurface. In either case the relative humidity increases as temperature drops. In either case the water becomes visible as liquid or solid when relative humidity arrives at saturation's 100% and temperature reaches the dewpoint. Again, the distinction lies in how the air is cooled to that dew point.

The names given various types of fog are good indications of what is involved. There are four basic kinds, with several other subdivisions thrown in for good measure. The four prime classes are termed *advection, radiation, frontal,* and *upslope.* A close look at each is now in order.

An advection fog is one formed by air cooling as it is moved sideways. The key is in the word *advection.* It refers to a *horizontal* motion. By contrast, convection suggests a vertical motion. So an advection fog results when air changes temperature sufficiently during a sideways motion. Here is an outline of the first of two ways this can take place.

Cold air moving sideways over warmer water meets the layer of warm air near the water surface. The result could be that the warm layer is cooled to the dew point and produces *steam fog* (Figure 97), a shallow, smoking vapor. Let a temperature inversion put a lid of warmer air on top of such a low-level formation and a very dense block of fog can develop. Likely regions would be over rivers and lakes. Likely times would be early hours in the day while the land around is still colder than the water surface. Should it occur over an ocean it would be termed *sea smoke.* Since the most likely ocean locale for cold air to be on the move is an arctic region, it can also be called *arctic sea smoke,* or just plain old *arctic smoke.* Attributed to western American Indians is another synonym, *pogonip.* But whatever the name and whether uttered on a bridge or in a hogan, the idea is the same: cold air moves sideways over a warm surface to cool a warm layer of air.

The second type of advection fog develops when warm, moist air moves over a cold surface. It is cooled when it meets the film of cold air lying

Figure 96. Fogbound as advection bank sweeps in. (*NOAA*)

near that surface. The result is the most common type, not only of advection fog, but of any kind. Nearly 80% of all marine fogs are said to develop in this manner. Since our concern is with weather as it affects the mariner, this kind of fog attracts our special attention.

The prime requirement of any advection fog is wind. Air must be moved sideways to warrant the *ad*vection part of its name, and the force causing the motion is wind. If the wind speed is too little, what fog forms will be very shallow. If the speed is too great, the fog can be swept upward to become a low cloud sheet. The least strength has been set as 4 or 5 knots, and the top speed has been pegged at 15 to 20 knots. But don't be too insistent when advising a deepsea mariner of those limits. The absence of contours on the ocean surface causes less churning or turbulence in the air, even when wind strength is 30 knots or more. Warm air driven by a moderate gale can stay low long enough to be cooled sufficiently by the cold surface. Advection ocean fogs do sometimes form in the presence of more than a fresh breeze.

Figure 97.   Destroyer in sea smoke as chilled air meets a warmer ocean. (*USN*)

Figure 98.   Advection fog requires wind.

In any case, advection fogs need wind. And the most common type also needs a cold surface over which its warm air mass flows. There must be a sufficient contrast between air and surface temperature. A likely place to expect such would be where a cold ocean current encounters a warmer sea. Air over the warm sea need only be shunted over the adjoining cold surface to make the fog bank appear.

Not often would we find a cold strip of land abutting a warm strip. At sea, though, such a contrasting surface cover is not at all so rare. Sometimes cold ocean water wells upward along a lee shoreline to form an inshore ribbon of cold. That is the story plot for California's coastal advection fog. Farther offshore, the cause can be the encounter of a cold horizontally flowing current with a warm one. In the North Pacific, the northeasterly flow of the Japan Current carries with it air warmer than that over the Arctic Ocean. Cold air funnels through the Bering Strait and has a showdown with the warm in the region of the Aleutians. The result? Advection fog of the densest variety.

Just as infamous is a counterpart which develops a continent away. In the North Atlantic, warm air moving northeast with the Gulf Stream meets cold air southbound with the Labrador Current. The rendezvous takes place in the region of Newfoundland's Grand Banks. What develops, particularly when the wind is from the southeast quadrant, is a thick, thick

Figure 99.   Advection fog seeps over Coronado while the main bank approaches San Diego's Point Loma. (*USN*)

advection fog. Similar conditions produce dangerous advection fogs on the west coasts of South Africa and South America. And common to all of them are the factors of wind to move the warm, moist air, and a cold surface over which it is made to flow.

The specifications for an advection fog can be summarized this way:

1. It is a wind-driven sea fog.

2. Development is not restricted to a certain time of day. A cold ocean current is cold compared to a neighboring warm strip at dusk as well as at dawn; and winds at sea can flow at noon as well as at midnight. A few of advection examples do seem to form at certain times of the day. San Francisco's variety tends to roll through the Golden Gate in late afternoon, but that is due to another circumstance. A few chapters back we read that in coastal regions air blows from sea toward land in the afternoon. That also happens in the San Francisco Bay Area. It is the afternoon sea breeze which fulfills the wind requirement for an advection fog. Coastal fogs of this type, wherever met, are subject to the same afternoon time frame. Not so, though, farther out to sea. So we'll include as a characteristic of this type of fog that it can form at any time.

3. This type tends to roll and pile up in banks, with no appreciable difference in thickness from bottom to top. Some other fogs seem to be denser in their bottom layers. That is not necessarily so for the advection type.

Here, then, is a one-sentence capsule describing what we have read to be the most frequent, by far, of maritime fogs: it is a sea fog which requires wind, can happen at any time, and can be of uniform thickness with altitude.

The next general kind of fog, *radiation* fog (Figure 100), has a personality almost exactly opposite to that of the advection type. It is described sometimes as a not-too-important maritime fog. But for those who travel coastal, and particularly inland waters, it can be a bugaboo.

The three cloud requirements of particles for nuclei, water, and a cooling process must still be met. A prime difference between advection and the radiation process is in fulfillment of the cooling essential. Rather than being moved sideways by wind from a surface of one temperature to a colder one, radiation's air mass stays put while the underlying surface changes temperature. For it to stay in one place, it cannot be in the presence of any appreciable wind. So, a first trait of radiation: little or no wind. In a flat calm the fog will be very shallow. A slight wind of up to 3 or 4 knots will cause enough mixing to build the fog to greater thickness. But should the wind be much stronger, the air mass will move off the base and not be cooled when the surface temperature drops.

This kind of fog would not be expected to form over an ocean. Such a surface would not change temperature fast enough before wind whisked the

Figure 100.   Shallow river fog blankets the surface. (*NOAA*)

air mass elsewhere. We've already read that water is reluctant to warm up or to cool off in a hurry. Land, though, will do so. By late afternoon it has absorbed the sun's heat and is warm. After sunset it begins to *radiate* its heat. And by the cold, dark hour before dawn, the land is cold. In turn, it will cool air in contact with its surface. If the temperature reaches the dew point and there are particles, then a surface cloud or *radiation* fog will form.

Since air closest to the cold land will have the lowest temperature, the fog occurs in a stable air mass with no inclination to convect or churn upward. So another detail is to be added: it tends to be thicker in the cooler bottom layers and thins out with altitude. Itemized, its traits are: (1) a land fog, (2) requiring little or no wind, (3) forming at night or early morning, and (4) tending to be thicker on the bottom.

As the day wears on, heat rays from the sun penetrate the fog and reheat the land. That heat reevaporates the water and by late morning the fog has begun to lift. The pattern is to burn off from the bottom up. If the day's warmth is not enough to dispel it all, then the fog becomes a daytime low cloud. Should a temperature inversion exist, cool lower air can be blanketed by a warm mass above. During the night the surface air can be further cooled by radiation to develop a taller pile of thick fog which will persist even through the succeeding day.

Where might this annoyance be most likely to appear? Wherever the land cover holds sufficient moisture to feed the air mass. That could be in such an area as a swamp, river, or delta. So, labels for this fog are swamp fog, river fog, or delta fog. Since tule grass grows in some such regions, it has also been termed a tule fog. And its tendency to hug the surface earns it the sometime name of ground fog.

The radiation type is closely related to dew, for the conditions to produce them are the same. Fog results when the cooling process causes condensation, not only on the ground as dew but also on the hygroscopic particles or nuclei in the air. Either dew or frost will also be present when radiation fog appears. And since clear nights accompany dew, the development of radiation fog can follow after such nights, with the expectation that settled weather will prevail for at least the greater part of the following day.

In the next chapter we'll meet the interaction of dissimilar air masses to produce weather fronts. And one of the results can be a *frontal fog* (Figure 101). Here we can preview what lies ahead and place this third species of fog in its proper niche.

Warm air tends to override cold in its path. Put another way, cold air can wedge under warm and cause it to rise. As the warm slides upward, it will cool. Clouds can then form in the warm mass. Any rain from those clouds will drop into the cold air beneath. And should that rain evaporate in the lower air, it will increase the water vapor content of the cold mass. When saturation is reached, a surface cloud can form in the cold air. That cloud is a frontal fog.

In this case, saturation is achieved in a manner different from that during the formation of the other fogs we've discussed. In both advection and radiation fogs, saturation happens by cooling air to the dew point. In the advection type, wind moves the air sideways over a colder surface. Radiation has the air stay in one place while the surface drops in temperature. A frontal fog develops when the water vapor in an air mass is actually increased. Moisture is added from the warm upper layer to the underlying cold wedge. When the cold has all the water vapor it can hold, condensation takes place and the fog appears.

The locale for this one can be anywhere that advancing warm air overtakes and climbs above a cold mass. Usually, though, it is expected more over a continental base than over a sea.

The last of our four types is an *upslope* fog (Figure 102). When air with high relative humidity slides upward over a rising land surface, it cools. Should the dew point be reached, fog will form on the side of the

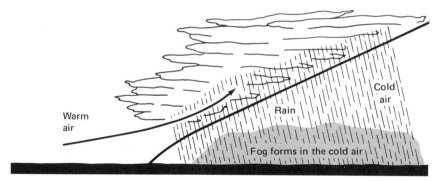

Figure 101.   Frontal fog as warm air overrides cold.

Figure 102.   Air rising over hillside forms upslope fog.

upsloping land. A mariner far at sea should have little problem with this, for gradual upslopes of the ocean are hard to come by. But inland waterways can be affected. Areas prone to receive this blanket are the ascending plains to the west of the Mississippi River. Moisture-laden air blown inland from the Gulf of Mexico can follow the slopes upward to reach its dew point. In wintertime the situation is aggravated by advection fog as well. In that season, the chilly land can cool warm air flowing in from the Gulf of Mexico. The combination of upslope and advection brings heavy and long-lasting fog to that region.

Set out here is Table A, which ranks visibility by code numbers. Extracted from the *International Visibility Code*, it appears in several editions of U.S. Coast Guard *Light Lists* to indicate what meteorological optical range might be expected of lighted aids to navigation. Its inclusion here is to specify what, internationally, is viewed as the progression upward from bare steerageway to full speed.

Understanding the mechanics of fog development is not complicated. And each mariner should keep in mind the basic principles when heading for a fog-prone region. *Coast Pilots* and *Sailing Directions* contain excellent summaries of where and when fog can be expected all over the world. Reading such guides, coupled with commonsense observation of prevailing atmospheric conditions, should provide valuable foreknowledge of what

TABLE A. METEOROLOGICAL OPTICAL RANGE

Code No.	Weather	Visibility
0	Dense fog	less than 50 yards
1	Thick fog	50–200 yards
2	Moderate fog	200–500 yards
3	Light fog	500–1000 yards
4	Thin fog	½–1 mile
5	Hazel	1–2 miles
6	Light haze	2–5½ miles
7	Clear	5½–11 miles
8	Very clear	11–27 miles
9	Exceptionally clear	over 27 miles

visibility might lie ahead. Old-timers retain a healthy respect for any kind of fog. It disorients the mind's eye as well as masking sight and muffling sound. Even the best-equipped vessel is just a power failure away from the old-fashioned days of casting the lead, streaming the log, and posting a sharp lookout. But now the sun is beginning to burn through and visibility is improving rapidly. Time to secure the fog signals, take our eyes off the radarscope, and look astern to see where we've been.

QUESTIONS

A moderate beam wind is moving warm air across our track, and the sea temperature has just dropped. We can expect to encounter another fog bank shortly. Don't expect, though, that the pesky radar willl be of much use. A few miles back it suddenly developed myopia and closed its all-round eye. Time to break out the old-timer's Three Ls of Lead, Log, and Lookout while we edge gingerly through a quiz.

1. Advection fog is considered prevalent in
   a. Aleutian waters.
   b. Newfoundland waters.
   c. California coastal waters.
   d. all of the above.

2. _____ is likely to develop during a cool, clear, calm night after a warm day.
   a. Advection fog
   b. Radiation fog
   c. Frontal fog
   d. Any of the above

3. Warm air rising over a cold hill is likely to produce
   a. an upslope fog.
   b. a frontal fog.
   c. either of the above.
   d. none of the above.

4. A(n) _____ never develops when the wind speed prevails at 20 knots.
   a. Advection fog
   b. Radiation fog
   c. Both of the above

5. When an air mass reaches saturation by the addition of water vapor, the type of fog likely to develop is called
   a. advection.
   b. radiation.
   c. frontal.
   d. upslope.

6. Mist is
   a. a very fine rain.
   b. another name for haze.
   c. both of the above.

7. Steam fog, sea smoke, arctic smoke, and pogonip are types of
   a. frontal fog.
   b. advection fog.
   c. radiation fog.
   d. none of the above.

8. When a radiation fog exists,
   a. air temperature increases with altitude.
   b. the air is said to be stable.
   c. both of the above.

9. According to the International Visibility Code, a dense fog is
   a. classified as Code 0.
   b. with visibility from 50 to 200 yards.
   c. both of the above.
   d. none of the above.

10. Most marine fogs are said to be caused by
    a. frontal conditions.
    b. upslope terrain.
    c. radiation.
    d. advection.

ANSWERS

This time we encounter a panel of four quizmasters. Each looks old enough to have sailed as ordinary seaman with Joseph Conrad. One mutters a singsong lyric as he hauls in the hand lead; another holds a coal-oil lantern to read the taffrail log. A third seems to be trying to fit an ear trumpet while he strains to listen for what might be ahead. The fourth? He is squinting at the International Visibility Code, ready to score your answers. As usual, 10 for each correct response. And the International Tally is as follows:

     100, Code 9, Exceptionally Clear
      90, Code 7, Clear atmosphere
      80, Code 5, Hazel (she didn't give her last name)
      70, Code 3, Moderate Fog with peasoup just ship-lengths away
  under 70, Code 0, Dense, and in the soup

1. d   6. a
2. b   7. b
3. a   8. c
4. b   9. a
5. c   10. d

Chapter 7

WEATHER FRONTS

When dissimilar air masses come together the encounter is not a friendly merger. Instead, each tries to retain its own personality and a sort of atmospheric war ensues. Along the front line of that battle, unsettled weather conditions develop. Wind shifts, clouds, and precipitation seem to follow a predictable pattern. The upshot can be a storm. Our next task is to analyze what transpires and why. Most of the factors have already been met. We must put to work our knowledge of wind, lapse rates, and cloud forms to interpret the melee.

Names have been given to the phases of this conflict. *Frontal analysis*, describing the whole discussion, is obvious enough. When the fracas is building up, the phase is called *frontogenesis*. The "-genesis" end of that term keys what is involved. As the jousting air masses square off, they generate an area of conflict. Then the frontal system grows and matures. Its full-blown phase brings us to *occlusion*. We meet this term too often in daily life. It suggests blanking off, as of an artery in a coronary occlusion. Weathermen use it to describe the blanking off of the fully mature storm center from the earth's surface. Thereafter the system begins to decay. Then the process is called *frontolysis*. Here the "-lysis" poop on the word tells the story. It comes from loosening or loss, and the connotation is disintegration or death. So, we have "paralysis" to speak of a kind of death. And meteorology has frontolysis to label the disintegration of a frontal system.

When -genesis and -lysis bob along in the wake of *cyclo*, the reference is to the building up and decay of a cyclonic atmospheric pattern. We might well consider *cyclogenesis* with its progeny along with *frontogenesis* and company; for most of the frontal battle seems to be associated with cyclonic cores.

Now that name dropping is out of the way, let's get to work. To start with we must try some three-dimensional thinking. Chapters ago we met Mr. Luke Howard. It was he who in the 19th century pinned names on clouds. And his vantage point in those years was the earth's surface. He knew, we can be sure, that the atmosphere had the third dimension of height; and it is a reasonable surmise that he also knew it twisted and churned vertically as well as left and right. But he didn't *know*, as do to-day's meteorologists with balloons and rockets and sundry related gear. Without shiploads of equipment we modern mariners are not very much better off. Yet, to comprehend the powers at work in fronts and cyclones we must conjure up that third dimension. A weather front is not a battle line drawn across the earth's surface. Rather, it is a no-man's land slanting upward as well as sideways. Our point of departure is an image of how such regions can develop.

Far back in Chapter 2 we read about the atmosphere's general pattern of circulation. Now we must revisit that discussion and add some more details. Air which has been resting over the earth's equatorial region will begin to rise and flow north and south away from the Equator. When that upper air has reached a latitude of about 30°, a pile-up starts to develop. The resulting increase in pressure creates the horse latitude regions. Concentrations have been marked in the North Atlantic as the *Azores–Bermuda High* and in the North Pacific as the *Hawaiian High*. Some of the air descending from high altitude flows back toward the Equator and is turned by Coriolis to the right in the northern hemisphere to cause the northeast trades. In the southern hemisphere a Coriolis left turn brings the southeast trades. In either case, that Equator-bound air will underrun the equatorial pile already rising. Such north–south migrations will obviously develop areas of contrast in specific regions. Figure 103 illustrates what happens in the tropics. The lines marked *ITCZ* represent the *Intertropic Convergence Zones*. There, rising air headed away from the Equator rides over Equator-bound air moving in nearer the surface. In such a region of convergence there is sufficient dissimilarity of the air masses to threaten atmospheric whirls and eddies. And we have tagged two areas where disturbances might develop: at the ITCZ in the northern and in the southern hemispheres.

The story doesn't end there. We've seen that at about latitude 30° some of the air which rises over the Equator and starts moving poleward will come down. But not all of it will then flow back to the Equator as a trade

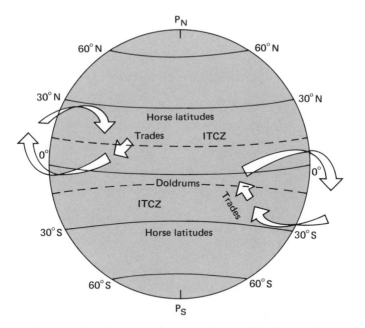

Figure 103. Atmospheric convection within the tropics.

wind. Other descending tongues will move along the surface *away from* the Equator. By the time Coriolis does its job, that flow will be toward the east and be named the *prevailing westerlies*. So between about latitudes 30° and 60°, atmosphere close to the surface will be made up of air which started near the Equator, ascended to a high altitude while it flowed poleward, and then came down to encounter the earth's influence and start moving from the west. Figure 104 shows that pattern.

There is more to the story, for we still have original equatorial air which has not yet descended. It will continue poleward, cooling as it goes. Above latitude 60° or so it will be so cold and heavy that it sinks toward the surface. There it will be forced by its pressure to start moving toward the Equator again. Coriolis senses this and makes it turn right in the northern hemisphere and left in the southern. The result in each case is a flow westward which we have learned is called the *polar easterly*. Figure 105 spotlights the contrast between the westward flow of that cold air and the eastward flow of warmer air adjoining, which makes up the prevailing westerly flow to the east. And the regions of contrast are marked *PF* for *polar front*. In Chapter 1 we read that polar, when referring to air masses, doesn't mean at the earth's caps; and here we see the polar fronts as at high latitudes, but not in Little America or riding Arctic ice floes. What we've

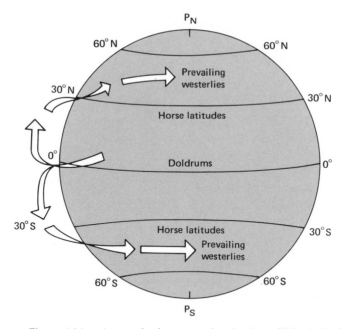

Figure 104.   Atmospheric convection in the middle latitudes.

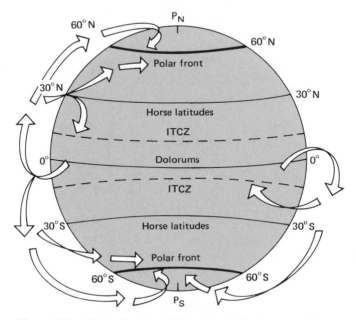

Figure 105.   Polar fronts and Intertropic Convergence Zones.

now gained is the concept of two more areas where dissimilar masses of the atmosphere can come together.

The upshot is that along an ITCZ and a polar front, the gauntlet can be thrown down. There, battle lines are drawn between massive blocks of dissimilar air to affect much of the world's population. They are not the only regions where contrasting chunks of atmosphere can meet, but they are the primary locations. Our survey of frontal activity must certainly concentrate on what might happen there.

We tend to live in a north-oriented world. It is the north point of a compass which displays a fancy flower. South is just *S*. We go *up* north and *down* south. In fact, some of us find it hard to accept that the Nile runs downhill from south to north. Where does this fit in the scheme of meteorology? Well, in discussing polar fronts we will adhere to custom and emphasize the northern hemisphere. There *is* a polar front in the southern, but it affects the smaller part of the earth's population. By contrast the northern zone, hovering between 30° and 60° latitude, influences billions.

In discussing the Intertropic Convergence Zones, though, we will become bihemispherical. Weather problems connected with the ITCZ disturb many people on both sides of the Equator. Let's take things in order. First up is the atmospheric commotion along the polar front in the northern hemisphere.

In Figure 105 we see air on one side of the front moving in a direction opposite to that on the other. Atmosphere in the belt of prevailing westerlies started out from the Equator to meander through the atmospheric sea. Its personality has been shaped by the region of its formative life. That might have been an ocean or a continent, but in either case it was warm. As the air rose and moved poleward it began to cool. In descending it warmed up again. The air on the other side of the front line also started near the Equator. And it cooled as it rose and warmed a bit as it came down. But by the time it reached one of the earth's caps it was colder and denser than that which descended to form the westerlies. So the polar front not only separates air moving in different directions; it also sets apart cold and high-pressure air from air that is warmer and of lower pressure. A region of discontinuity marks the separation zone.

Front is the name for the boundary when traced at ground level; *frontal surface* is the term to describe it as a three-dimensional area. And it is not a vertical bulkhead. Warm and low-pressure air can be expected to lap over the top of a pile of cold and high. Any gradual drop in temperature with height is now lost. From the surface upward, temperature drops within the cold mass until the level of contrast is reached. Then the temperature can begin to rise for a while before it again begins to drop. Following along will be pressure differences and contrasts in humidity. All

Figure 106. Perspective view of
warm air rising over wedge of cold.

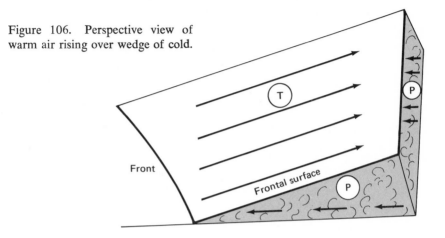

this is reasonable, for there are two different air masses now piled in the
sky. Figure 106 tries to illustrate the story, and "tries" is an apt verb.
Fronts and frontal surfaces extend horizontally for hundreds of miles and
vertically for thousands of feet. No page can show the true picture. With
allowance, then, for such limitations, view Figure 106 as a kind of example.
We are looking north, with east to the right and west to the left.

The frontal surface is not a neat line. Rather, it is a zone within which
some mixing of air takes place. Its depth can be measured in hundreds or
thousands of feet. But to the south and west, far back on one side, stands
undiluted warm air while on the other side waits just as unsullied cold air.

To identify this line of discontinuity as if it were a parallel of latitude
is faulty. In summertime the sun's warmth displaces it away from the tropics.
Then the battle line might be drawn as far north as 60°. In winter, cold
air breaks out of its icy confines and bullies its way south. Then the polar
front might even approach the tropics. Nor is the frontal region a continuous unbroken barrier. When the transition from tropical air to polar is
gradual, there might be breaks in the line, with no polar front at all in
the region. Usually, though, it is looked for in the midlatitudes, and it
appears as an undulation wedging wave-like toward the pole at one point
and toward the Equator at another. Figure 107 centers on the North Pole
and shows the general northern hemisphere picture.

Oversimplification must be risked again. This concept is so important
that we must not fog it with too much scientific nicety. Figure 108, in
several panels, presents a capsuled biography of a cyclone from birth to
extinction. We can view it as an area along the polar front which is begin-

Figure 107.   Polar front line as seen from above the North Pole.

ning to wrinkle into a crest. We can also consider that it is any region where warm abuts cold under circumstances when a wave pattern might form. Since, though, the polar front is such a prolific source of such agitation, let's assume we are examining one of its sectors. In Panel A, air on each side is flowing in a normal manner: cold from the east and warm from the west. In Panel B, though, increasing pressure of the cold air causes a bend or kink in the dividing line. That deepens in Panel C and becomes an unstable cresting wave in Panel D. In Panel E the warm core is now completely surrounded by cold and is beginning to lift off the surface as an occlusion. And Panel F shows the dénouement. By then the warm center is just a weakening eddy and the two masses revert to business as usual on their respective sides of the front.

Figure 109 is a zoom-view of the wave pattern we've just seen. Our vantage point has us looking toward north at the top. The broken line indicates the more-or-less northeasterly direction followed by the wave crest over the earth's surface. And isobars show what could be the pressure distribution in the region. Since pressure decreases toward the low center

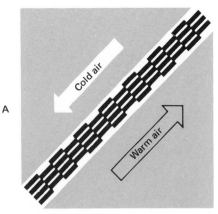

A. Opposite air flow while equilibrium still exists.

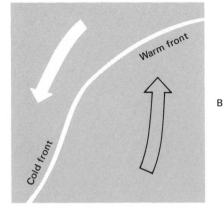

B. Increased cold-air pressure bends the front line.

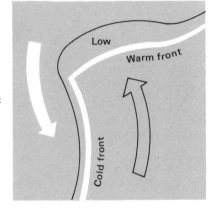

C. A pocket of warm air begins to form.

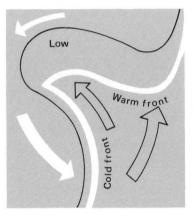

D. The warm air core deepens.

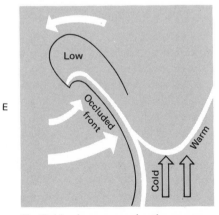

E. Cold air surrounds the warm sector.

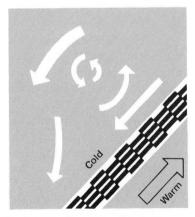

F. Warm air core disappears as equilibrium is restored.

Figure 108. Life cycle of a cyclone.

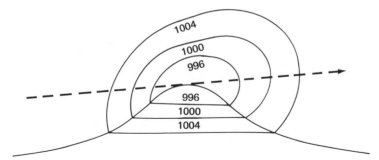

Figure 109. Pattern of isobars
in an extratropical cyclone.

of the system, we call this a *cyclone*. And since the geographical region is
outside the tropics, we call it an *extratropical cyclone*. And once born it
will be carried off by prevailing winds and the earth's easterly rotation to
bother areas in its path.

The advent of such a pattern is not heralded by comets or rolls of distant
drums. Weathermen must pore over data furnished them from widespread
observers to detect any telltale signs. Notice how the isobars seem to bend
or kink at the line of the wave in Figure 109. This is a characteristic trait
of such a formation. When trying to flush out the development of these
storms, meteorologists look for such indicators. But first they must know
what the barometer reads at various positions throughout the area before
they can plot isobars and look for kinks. Since few polar bears or migrating whales carry instruments, they rely heavily on mariners' reports to supplement their own precise but all-too-sparse observations.

We'll start from the premise that our weather watchers have discerned
the pattern of a maturing wave as seen in Figure 109. Now we must add
factors, one by one. In Figure 110 we consider wind direction at four separate positions in the system. We selected the four cardinal points of the
compass: north, south, east, and west. Each time we invoke our venerable
recipe of "high to low with a Coriolis twist." At Point 1, north of the
center, the wind will be from a northeasterly point. At Point 2, east of
the center, it will be southeasterly. Point 3 is south of the center and shows
wind from the southwest quadrant. And Point 4, west of the center, has it
from a northwesterly direction. Each time we found the wind by saying
"high to low with a (northern hemisphere) right turn."

As the wave moves along its line of progression the pressure will change
for regions in its path. Figure 111 focuses on that. At Point *A*, ahead of

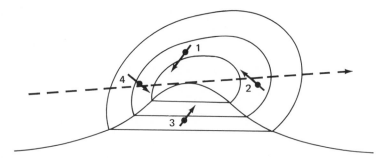

Figure 110. Wind directions within an extratropical cyclone.

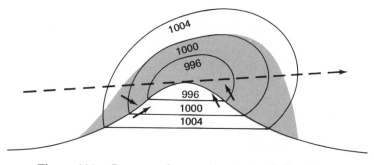

Figure 111. Pressure changes in extratropical cyclone.

the crest, the pressure will be dropping as the low core moves closer. At Point *B* pressure will be rising as the core moves away.

Figure 112 concentrates on surface temperature. At Point *A*, as the warm core approaches temperature could be expected to rise. At Point *B*, as the center moves by to the eastward temperature could be expected to fall.

Figure 113's subject is humidity, and thus precipitation and clouds. The core tends to have a greater absolute humidity than air ahead and behind. That means it actually contains more water vapor. Then, as the center is lifted by air ahead and behind, it begins to cool. Its relative humidity will now increase. And when the dew point is reached with particles present, clouds will form. Let them get too soggy and precipitation will begin to fall. Should the clouds hover close enough to the earth, a frontal fog could result. The shaded portions of Figure 113 show the areas of cloud and probable precipitation.

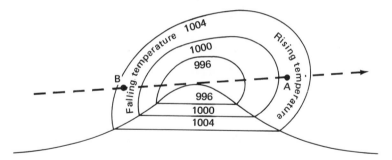

Figure 112.   Temperature contrasts in extratropical cyclone.

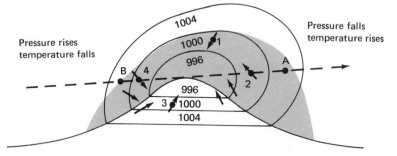

Figure 113.   Regions of clouds and rain in extratropical cyclone.

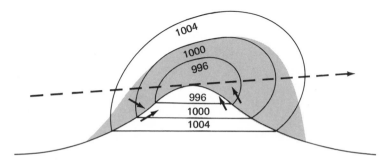

Figure 114.   Review of basic patterns in extratropical cyclone.

In Figure 114 we see it all put together in a single downward or plan view. We must bear in mind, though, that such a system is constantly changing shape and size as it progresses from frontogenesis through occlusion to frontolysis. More of that to come.

What is missing from this series of sketches is the third dimension of height. It is time now to remedy that situation. To do so we'll consider

Figures 115 and 116 as being different views of the same situation. Eight points are marked on each. They fix a latter-day Luke Howard prone on the earth's surface as the frontal system travels by. It would take too many sketches to show his progressive position during the fly-by. Instead, we'll let the cyclone stay put and mentally move our observer from right to left. Both Figures 115 and 116 place him on the storm's track. He will experience the full sequence of changes as the cyclone's center moves toward him, passes over, and then travels onward to the east. This is a limitation, for his observations are true only for such conditions. Were he north or south of the track, the scenario would change. Even so, following the script along the track gives us the most complete survey of what might transpire.

A mass of warm air is moving eastward and invading colder regions in its path. As it moves along, cold air in the rear stands ready to flow into its wake. The location could be near the Aleutians, offshore from Puget Sound, near one of the Great Lakes, north of Cape Hatteras, or, perhaps, in the Mediterranean. Wherever our observer might be, the time is winter in the northern hemisphere. At Point 1 he is under a uniform air mass with traits usual for the time of year. Temperature and humidity would be

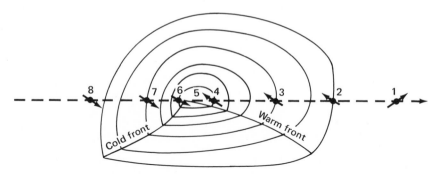

Figure 115.   Looking down on the passage of a frontal system.

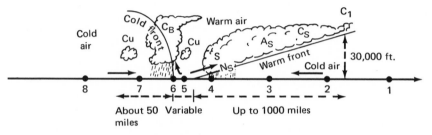

Figure 116.   Passage of a frontal system in profile.

on the low side with pressure on the high. His wind would probably be prevailing westerly. There is no reason yet by instrument or natural senses for him to expect any change. But to the westward is a depression, a pressure hole in the atmosphere. And it is coming toward him at a speed of, perhaps, from 10 to 20 knots.

Somewhere between Points 1 and 2 he looks up toward the west and sees curls of cirrus clouds. They seem to be shredding into mare's tail strands. From now on the clues will begin to appear. Those high wisps betray winds caused by the oncoming warm air starting to overrun his cold mass. At Point 2 he is under the edge of the warm front. Cirrus has now thickened into cirrostratus layers and the lowering trend promises to continue. His wind has shifted. The prevailing westerlies have given way to a new influence. His cold mass has learned of the depression to the westward. High blows to low with a right turn, and the wind is now southeasterly. Temperature is going up, pressure is falling, and the humidity is on the rise.

At Point 3 the evidence is all in. Cirrostratus has become altostratus. The trends of temperature, pressure, and humidity continue. The wind stays from the southeast quadrant. The warm frontal surface is lowering steadily and his atmosphere is no longer a uniform cold air mass. Now there are two layers above, with a frontal zone between them. In Figure 116 we see the superior warm air sliding up the incline while the lowdown cold flows westward toward the center.

By the time Point 4 has been reached the cloud ceiling has dropped very low. Stratus layers shroud the sky and nimbostratus are wetting him down. And something else might take place. Water transferred from the warm air down to the cold might increase the relative humidity to 100%. The result could be a frontal fog. In any case, temperature, pressure, and humidity progress as before and the wind remains southeasterly.

Point 5 shows him in the depression, with the warm front moving steadily farther eastward. Let's stop the action for a moment and review what we've seen. This has been the passage of a *warm front*, for the label depends on the kind of air moving in. The horizontal span of this surface can be from 750 to 1000 miles. Assuming a speed of 15 knots, we calculate that it might take two or three days for it to pass by. During that time our observer notes a regular progression of atmospheric change. Clouds start out high; then they lower and thicken until they almost reach the surface. Temperature and humidity go up; pressure goes down. The wind blows toward the low center. For the moment we'll identify the cloud forms as stratus type. They need not always be such on a warm front, but we must start someplace.

Back to our friend supine at Point 5. There he is in the low center, and things become variable. While he is covered by that depression temperature,

Figure 117.   Roll cloud of squall line passes over Jacksonville Naval Air Station. (*USN*)

pressure, and humidity will tend to stabilize. And the wind will be fitful, following the whims of local contrast. Even the width of the low is variable. It might be 100 miles across; it might be only 10. But its width, in any case, is shrinking. We'll add that discussion to our list of things to come.

Between Points 5 and 6 the observer could encounter a *squall line*. Coming fast from the west is a cold front, and it rolls along like a breaking sea. Just as ahead of a breaker there can be backwashes and rips, so leading the cold front can be dangerous atmospheric eddies. Squall lines forerunning the onset of a cold front could spell serious trouble.

The observer muddles through and gets to Point 6. Now the game plan changes dramatically. Cold air tagging along behind the eastbound warm is ready to surge along the surface. Since it is now moving in, the line between them is called a *cold front*. The warm core finds itself upended and propelled aloft. The combination of sudden cooling and upward motion

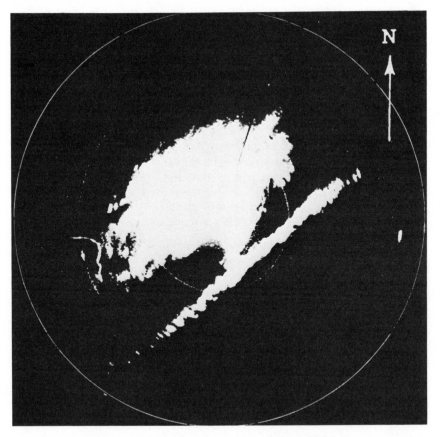

Figure 118. Radar view of squall line. (*NOAA*)

produces vertically developed clouds. In fact, at the front line it might well produce a cloud with great vertical development: cumulonimbus. And from it can come thunder, lightning, and hail. So common is this expectation that cold front and cumulonimbus are almost synonymous. Spun off from this sudden uplift can be clumps of cumulus clouds. And from Point 6 through Point 7, our observer would note a sudden drop in temperature. The pressure would begin to rise. For a while clouds would show, but shortly the air would clear and the humidity would drop. At Point 6 he would also observe a marked change in wind direction. Now "high to low with a right turn" has the wind blowing out of the northwest quadrant. Where the cold frontal surface touches the earth is called a *wind shift line*. And the change can be as much as 180° from one side of the low center to the other.

At Point 8 the observer is again in the clear. The normalcy of a uniform air mass overhead is ready to be restored, with temperature and humidity low, pressure high, and wind prevailing from the west. He has now lived through the passage of a cold front. Let's pause again to recap what happened.

As the cold air came pushing in along the surface, he noted with no surprise that the temperature dropped. No more unusual was the fact that the pressure rose. The warm air spurting upward caused towering accumulated clouds. And they might have provided him with frightening, but still fascinating, displays of nature's power. Figure 116 shows that the horizontal span of the cold front is about 50 miles. That steep plow blade of atmospheric change tends to move faster than the warm front ahead of it to the eastward. It will pass by in just a few hours.

There are some other truisms to be stated about all this. Polar front activity tends to develop in the midlatitudes, that is, in the region of the prevailing westerlies. These systems move from west to east over the earth's surface in each hemisphere. They are more pronounced in the wintertime, for then the icy air from the earth's cap is more likely to muscle in on temperate climes. When a wave in the polar front grows into a cyclonic pattern, it is like a vortex. And it need not be an isolated fluke: there can be a succession of such swirls moving eastward across the earth. So our observer at Point 8 in Figure 116 should not be lulled into complacency. Still farther west can be another front, and yet some more others, ready to repeat what he has just been through. On occasion that icy air can break through the defenses of the warm mass to send a chilling blast of cold into "enemy" territory dominated by dissimilar air. When such a breakout occurs, the action will be short-lived but energetic. Like a scouting party, a core of cold and dense air can enter warm air space. It will be overwhelmed eventually by the legions of warm all around; but while the foray is on, bluster and fuss will be the order of the day.

Our observer has by no means had a unique experience. Most of us, one time or another, have observed this parade of air masses. So common is the sequence that rules of thumb, jingles, and even reference tables have been fashioned as guides. When the wind hauls into an easterly quadrant and the barometer begins to fall, says one official table, rain is not too many hours away. When the wind goes westerly, says the same table, fair weather pends. "Wind from the east, 24 hours at least" says a jingle. Another might change the time base, but the prediction of rain to come remains unchanged. "Mackerel sky and mare's tails make tall ships take in small sails" is another ditty. Someplace between Points 1 and 2 in Figure 114 our observer might have seen not only shredded cirrus, but also the fishscale underside of thickening high clouds. On a sailing ship with lofty masts it would be high time to send sailors aloft, for in not too many hours some dirty weather might make sail-shortening a slippery chore.

Figure 119.   Cumulonimbus blooms on a cold front. (*NOAA*)

Figure 120.   Satellite view of wintry
air invading the Midwest. (*SDS, NOAA*)

Even rainbows have been included in the poetry. "Rainbow in the
morning, sailor take warning; rainbow at night, sailor's delight" is one
version. A rainbow is the spectrum of sunlight refracted by water droplets.
In the morning, with the sun to the eastward and clouds to the west, the
prudent seaman takes heed. A rainbow appears in the clouds to the west
and heading his way. As night approaches, though, he relaxes. Now the
sun is in the west and the rainbow will develop in clouds to the east. With

Figure 121.   A day later, satellite records a breakthrough to the Gulf of Mexico. (*SDS, NOAA*)

delight he waves adieu to the eastbound clouds while enjoying stabilizing weather.

We've bitten off quite a chunk of weather in this sitting, and more of frontal analysis remains to be served. For now, though, we are better off to exercise discretion. Mare's tails are riding rainbows while being chased by thunderheads. We should pause to reconsider where our discussion has led.

QUESTIONS

Over the western ocean stands a bewildered air mass. Not too long ago it enjoyed the balmy atmosphere of the tropics. Now, by nature's laws, it has been forced to face the reality of the other world. Whether it can cope or not depends on our understanding of its trauma. Every instinct cries that we recognize its plight. Here, then, is the cure:

1. Frontolysis refers to
   a. the building up of a front.
   b. the decay of a front.
   c. either of the above.
   d. none of the above.

2. A warm front defines the dividing line between
   a. oncoming warm air and cold air to the eastward.
   b. oncoming cold air and warm air to the eastward.
   c. neither of the above.

3. An extratropical cyclone develops
   a. out of season in the tropics.
   b. outside the tropics.
   c. neither of the above.

4. In the northern hemisphere, ahead or east of the low core of an extratropical cyclone,
   a. the pressure is dropping.
   b. the wind is from an easterly quadrant.
   c. both of the above.
   d. none of the above.

5. _____ is associated with the passage of a warm front.
   a. Decreasing pressure
   b. Increasing pressure
   c. No pressure change

6. _____ are associated with the passage of a cold front.
   a. Stratus-type clouds
   b. Cumulus-type clouds
   c. Both of the above
   d. None of the above

7. The horizontal span of a warm front is
   a. greater than that of a cold front.
   b. less than that of a cold front.

8. Mare's tails are associated with the onset of a
   a. cold front.
   b. warm front.

9. You are south of an extratropical cyclone in the northern hemisphere. The wind direction would be
   a. from the NE quadrant.
   b. from the SE quadrant.
   c. from the NW quadrant.
   d. from the SW quadrant.

10. At the cold front the wind shifts to a
    a. westerly quadrant.
    b. easterly quadrant.

ANSWERS

That air mass is eyeing us nervously! Whether its future is to beam benignly on Bahama bikinis or shroud a bunch of walrus tusks depends on our score. The pattern? As usual, 10 for each correct response. Then,

      100, Nassau bound
       90, Enjoying the Gulf Stream
       80, Edging the Bermuda Triangle
       70, Sargasso Sea on the starboard bow
    under 70, Want to buy a walrus tusk cheap?

1. b   6. b
2. a   7. a
3. b   8. b
4. c   9. d
5. a   10. a

Chapter 8

MORE ON FRONTS

In the last chapter we tagged a few items for later discussion. One of those had to do with the type of cloud expected during the passage of a warm front. We were told that the general form is stratified which will thicken and lower from cirrostratus through altostratus to low-level stratus and nimbostratus. But there can be exceptions.

Figure 122 repeats what we've already seen about the stratified procession. Such is the case when the oncoming warm air is moist and stable. The adiabatic lapse rate remains greater than the existing lapse rate. The air is wedged upward by cold air ahead and will drop in temperature at a rate greater than that existing in its air mass level for level. The rising air will be colder than its surroundings and so will resist any lift. Were it not for the slant of the cold wedge forcing it upward, that air would not rise at all. Chapters ago we saw this meant stability. And the cloud form resulting when such air reaches the dew point is a layered stratus type.

In Figure 123 we see a different picture. Imbedded in the warm front clouds there can be some of the cumulus type. The warm air climbing the frontal slope is moist and conditionally unstable. Its adiabatic rates switch from more to less than the existing rate. Early in its upward trip while still dry air, it cools faster than the surroundings. But when the altitude of dew point is reached and condensation begins, it will thereafter cool at a slower, moist adiabatic rate. It will flip from stability to instability. Condensation will take place while it is rising, and the result will be cumulus-type clouds. In fact, some of those cumulus might be cumulonimbus, producing thunderstorms on a warm front.

Of what value is this knowledge to a surface mariner barren of instrumentation? Perhaps on two scores. First, his struggle with adiabatic and other lapse rates several chapters ago can now be justified. At least the prospect can be viewed with some understanding. Second, he is reminded that weather patterns don't always wear unambiguous insignia. To meet a thunderstorm as a cyclone moves eastward over your position does not mean that somehow you slept through a warm front which has already passed by. You might be under it at the moment, with warm, unstable air aloft.

We can also now clear up a few murky points left over from the chapter on clouds. There we learned that altostratus forms are reliable indicators of warm front activity. That makes sense. Figure 122 shows them as layers in warm, stable air sloping up the frontal surface. We also read that cirrocumulus and altocumulus can be more ambiguous. Sometimes the prospect is fair weather, but sometimes not. Figure 123 suggest a "not" circumstance. Geography and the company they keep can vary the prediction. Arranged in a lowering mass of clouds as seen there, they can suggest warm, unstable air bubbling upward along a warm front.

Still another puzzle can now be unraveled. *Mackerel sky* is a name for cirrocumulus as seen from below. It is also a suggestion of warm front problems. Logic now requires that cirrocumulus have some association with a warm front. Logic is served by Figure 123. When the warm air has instability, cirrocumulus can appear. Seeing the fish-scale underside of mackerel sky, the sailing master breaks out all hands to take in small sails.

Figure 122.   Cloud patterns along a warm front.

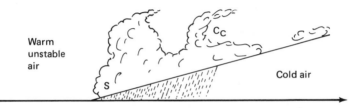

Figure 123.   Warm front clouds when air is unstable.

Following in the wake of the low core is a cold front. What clouds it breeds depends on such factors as stability of the air and the front's rate of advance. Fast-moving ones, particularly in winter, have been known to chase after a low at more than a mile a minute; but usually the speed is less than half that rate. Friction with the earth tends to hold back the front at the surface and steepen the slope. If the warm core develops instability, the upshot might be Figure 124. A *squall line* of thunderstorms can precede the front by many miles and produce very turbulent weather.

A slow-moving cold front has a more gradual slope. If the warm air in its path is stable, then the clouds are stratus in form, as shown in Figure 125. Unstable warm air brings the cumulus type prone to build into the thunderstorms of Figure 126.

Our next project is to follow the extratropical cyclone along through the other stages of its life cycle. Coming up is occlusion, with frontolysis close behind. As the low core slants upward over the warm front, it is pursued by the cold front astern. Figure 127 repeats what we've already seen as a cross-sectional view. Both fronts are traveling eastward, but the cold front has

Figure 124.   Turbulence along a squall line forms churning roll clouds over Florida. (*USN*)

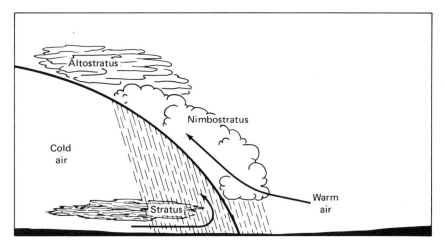

Figure 125.   Clouds at a cold front when air is stable.

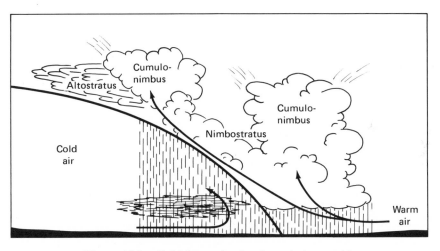

Figure 126.   Cold front clouds when air is unstable.

Figure 127.   Profile of warm and cold fronts in extratropical cyclone.

greater speed. It is catching up with the warm front; and in the process it narrows the low core's contact with the earth's surface. Figure 128 shows a panel of sketches to illustrate the progression.

In Figure 128C the low core is about ready to lift free of the surface. The cold air ahead and behind will very soon block it off entirely from contact with the earth. That is the point of *occlusion*. The cyclone's center-piece of low will soon become an elevated swirl. Filling in beneath is air not sufficiently different to maintain the cyclonic pattern. As that filling process continues, the system will decay. Occlusion ushers in *frontolysis*. Our next subject considers how occlusion and its aftermath can come about.

Until now the cold air ahead and that behind had little concern for how they compare. The warm center was a buffer zone of separation. But now the buffer has eroded and the two cold masses are directly at odds. What happens next involves a comparison of those two.

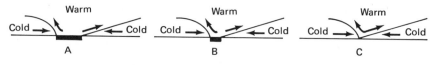

Figure 128.   Development of occlusion.
A. Cold air ahead and behind separated by mature warm sector.
B. Buffer of warm core narrows as occlusion approaches.
C. Occlusion begins when warm sector lifts free of surface.

In Figure 129 we see one possibility. The cold air to the west, or behind the cold front, is colder than that ahead under the warm front. It has the least inclination to rise, and so it won't. The cold front will continue to move along the surface, forcing all the air ahead to go up. This would be a *cold front occlusion*, or a *surface cold front*, or an *upper warm front*. Since occlusion can also be named by what happens to the cold front, it is some-times called a *surface occlusion*.

In Figure 130 some cloud forms have been added. Early in the occluding process the clouds ahead of the cold front are more like those expected in warm front regions. Both clouds and weather near the surface are then similar to that at a cold front. As the occlusion progresses, the warm air is lifted so high that clouds along its front tend to disappear. Then both weather and clouds bear resemblance only to cold front conditions. This cold front occlusion has been described as the more common type. Moreover, it is said to develop more frequently over continents and along their eastern seaboards. Again, our attention to background pays dividends. As a warm core would pass over a continent bound for an ocean surface to the east-ward, it would be chased by cold, continental air. We could expect that to

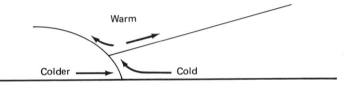

Figure 129. When air behind the warm sector is colder than that ahead, the result is a cold front occlusion.

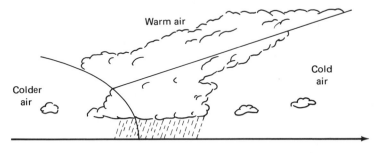

Figure 130. Cloud forms at a cold front occlusion.

be colder than ocean air ahead. So the continental air stays near the surface and forces everything in its path to ascend.

Figure 131 shows the other possibility. Now the cold air behind the cold front is not as cold as that ahead under the warm front. It and its cold front will be forced aloft to chase the warm air core to extinction. The name

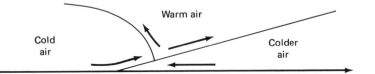

Figure 131. Warm front occlusion results when a cold front moves upward over colder air ahead.

now is *warm front occlusion,* or *upper cold front,* or *surface warm front.* Since the cold front now goes up, the name can also be *upper occlusion.*

Figure 132 adds cloud forms. The surface situation is like that at a warm front, and cold front tendencies will be noted at altitude. As the warm core reaches high altitudes, the frontal activity will diminish. Beforehand, though, if the warm air is moist and unstable, thunderstorms may develop. The locale would not be expected to be continental. Rather, it would be off the west coast of large land masses. Background, again, preens its feathers.

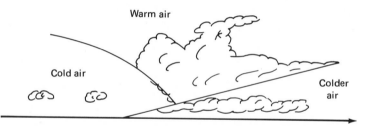

Figure 132.   Cloud forms at a warm front occlusion.

Cold maritime air moving behind a warm core heading inland would encounter colder continental air ahead. It would be wedged upward to pursue the warm center over the base pile of continental air staying at the surface.

Sooner or later the core of the cyclonic system will decay so much that little difference will remain between air ahead and behind and in between. When that happens, uniformity is being restored. And with it comes frontolysis, the death of the pattern. Looking westward, the warm core might see cold pursuing it up the warm front slant toward upper occlusion. Perhaps, though, it might observe a pile of cold bullying its way along the surface toward a surface occlusion and shoving upward everything in its path. Either way, the warm center knows the jig is up. Its depression will be filled in and the atmospheric low essential for other air to cycle around will disappear.

At this stage of the drama a troublesome sideshow might make an appearance. Sometimes another depression will form on the flanks of the primary disturbance. This *secondary low* can show up near the original warm front (to the southeast in the northern hemisphere) or along the first cold front (to the southwest in a northern cyclone). It can build up quickly and seems to have a mind of its own. Sometimes its course is the same as the parent; at other times it follows a different path. In every case, mariners should be alert to the possibility that a dying storm might spawn this bumptious offspring.

Both warm and cold fronts are related to movement of discontinuities across the earth's surface. When warm air moves toward cold, we've seen that the result is a warm front. Should cold move toward warm, then what appears is a cold front. But what happens when there is a standoff, with neither pile able to nudge the other one way or the other? Weathermen call that a *stationary front*, and watch closely for future developments. While the sparring around continues, weather conditions seem to resemble those expected at a warm front. But the situation can change suddenly and without much evidence for prediction. Enough to add stationary front to our growing roster of terminology and to view it as the overture to an un-predictable First Act.

Absent so far from our frontal analysis has been a discussion of anti-cyclones. That omission must be remedied. Our attention has been on weather patterns which, while migrating eastward, bring bad weather to earthlings in their paths. They are revolving forms swirling around low cores. And for so long as the core can remain of sufficiently low pressure compared to its surroundings, the cyclone can live out its life cycle from -genesis to -lysis.

Anticyclones, though, have a *high*-pressure core. The centerpiece is a mass of subsiding dense air from which the swirl is outward at the surface. Many pages back, when meeting Coriolis for the first time, we viewed sketches like those in Figure 133. The northern hemisphere drawing shows a clockwise twist; in the southern hemisphere the turn is counterclockwise.

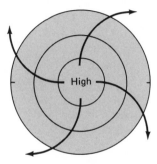   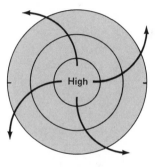

Northern hemisphere   Southern hemisphere

Figure 133.   Patterns of air flow in an anticyclone.

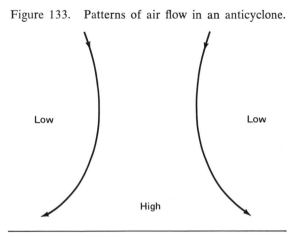

Figure 134.   Anticyclonic air flow in profile.

In profile an anticyclone of either hemisphere resembles the sketch in Figure 134. The central column is piled more fully with air because of the inward or converging flow at altitude. The result is a flow outward, or divergence, at the base. As the air within the column subsides, it will warm adiabatically. That will cause the relative humidity to decrease and move drier air out from the center's base. We can anticipate what kind of weather to expect: fair and dry with clear skies. As for wind strength, it is usually less in anticyclonic weather than when a cyclonic pattern is moving by.

Although more bland than cyclones, these high-centered forms can cover more geography. The long diameter of their elliptical shapes can be from 200 to 2000 miles. And they can be divided into two kinds: cold and warm. A *cold anticyclone* has its central core colder, level for level, than surrounding air. Some of them seem to have a semipermanent location in the wintertime. Those parked over Siberia and North America act as sources for continental polar air masses which, as we've seen, function in the development of low-pressure cells. They supply part of the cast for the drama of our winter extratropical cyclones. We need not be overly inquisitive about their internal workings; but this we can note. The pressure contrast between the core and its surroundings decreases with altitude so that the activity is primarily near the surface.

Throughout a *warm anticyclone*, the temperature, level for level, is greater than that of its environment. It is like a mass of tropical air trapped in alien territory. Air aloft in its core is dense enough to cause subsidence and a greater pressure at the base; so it still has a high center within itself. This kind also tends to have semipermanent locations, and they are usually associated with the horse latitudes. There, as we've read, the wind is slight and the weather is fair. These regions serve as origins for tropical maritime air to feed low-pressure cells traveling nearby. And a more specific definition has been given a few of those locales. We read of the Azores and Bermuda Highs in the North Atlantic, and of the Hawaiian High in the North Pacific. They are labels for such formations of particular interest to North America. Figure 135 illustrates the average concentrations of high and low cells in January; Figure 136 shows them for July.

The highs are not always so benign, however. In wintertime, the buildup of pressure on the pole side of the polar front can produce a break in the battle line. Such a *polar outbreak* will allow chilly air masses to penetrate deeply into warm regions. The pressure will rise rapidly, the temperature will plummet, and the Gulf of Mexico might be in for a *norther*. Should such a breakthrough of arctic or polar air occur in northern Europe, Great Britain would be chilled to the bone.

What we've done by this time is gain more than a passing acquaintance with the outcome of conflict between massive piles of dissimilar atmosphere.

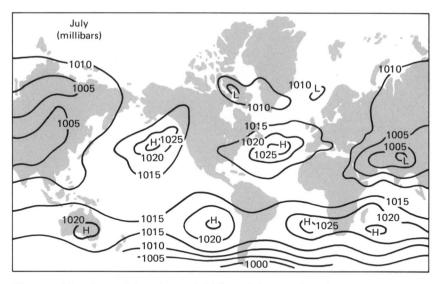

Figure 135. General locations of high and low regions in January. (*From* Aviation Weather; *Washington, D.C.: F.A.A., 1965, p. 14*)

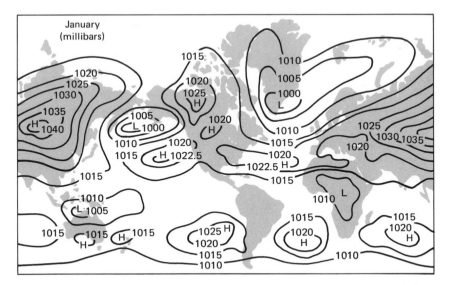

Figure 136. General locations of high and low regions in July (*From* Aviation Weather; *Washington, D.C.: F.A.A., 1965, p. 14*)

It all seems to be on a grand scale, and its northern hemisphere perform-ance affects much of the world's people. Yet the design seems as intricate as the workings of a fine timepiece. And it serves to transfer heat away from the Equator, to distribute moisture around the planet. History has deep concern for how the patterns appeared long centuries ago when the Sahara was green and Myceneae flourished. What the future holds might well depend on where and how the lows and highs should wander. All that, though, is "by the way" speculation for the mariner. Based on what we have discussed, he should be able to achieve a practical understanding of what might transpire for his lifetime of heres and nows.

Before we close this chapter we should get behind us a weather rule for estimating the direction of a nearby low. It has been named the *Law of Buys-Ballot*, after a chief of Holland's meteorological service; and, contrary to indications, he was not a dealer in illegal votes. This eminent scientist of the 19th century is remembered for a simple means to translate wind direction into the bearing of a low. One statement of the rule is this: *Face the wind and the low will be 8 to 10 points to the right when in the northern hemisphere and to the left when in the southern.* To speak in points is going out of style, so a conversion to degrees is in order. The 8 to 10 points trans-lates to an arc of 90° to 112.5°. Sometimes the span is widened to from about 75° to as much as 135°.

One reason for the angular difference, however described, is this. At altitude wind is less affected by the earth's frictional drag and tends to flow parallel to the isobars. Another deals with the fact that such drag is greater over land masses than over the sea. Still a third takes into account the fact that as wind speed increases, centrifugal force bends wind flow out more from a direct high-to-low pattern. In Figure 137 we see a low to the east of an observer aloft in the northern hemisphere. Facing the wind, he would reckon the center to be about abeam to starboard, or 90° from the wind. But were he closer to the surface he would not expect the wind to follow the isobars. Instead, it would cross them at an angle. Figure 138 has the observer facing a surface wind. Now he would measure the center to be abaft his starboard beam, or more than 90° from the wind direction.

Another version of this law has you with your *back* to the wind. Then the northern hemisphere application would have the low to your left, and in the southern hemisphere it would be to your right. Familiarity with only one of these recitals brings no confusion until the existence of the other is dis-covered. Then they might appear as two conflicting laws. But a glance at Figures 137 and 138 seems to indicate that the result is the same whether the wind is on your chin or on your shoulder blades. There is, though, a difference. With wind ahead, you will find the center is 90° or *more* from

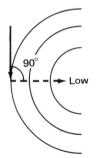 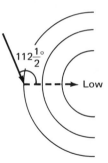

Figure 137. Buys-Ballot Law applied by an observer aloft near a northern hemisphere low.

Figure 138. Buys-Ballot Law applied by a surface observer near a northern hemisphere low.

the direction you face. With the wind on your back, that bearing will be 90° or *less* from the direction you face.

Which declaration Buys-Ballot himself might have preferred is not significant. Mariners, though, have made a customary selection. Putting our stern into the weather can sometimes be risky, so we choose the face-to-the-wind account. Airmen, it seems, favor the back-to-the-wind rule. Perhaps their reasoning is as simple as this: aircraft prefer a tailwind. We should be aware that there are two ways the rule can be stated. Then we should leave airmen waving their rudders at the wind while we perpetuate our own surface-bound view. In the process we have protection against unnecessary concern should we encounter the airmen's description.

Time for us to take all way off the ship, poke a wet finger skyward, and take a bearing. The next chapter will have us gingerly sampling the mysteries of tropical cyclones. Beforehand we should make certain that what is now on board is well secured to handle the onslaught.

QUESTIONS

Life, they say, is a succession of highs and lows. Some quarters recommend that when we perceive the peaks and troughs of our biorhythms, coping can be a breeze. Who are we to say nay? Seamen have no call to criticize the buoyage system until after they've tried the channel. Let's test some ups and downs to learn whether our present phase is on the -genesis side or sliding into a -lysis lurch.

1. A warm front thunderstorm might occur when the warm air
   a. is unstable.
   b. has an adiabatic lapse rate less than the existing lapse rate.
   c. both of the above.

2. _____ is the term describing a situation during occlusion when the warm front stays in contact with the earth's surface,
   a. Surface warm front
   b. Surface cold front

3. _____ is the term describing a situation during occlusion when the cold front stays in contact with the earth's surface.
   a. Surface warm front
   b. Surface cold front

4. A cold front occlusion
   a. is the more common type.
   b. develops more frequently on the eastern coast of a continent than on the western coast.
   c. both of the above.
   d. none of the above.

5. Weather conditions at a stationary front resemble that at a
   a. cold front.
   b. warm front.

6. Anticyclones
   a. are associated with fair weather.
   b. rotate counterclockwise in the southern hemisphere.
   c. both of the above
   d. none of the above.

7. A semipermanent high-pressure region located over Siberia would be
   a. of the warm type.
   b. of the cold type.

8. A norther in the Gulf of Mexico is associated with
   a. a polar outbreak.
   b. a Bermuda outbreak.
   c. a surface warm front.
   d. none of the above.

9. You are in the northern hemisphere near an extratropical cyclone. The wind is north. By applying the Law of Buys-Ballot, mariner-style, you would estimate the low center to bear
   a. west to northwest.
   b. south to southwest.
   c. north to northeast.
   d. east to southeast.

10. You are in the northern hemisphere and due north of the center of an anticyclone. The wind direction to be expected would be from the
    a. northwest quadrant.
    b. southwest quadrant.
    c. northeast quadrant.
    d. southeast quadrant.

ANSWERS

Crests are better than troughs, says the quizmaster. He has prepared a graph and waits with pen at the ready to plot your wave along the front line. The usual 10 for each correct response, and here is how he weights the isobars:

> 100, Warm anticyclones prevail
> 90, A lone Siberian high joined the train
> 80, Two lows, but no cause for great concern
> 70, Pressure dropping and heavy clouds!
> under 70, The warm front thunders from too many blunders!

1. c   6. a
2. a   7. b
3. b   8. a
4. c   9. d
5. b   10. b

Chapter 9

TROPICAL CYCLONES

Even the arctic mariner is inquisitive about a tropical cyclone, for it is without peer as the greatest natural show on earth. The emotions of observers in its path are, understandably, less detached. This storm is a vicious, almost unbelievable, affair. *Bowditch*, the seaman's bible, is seldom noted for extravagant prose. Yet it speaks of the tropical cyclone in these words:

As the center of the storm comes closer, the ever-stronger wind shrieks through the rigging. . . . Even the largest and most seaworthy vessels become virtually unmanageable. . . . Less sturdy vessels may not survive. . . . The awesome fury of this condition can only be experienced. Words are inadequate to describe it.*

That sort of introduction impels us to a very close look.

A dividend of this study is that in one session we can dispose of a cluster of atmospheric torments. *Tropical cyclone* is the general name for such beasts, but regional labels have been applied here and there. The term *hurricane* describes one in the western North Atlantic, Caribbean, and the eastern Pacific. *Cordonazo* and *Lash of St. Francis* are local names for fierce southerly winds of a tropical cyclone on the west coast of Mexico (St.

* *American Practical Navigator (Bowditch)*, Publication 9 (Washington, D.C.: Defense Mapping Agency Hydrographic/Topographic Center, 1977), 1:902.

Francis is held accountable because the likely time for the coast to be pummelled is around his October 4 feast day). *Typhoon* is applied to those in the western Pacific, with *baguio* as an alternate in the Philippines. The Bay of Bengal calls it a *cyclone*, as do most areas of the North and South Indian Oceans. When one visits the region north of Australia it can be tagged a *willy-willy*. Each monster, though, regardless of name, is essentially the same powerful cycle around a low-pressure vortex originating in a tropical region.

By no means does that infer they are confined to the tropics. As they spin across the earth they follow tracks which go westward for a while, change course toward the nearest pole, and then recurve to rumble eastward at higher latitudes. The litter in their wakes can stretch from the West Indies to Manhattan, from Mindanao to Kobe. And for much of that time they were accepted with the resignation accorded sudden death and imperious taxation. Barely more than a century ago the first system of hurricane warnings was instituted in the United States, and for the next 80 or so years, the network was expanded and polished. But not until the late 1950s was a concentrated effort made to learn exactly what makes

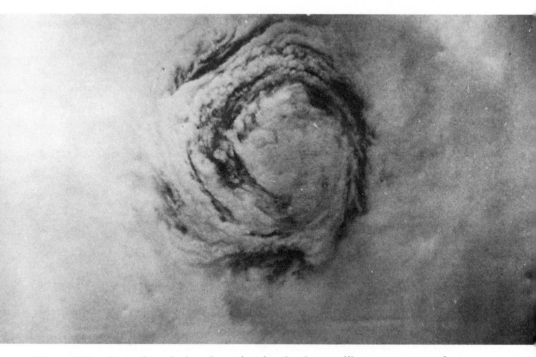

Figure 139.   Core of tropical cyclone rips the cloud cover like an open wound. (*NOAA*)

tropical cyclones tick. In the past 20 years more has been discovered about their makeup than in the previous 2000. Aircraft, submarines, and surface vessels were involved to reconnoiter on the flanks and to probe deeply into the heart of their mysteries. Nowadays, much sophisticated instrumentation is applied to the task. Satellites, radar, and widespread surveillance by air and sea are working to solve such puzzles as how, why, and when nature erupts in these titanic rages. There are still regions of solitary ocean where these atrocities can build up unobserved; but, for the most part, mariners have data at hand to signal in advance what might be in the wind.

The more information is compiled on specifics, the more interest we might have in banishing these horrors from our sight. *Weather modification* deals with the mechanics of altering circumstances so that no more need we have concern for such devastation. And devastation, indeed, is the aftermath of a tropical cyclone. But conservative action is still the guiding principle. We've all learned the hard way that tinkering with natural forces requires the utmost care. Tropical cyclones serve a good purpose despite the price in lives and property damage. Until there is certainty that the cure is not worse than the disease, modification takes a back seat to observation.

We've already read that the tropical cyclone is spawned in the tropics while the extratropical variety breeds at higher latitudes. But they differ more than by geography. The tropical one is smaller and much, much more intense. And there are more basic contrasts. The extratropical, we've seen, is the result of conflict between two *dissimilar* air masses. The tropical one is a violent commotion within a single pile of more or less uniform air. Absent from it is a true frontal pattern such as we analyzed in the last chapter. To examine the workings of a tropical cyclone is to mix hypothesis with proved laws, for there is no uniformity of thought on the exact recipe nature uses to concoct these fierce storms. Much has been learned, but some remains unsettled on the hows and whys. We should, of course, discuss the general principles involved; but we should also retain the perspective of seamen. Our concern is with recognition and avoidance. To plunge deeply into theory would not really serve our aim. It is better, by far, that we recognize generalities about causes but concentrate on the more practical aspects of effects. First, then, to sample some of those hows and whys.

On the poleward sides of the equatorial doldrums, trade winds stand ready to invade from either side. The inflow from northeast and southeast produces a convergence of air into that low region followed by convection. The result can be heavy clouds and rainfall. The name given the area is *Intertropical Convergence Zone* or *ITCZ*. It vacillates north and south in latitude, lagging somewhat behind the sun's seasonal course. What it does,

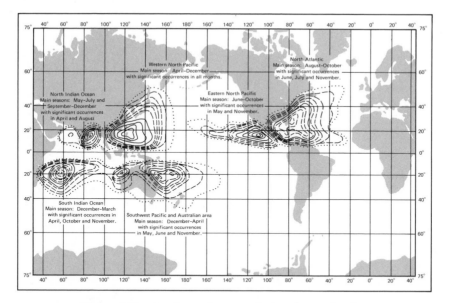

Figure 140. Regions where tropical cyclones develop.

Figure 141. Hurricane drives 10-foot plank through royal palm. (*NOAA*)

Figure 142. Camille makes toy boats of large freighters . . . (*NOAA*)

in any case, is create a surface inflow and an upward convection. The lower part of Figure 144's satellite view reveals a line of clouds stretching westward from the Gulf of Panama. This marks the ITCZ within the tropics in the North Pacific.

Another influence must be considered. On the Equator side of semipermanent subtropical highs (such as the Azores–Bermuda High in the North Atlantic), a trough of low-pressure air can begin to drift westward. Its undulating pattern is called an *easterly wave*. Ahead of it there is good weather with rows of cumulus clouds. In the northern hemisphere the prevailing trades become more north than northeast. Behind it, though, the wind moves around (in the northern hemisphere) to become southeasterly. Heavy piles of cumulonimbus clouds bring poor visibility, rain, and even thunderstorms. What is happening is that air is converging behind the trough and producing another likelihood of updrafts and convection. In the North Atlantic these easterly waves seem to appear from May to November and become almost a daily occurrence during the peak of the hurricane season. Figure 145 shows what might be expected in that ocean.

Figure 143.   ... and chooses an unusual berth for a Mississippi trawler. (*NOAA*)

So far, then, we have a wavy region of converging trade winds within the tropics and the periodic passage of a low-pressure trough from east to west. Let the two of them coincide and it is no wonder that central lows can form, around which cycling winds develop.

These storms have been described as atmospheric heat engines. As such they require fuel, and the ocean is the source. When the ocean surface is about 80° F or more, warm air well laden with water vapor is moved upward by all this convection. Should the latitude be at least 5°, there will be sufficient Coriolis effect to bend the inflow away from a direct high-to-low path. A vortex of warm, moist, and ascending air can form. When that takes place there is a *tropical disturbance*, the first phase of this cyclone's life.

As the ocean feeds more and more water vapor into the center, the warm core accelerates upward and out from the top of the chimney. In going up it cools to the saturation point. Then comes condensation, and with it outlandish transfers of heat to power the engine. Isobars, the lines of equal pressure, close around the center to indicate rotary circulation at the earth's

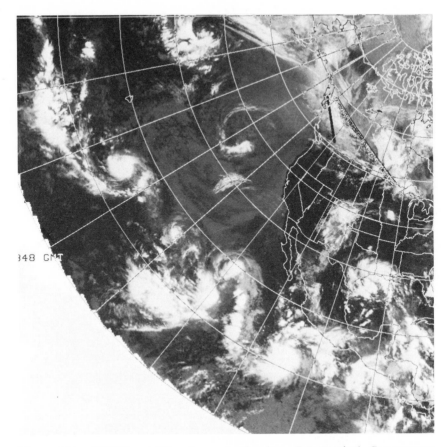

Figure 144. TIROS satellite views clouds along Intertropical Convergence Zone in North Pacific. (*NOAA*)

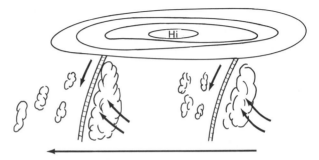

Figure 145.   Low-pressure troughs travel through the ITCZ as easterly waves.

Figure 146. Satellite records a North Pacific trio. Kate, just to the left of center, is a tropical cyclone. Liza, on the right, is still a depression but destined to become a killer. Between them is an unnamed sister who never grew up. (*NOAA*)

surface. The wind builds, but is still below 34 knots. Now the pattern is called a *tropical depression*.

Were it not for one more influence, the rising air would tend to settle around the core. Sooner or later the inflow would fill the core and the cycling form would cease. But this atmospheric engine is equipped with a pump. As the central air rises it is sucked out by high-altitude winds and whisked away to descend hundreds of miles distant. The result is an extreme drop in the core's air pressure, aggravation of the inflow, and continued life for the chimney. As the speed of inflow increases, the chimney effect intensifies. When the wind is more than 33 knots, but no more than 63, the condition is called a *tropical storm*. When the wind mounts to 64 knots or more the result is a *tropical cyclone*.

The developing stages of this weather are signaled by storm warnings. As an aside, we can recognize an accidental correlation between the night signals displayed for those warnings and Rules of the Road. When the wind is no more than 33 knots the signal is a red light over a white. That is a *small craft advisory*. By Rules of the Road it can mean "fishing," and you might do so for a while in a tropical depression. Wind from 34 through 47 knots is warned by white-over-red and means *gale*. Rules of the Road say it tells of a "pilot ahead." When the wind speed is 48 through 63 knots, storm warnings tell of a *storm* by showing two vertical red lights (by Rules of the Road the meaning is "not under command"). During a tropical storm, with winds 34 through 63 knots, you might well need a pilot or even be out of command. And when the wind reaches 64 knots or greater in a tropical cyclonic pattern, storm warnings say *hurricane* by red-white-red lights in a vertical line. One Rules of the Road use for that display is "engaged in an underwater operation." At that stage of the game, the suggestion could be all too apt!

Back, though, to our consideration of the tropical cyclone. Its growth from disturbance to cyclone follows an ascending order of intensity, but not all disturbances make the full transition. An estimate is that barely one in ten reach the cyclone stage. That 10%, though, is far more than enough.

Since one requirement is a very warm ocean, the likelihood of occurrence is the time of year when oceans might become very warm. That is late summer. So these are storms of the late summer for the hemisphere. May to November is the northern season, with August to September the peak time. Out of this has come a not-too-valid ditty:

> June, too soon; July, stand by; August, beware you must;
> September, remember; October, all over.

The residents of Galveston or Brownsville in those years when November blows down power lines and floods the streets are not impressed. The North Atlantic hurricane more or less follows this rule, but we had better consider the season as fully May to November. The same is true of tropical cyclones in the eastern North Pacific. Typhoons of the western North Pacific have appeared in every month, for they are the most capricious of these storms. Even so, late summer peaking is the rule. Cyclones of the Arabian Sea seem to have two peaks: one in June and another in October.

In the southern hemisphere the season is from about November to May, with January through March the most active months. Again, the late summer rule is followed. You should note, though, that there is no mention of the South Atlantic. That is for good reason: there are *no* tropical cyclones in that ocean. Two factors have been suggested for this. First, the ITCZ doesn't visit the South Atlantic; instead, it hovers north of the Equator. The southeast trades cross the Equator before they intrude on the equatorial low, so there is no south latitude place for inflowing wind

Figure 147.   Ava reveals her near-perfect core to a satellite. (*NOAA*)

to capture a warm core in that region. The second factor is that the ocean temperature remains too cold to provide sufficient water vapor for fuel.

So far, then, we can summarize the fundamentals of these storms in this way:

1. They occur in the late summer for the hemisphere,
2. They develop, usually, no closer than 5° latitude from the Equator, for Coriolis must be sufficient to start a cycling motion.

The form of their isobars is more nearly circular than that shown by other cyclonic patterns. A downview emphasizes that they are, indeed, deep pockets of low pressure with higher air whirling all around. Once started, they are carried by the prevailing trade winds to follow an initial westward track. Their forward progress is then usually no more than 15 knots. Next, Coriolis goes to work, for the vortex is in motion over the earth's surface. In the northern hemisphere the track curves to the right; in the southern hemisphere it curves to the left. In either hemisphere the curve is away from the Equator. For a while the forward progress might slow down; sometimes it even seems to stall. But when the storm reaches a latitude of about 25° to 30° it begins to recurve to the eastward. Coriolis begins the course change and the influence of prevailing westerlies finishes the job. After recurving, the forward progress accelerates. In fact, sometimes it can exceed 50 knots! As the tropical cyclone heads eastward into higher latitudes it can begin to change into an extratropical storm. Figure 148 illustrates the general idea for storm tracks in both hemispheres.

It must be noted that the sketch speaks only in generalities, for no two tropical cyclones have been known to be exactly alike. They seem to be steered over the earth's surface by the flow of air within which they drift. In that environment they can be shunted by concentrations of high pressure, and that not so high as to deviate greatly from a standardized track. Some North Atlantic hurricanes might bend sharply after roaring over the Lesser Antilles and curve northeastward toward open ocean. Others might forge westward over Cuba, race across the Gulf of Mexico, and ravage the coast of Texas. They can lunge and feint, make a loop or two, and might even suddenly reverse field. Typhoons can be particularly erratic. Enough for us to recognize that they follow no fixed roadbed.

But let's focus on clues useful to a mariner when beset by a tropical cyclone wherever met and following whatever serpentine track. He would like to have the assistance of radio reports from professional weathermen.

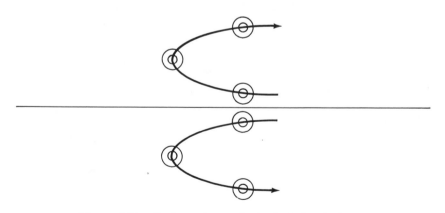

Figure 148.   Basic storm tracks in both hemispheres.

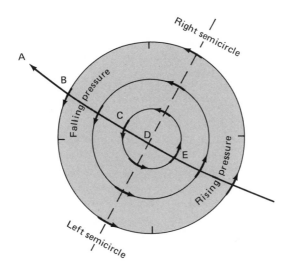

Figure 149. Northern hemisphere tropical cyclone detailed by semicircle and pressure change.

Based on data collected by intricate devices observing a wide region, such warnings are priceless when they can be received. He would also like to use his own radar to tell him what disturbances are around. But he must be ready for the time when aerials and antenna have been blown overboard by the fury of the wind. When there is any likelihood of a tropical cyclone visiting his area he should be able to determine what to do with a barometer, a wet finger, and a cool head containing basic information. Even so ill-equipped he need not give up the ship.

Figure 149 is a downview of a northern hemisphere tropical cyclone. There we see it straddling its track and heading in a northwestward direction. The locale is within the tropics, before much curving poleward has begun. The track divides the storm into two parts. Looking in the direction of progress we see them named as the *right* and *left* semicircles. Through the center, and perpendicular to the track is a broken line to show the regions of falling and rising pressure as the storm moves along. The combination of track and broken line creates a pattern of four quadrants: in each semicircle one is forward of the center with falling pressure and one behind the center with rising pressure.

Note the wind arrows, telling us that the high-to-low path has been influenced by Coriolis and centrifugal force to create a truly cyclic flow around the center but not into it. In the right semicircle wind flow can be in the same direction as the course of the storm along its track; in the left portion that flow can be opposite. Sea and swell are wind-driven and depend on such factors as wind strength, fetch, and duration. We've already met fetch as the distance that wind blows with unchanged direction over a water surface. As the storm progresses it keeps moving over different surfaces, so duration and fetch at any one point in the pattern are short. Even so, Figure 149 shows that in the right semicircle, particularly near the dividing line between falling pressure in the front quadrant and rising to the rear, those two factors can be greater than in other areas. There, a 100-knot wind within and traveling in the same direction as a 15-knot storm has a longer opportunity to whip the sea into less changeable contours. There, the waves will be higher and the swell created will be propelled along the track. That swell reaches such a speed that it outruns the storm and becomes advance evidence of what is churning along behind it.

Days before the storm appears, long-crested swells should be expected in the region of Point A in Figure 149. Eight per minute is an average rate for normal swells in a deep ocean. Those generated by a tropical cyclone pass at about half that rate and are about twice as long. Swell direction is a clue to the bearing of the storm itself; but the observer must keep in mind some other factors. The direction from which swells come indicates the direction of the storm *when they left its influence.* But while they are enroute, the storm will be following its curvy track. Moreover, the swell patterns change in shoaling water. The lines of their crests will be altered by bottom contours. The hint is more reliable in deep water than in shallow, and, at best, it reports the history of where the storm has been. Swell action should be noted, for it does warn that a tropical cyclone is in the offing. But building too many specifics on its testimony might be dangerous.

When the center is still more than 500 miles away the barometer often rises a bit and the skies are quite clear. Soon, though, the barometer gets fidgety and begins to pump up and down. Next to appear will be a cloud sequence somewhat similar to that heralding the approach of an extratropical warm front. Mare's tails string out from the storm and can be used as another pointer to the cyclone.

Now the barometer begins its long fall. Cirrus is replaced by cirrostratus and then altostratus, to be followed by stratocumulus. The cloud forms thicken and rain begins to fall. The wind would now be from 20 to 40 knots and the storm center is still several hundred miles away. But ready to appear over the horizon is its actual body. A murky barrier of heavy, dark clouds becomes visible. This wall of cumulonimbus is called the *bar,* indicated by Point *B* in Figure 149. Patches of it rip off to bring squalls and sudden gusts of wind.

Now the barometer speeds up its fall and the wind increases. Seas run

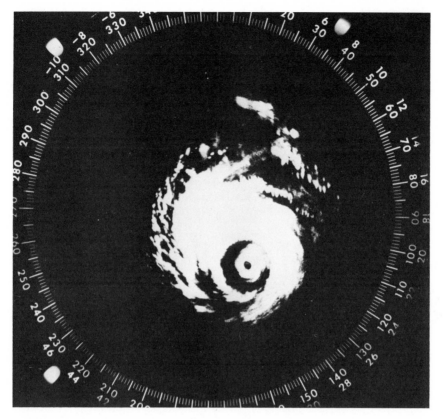

Figure 150.   Radar captures Beulah's eye near Brownsville. (*NOAA*)

high and squall lines roar past. In daytime the sun is darkened by heavy overcast as the barometer tumbles and the wind grows stronger. And still the center can be up to 200 miles away. What happens next is more of the same with mounting intensity. The noise of the wind becomes a distinct rumble and rain pours from the sky. There seems to be a pattern of bands of heavy clouds spewing torrential rain separated by areas of little or no rain.

At point *C* in Figure 149, the *wall of the eye* makes its appearance. This is a frightening pile of clouds from which the rainfall is heaviest. The wind reaches maximum speed. There is no firm statistic for velocity at this inner band, for instruments don't stand up under the blast, but estimates of nearly 200 knots and even more are not out of line.

Point *D* is in the *eye of the storm*. There the fast-ascending air creates an eerie, vacuum-like core. Cloud cover diminishes; often, clear sky is visible. The wind drops below 15 knots, but the seas don't lie down. Instead, they are a confused mass colliding every which way. Point *E* is on the rear side of the eye, within the back part of the wall. The wind howls again, but now from the opposite direction. Rain falls in torrents from masses of cumulonimbus clouds and the sequence is the same as that from B to C, but in reverse. This rear portion passes over more quickly since the storm patterns are not as wide in the rear as in the forward regions.

Although a tropical cyclone is not as large as an extratropical one, its dimensions are still impressive. For a radius of 200 miles from its center winds will be of gale force. For a radius of 50 miles they are at hurricane speed. The eye's size is not standardized, but about 15 miles across is an average diameter. The life of a North Atlantic hurricane can be from about 8 days early or late in the season to about 12 days at peak times. Air pressure in the eye might average 2 inches (or nearly 68 millibars) below normal and has been known to fall almost twice as much. The water level can rise from 1 to 4 feet into this low.

The energy spent during its lifetime exceeds man's electrical needs for many weeks. But that energy still needs fuel. When a tropical cyclone moves inland it loses its supply; then it begins to decay. Moreover, an increase in frictional drag helps the process of filling in the core. Rain still falls in crippling amounts, but the whirling vortex disappears.

Here is a recap of the clues so far available to a mariner. A long, slow swell precedes the storm and points generally to its location. Thickening and lowering clouds couple with a falling barometer to give evidence of its arrival. Bands of dark, heavy clouds alternate with thinner spirals as the wind increases, the barometer plummets, and the center approaches. Around the center the greatest violence is met, and in the eye is a relative calm with lowest pressure. But there are still more hints to be found by the mariner. Figure 151 is another view of a northern hemisphere tropical cyclone. This time several positions are marked on the sketch as Points 1 through 6. If our harried observer were stationary at Point 1 with the storm traveling along the track over him, he would appear to move, relative to the storm, through those six points. What would he note? From Points 1 through 3 the pressure would be falling and the wind would be nearly unchanging in direction. After the center passed he would find himself progressing from Points 4 through 6. The pressure would be rising and the wind would have switched to a still unchanging but opposite direction. From Points 1 through 3 the wind would be increasing in force; from Points 4 through 6 it would be decreasing. When wind direction doesn't change appreciably, he is on the track. When the barometer is falling and wind speed increasing, he is ahead of the center. When the barometer rises and wind speed diminishes, he is behind the center. Don't ask him how he can judge an alteration in wind speed. His anemometer might tell the difference between 150 knots and 130, but that loyal instrument fell overboard

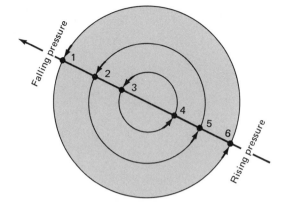

Figure 151. Pattern of pressure change during passage of northern hemisphere tropical cyclone.

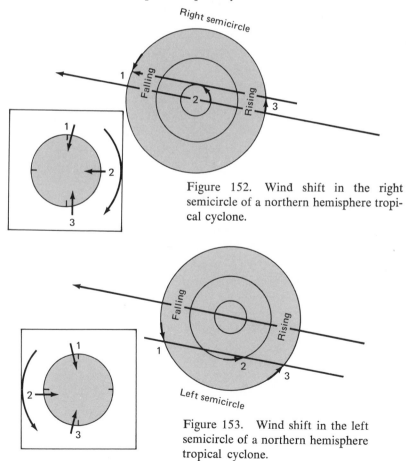

Figure 152. Wind shift in the right semicircle of a northern hemisphere tropical cyclone.

Figure 153. Wind shift in the left semicircle of a northern hemisphere tropical cyclone.

some time ago. He should, though, treasure his barometer more than his life jacket.

In Figure 152 we see the same storm again, but now different positions are marked. This time the observer is not on the track; instead, he is in the right semicircle. As the storm travels by, he moves from Points 1 through 3. The pressure falls at first and then begins to rise, as before. But the wind pattern is not the same. At Point 1 it is almost north. Point 2 shows it as east and at Point 3 it is nearly south. The inset in Figure 152 plots the successive wind directions and reveals that the shift is *to the right*. This is a *veering* wind.

Figure 153 displays the storm another time. Here the observer is in the left semicircle and, relative to the center, moves from Points 1 through 3. The wind is now almost north at Point 1, westerly at Point 2, and nearly south at Point 3. The inset shows the shift as one *to the left*. The label for that is a *backing* wind.

The combination of the last two sketches brings more hints. When, in the northern hemisphere, the wind shifts right, the observer is in the right semicircle. When it shifts left, he is in the left semicircle. Of course, it is somewhat impractical to ask how to determine wind direction when the force is extreme and the air is full of spray. The pessimist abandons the task to cringe in the lee of a bulkhead. But those stouter of heart could invoke this suggestion: watch the motion of lower clouds.

We should look again at Figures 151, 152, and 153. In the right semicircle of a northern hemisphere tropical cyclone more severe conditions can exist. There, wind and storm run in similar directions. This can mean stronger winds, higher seas, and a tendency to be swept toward the track in the path of the oncoming eye. By contrast, winds in the left semicircle can be opposite to track motion, bringing less strength, smaller seas, and a tendency to be thrown to the rear of the eye. So names have been given to the right and left portions. The right semicircle in the northern hemisphere is called the *dangerous semicircle*; the left is called the *navigable*. Neither one is particularly safe, but relative to each other they can be ranked.

One more factor stands between us and a recap of traits of the northern hemisphere tropical cyclone. In the last chapter we met the Buys-Ballot Law. It can serve to tell something more about this storm. By the mariner's version we are told to face the wind and the low pressure center is from 8 to 12 points (90° to 135°) to the right in the northern hemisphere. Figure 154 repeats our storm again and applies this law. At the four points shown, the rule holds up. The center in each case is about abeam to starboard.

Now for the promised recap of a northern hemisphere tropical cyclone. It is a late summer storm which originates at no less than 5° latitude. Early

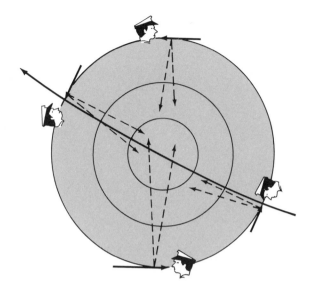

Figure 154. Buys-Ballot Law applied in a northern hemisphere tropical cyclone.

in its life it moves westward with the trade winds and then curves to the right away from the Equator. Next it recurves to the eastward. Its right half, looking along the direction of travel, is called dangerous; its left half is termed navigable. In its dangerous part, the wind veers to the right; in the navigable, the wind backs to the left. For an observer on the track, the wind maintains one steady direction when he is ahead of the center and an opposite, but still steady, direction when behind it. The pressure falls as the eye approaches and rises as it moves beyond. According to the Buys-Ballot Law an observer facing the wind should consider the center to bear from 8 to 12 points (90° to 135°) to the right.

Our jury-rigged observer, then, is not beyond aid when electronics jump ship. Figure 155 has a panel of sketches to depict his plight when all he has left is a barometer, wind direction, and Buys-Ballot. In Figure 155A the wind is from about northeast and the barometer is falling. At least he can surmise he is ahead of the center and the eye is someplace to the southeast. In Figure 155B, a while later, the wind is from about southeast and the barometer is still falling. The wind shift has been to the right. That tells him that he is in the right or dangerous semicircle. Now the center is probably from south to southwest of him. In Figure 155C the barometer has begun to rise and the wind is more nearly from the south. He's still in the dangerous semicircle, but now he is in the rear of the storm. And the center, says

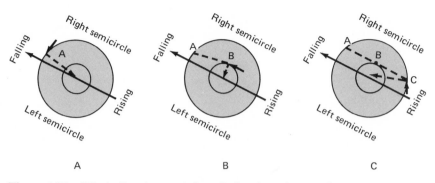

Figure 155. Wind direction and Buys-Ballot Law locate observer relative to center of northern hemisphere tropical cyclone.

    A. In right semicircle ahead of center in northern hemisphere.

    B. In right semicircle abeam of center in northern hemisphere.

    C. In right semicircle behind center in northern hemisphere.

Buys-Ballot, is somewhere to the west of him. Not scientific, but in his condition it's the only game in town. The comment has already been made that short-circuits are the downfall of marine electrons. And in the teeth of a tropical cyclone, much more than a short-circuit can immobilize modern aids.

It is one thing to know where you are in relation to a tropical cyclone; it is another to do something about it. Maneuvering in the presence of such an ogre is a perilous task. It must be accepted at the outset that precise navigation is impossible. Mountainous seas and Force 12 winds allow little more than bare steerageway. Even if you have the facility to change position with some will, the whims of the storm track must be considered. To head off in one direction might just mean crossing the track in front of the eye after the storm has decided to loop or hook. There are classic maneuvering rules, and we will review them. But we should recognize that they presume all other things to be equal. To put 40-foot seas on the quarter with 3 feet of freeboard might not be too intelligent. One reaction is to batten down everything and let her ride as best she will until the fury is past. Even so, the classic rules bear attention. Assuming, then, we can go bow-on or stern-to, here is the idea.

First of all, don't forget common seasense. Secure *everything* which can be secured. The storm's power far exceeds imagination. What can work loose will do so. Even the most basic requirements of stability should not be overlooked. Liquids sloshing in a tank can move so quickly that much weight is transferred from here to there almost in an instant. This is called *free surface effect*, and can act as if the center of gravity of the entire vessel were suddenly raised. If you can, leave no tanks partly filled

Figure 156. Satellite view of Viola east of the Philippines as received aboard M/V *Glomar Challenger* while within the storm. (*Courtesy Captain Joseph Clark and Global Marine, Inc.*)

with liquid. Combine two partly full tanks into one completely filled; pump some contents overboard if you dare. But at least remember that 300 gallons of fuel can be a ton of weight. Let it start splashing port and starboard in a slack tank and basic stability will soon be impaired. Be sure the scuppers are free. Should rainwater pocket on deck, you might have an unexpected "tank" adding up to more tons. A tropical cyclone has been known to dump nearly 4 *feet* of rain in a day. Not all of it falls in one place and you would never expect that much to come aboard. But no chances should be taken. The idea is to make weights stay put as much as possible.

Having attended to the precepts of seamanship, we can move on to some general guides for the northern hemisphere. As you read them, keep in mind how very general these maxims are. They must presume that under actual conditions data can be observed and recommended measures are feasible. At night in the black heart of a raging hurricane there will be scant chance to note cloud motion or to learn much about the sea other than that it is incredible. And with just a few feet of freeboard aft, to place one's stern to skyscraping waves could be insane. Yet these are rules which have evolved from centuries of seafaring to be applied with liberal amounts of common sense. Figure 157 illustrates what is involved.

> **1. When in the dangerous semicircle ahead of the center, put the wind broad on the starboard bow (045° relative) and make all way possible.**

In Figure 157 that mariner would be at Point *A*. There would be a temptation to dart across the track to make for the navigable semicircle. But with the storm moving at many times his progress in tumultuous seas, he would too often reach the track at the same time as the wall and the eye. Discretion prevails, and he tries to bull his way toward the outskirts.

> **2. When on the storm track ahead of the center, put the wind two points on the starboard quarter (about 157.5° relative) and make all way possible.**

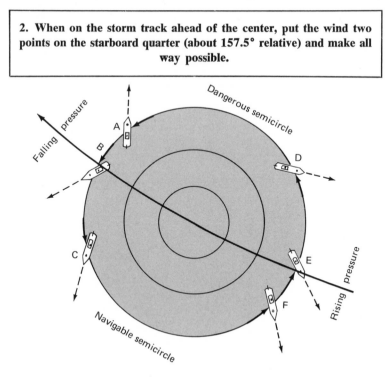

Figure 157. Recommended maneuvers in a northern hemisphere tropical cyclone.

Now, in Figure 157 he is at Point *B*. Since he is already on the track he has no option but to get away from it. And heading into the navigable semicircle, if he can, is the best idea.

---

3. When in the navigable semicircle ahead of the center, put the wind broad on the starboard quarter and make all way possible.

This mariner is at Point *C* in Figure 157. With the wind 135° relative to his bow he is trying to claw his way toward the fringe in the region of lesser storm violence.

---

4. When in the dangerous semicircle behind the center, put the wind on the starboard bow and remember the possibility of recurving.

The position now is Point *D* in Figure 157. Pressure is rising and the worst is over, provided the mariner doesn't blunder into an encore should the cyclone curve eastward toward him.

---

5. When on the track behind the center, avoid it by all practical means.

When at Point *E* in Figure 157 the mariner should, obviously, not start chasing the eye. He should probably put the wind on the starboard bow while moving into the navigable semicircle. And, again, recurving should be considered.

---

6. When in the navigable semicircle behind the center, put the wind on the starboard side and make all way possible.

The mariner is now at Point *F* in Figure 157. Whether he puts the wind on the bow or quarter can vary as wind direction changes. But the plan is to move farther to the rear of the storm at increasing distance from the track.

---

7. When obliged to heave to, do so head-to-sea when in the dangerous semicircle and stern-to-sea (freeboard permitting) when on the track or in the navigable semicircle.

Apparently the rationale is this. In the dangerous semicircle, wind and sea will move the hove-to vessel toward the track inevitably; but there is no reason to make the task easier for the storm. Keeping your bow into the weather is usually safer, and the movement downwind will not be so rapid. In the navigable semicircle, wind and sea will move the hove-to vessel away from the track, and that welcome influence should be assisted by pointing the bow downwind. There is another approach recommended for this predicament. By it, the mariner is advised to secure all he can and let the vessel attain her best riding attitude in her own way. With the limited options available in practice, that might often be the unchangeable outcome.

Maneuvering near the center of a tropical cyclone makes more demands on cool exercise of common sense than any other phase of seafaring. The best tactic is the one which succeeds the first time, for no escapee from such confusion purposely revisits the scene to try another. But we need not view these recommended canons as only applicable when the ship is caught up in the total fury of the storm. As preventive measures when the mariner finds himself in the suburbs of such power, they are of at least equal value.

We cannot overlook the southern hemisphere. Yachtsmen on a dream voyage through Polynesia might well become involved; and large vessels bound from Chile to Japan could meet hurricanes plus typhoons all in one passage. Tropical cyclones south of the Equator differ from the northern kind, but in an almost exactly opposite manner. Such elements as swell, bar, wall, and eye are similar. So is the idea that first they move westward with the trades, then curve poleward and recurve to the east at higher latitudes. Here, though, the key word is *left* instead of right.

Figure 158 shows the classic track of a tropical cyclone in the southern hemisphere. The start is in an ITCZ. Next follows a not-too-speedy drift westward in the southeast trade winds. Now, though, Coriolis curves the track to the left. At an even slower speed the cyclone heads south for a while, toward the pole. At between 25° to 30° latitude, Coriolis bends it to the left. Speed on the track increases as the storm climbs southeastward to even higher latitudes.

The wind arrows reflect the Coriolis left turn from a direct high-to-low direction. It is in the left semicircle, says Figure 158, that wind flows with the storm instead of against it. So, semicircle safety is reversed: left is dangerous and right is navigable.

Point by point, the pattern of opposites continues. For example, the Buys-Ballot Law now states that when we face the wind the low center is

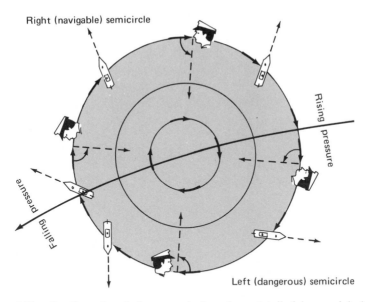

Right (navigable) semicircle

Rising pressure

Falling pressure

Left (dangerous) semicircle

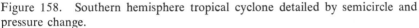

Figure 158. Southern hemisphere tropical cyclone detailed by semicircle and pressure change.

to the left. And maneuvering requires that we put the wind on the left side whenever in the northern hemisphere it should be on the right.

Figure 159 points out the windshift patterns. For Point *A* in the dangerous semicircle, the shift is to the left; for *B* in the navigable semicircle, it is to the right. That, as we should expect, is exactly opposite to the northern hemisphere. Now, though, we encounter something left foggy in many weather discussions. North of the Equator the wind is said to *veer* to the right and *back* to the left. That statement should not be disputed, for it conforms to international usage. Confusion can stem from it, though. An older practice described a veering wind as one which shifts to the right in the northern hemisphere, but to the left in the southern. And by that view a backing wind was just the opposite. That outlook is waning, but it still might have sufficient life to be troublesome. We should scrub up the definitions this way:

Veering is a wind shift to the right. It describes the movement in the dangerous semicircle of a northern hemisphere tropical cyclone and in the navigable semicircle of one in the southern.

Backing is the name given to a wind shift to the left. It refers to change in the navigable semicircle of a tropical cyclone in the northern hemisphere and in the dangerous semicircle of one in the southern.

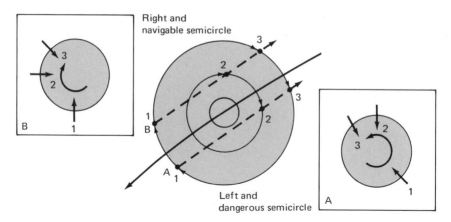

Figure 159.   Windshift patterns within southern hemisphere tropical cyclone.

Bewildering? And more so. During a period while terminology changes this can also be risky, for more than purity of expression can be involved. A resident of the north while in a southern hemisphere tropical cyclone might hear just a snatch of a radio message from a nearby ship crewed by residents of the south. If all he caught was "Wind is veering" and if he wasn't sure which definition was followed, his image of the storm could be topsy-turvy. Were he to understand that as a wind shift to the left, he might assume the reference was to the southern hemisphere's dangerous semi-circle. In fact, though, the other ship could be speaking of the navigable semicircle and its wind shift to the right. All this might seems to be building problems out of all proportion, but such is really not so. Precision of expression increases in value with the seriousness of the crisis. What seems a very attractive alternative is to throw overboard such catchwords as "veering" and "backing" whenever possible, and to be sure their meanings are the same at both ends of the message whenever they are put to use.

Matters nautical seem very resistant to change. Magellan's fo'c'sle hand measured water depth with a weighted line while we do it today by sound wave. But we still make use of water depth in navigation. The basic principles of getting from departure to destination in safety are surprisingly unaltered. Certainly this is true for the pleasure mariner. Instrumentation, it's been said, varies directly as the size of the vessel. From that it follows that the need for fundamental knowledge works in reverse. When bridge devices are meager, the mariner relies much more heavily on basics. Table B recaps the bedrock details of a tropical cyclone. In fact, it should be viewed as almost indispensable when there is any anticipation of encounter with such a storm.

As you read it, note the importance of the word *right* in the *northern* hemisphere and the word *left* in the *southern*. It seems that everything significant and foreboding north of the Equator is related to right, while in the south the key is left. When the winds are howling in a tropical cyclone, when the whole vessel is in disarray, remembering the importance of right and left could mean the difference between salvation and disaster. These general statements, true for both hemispheres, should be added:

1. In the dangerous semicircle, put the wind on your *bow;*
   in the navigable semicircle, put the wind on your *quarter.*
2. When the wind is steady in direction, you are on the storm track.
3. When the wind changes direction, you are not on the track.
4. When the barometer falls, you are ahead of the center.
5. When the barometer rises, you are behind the center.

TABLE B. TROPICAL CYCLONE CHECKLIST

	Northern hemisphere	Southern hemisphere
The storm track curves to the	Right	Left
Looking in the direction of the storm track, the dangerous semicircle is to the	Right	Left
In the dangerous semicircle, the wind shifts to the	Right	Left
Buys-Ballot's Law says face the wind and the center is 8 to 12 points to the	Right	Left
By Coriolis effect, high blows to low and turns to the	Right	Left
In the dangerous semicircle, place the wind on the	Right bow	Left bow
On the storm track ahead of the center, place the wind on the	Right quarter	Left quarter
In the navigable semicircle, place the wind on the	Right quarter	Left quarter
In the dangerous semicircle, sailing vessels keep close-hauled on the	Right or starboard tack	Left or port tack
In the dangerous semicircle, sailing vessels heave to on the	Right or starboard tack	Left or port tack

We have given the tropical cyclone great attention, and some mariners might wonder why. Operation in the Gulf of Mexico, the Caribbean, or along the Eastern Seaboard requires some knowledge of these monsters; but what about the mariner in Puget Sound or coastal California? In rebuttal we could say that this discussion rounds out our treatment of weather for all hands, tying in some other principles encountered along the way. But there is more to it than that. Seamanship and "Be Prepared" are synonymous. The occasions to don a life jacket or use artificial respiration are very few in a lifetime. But a mariner must still know how to wear the life jacket and how to revive a drowned person. Moreover, the sea is addicting. Not just a few sailors from the West Coast venture, sometime, into Intertropical Convergence Zones.

Figure 160.   A frightening foursome arches eastward over the Pacific. (*NASA*)

What we have yet to discuss is the matter of names given individual tropical cyclones. Centuries ago they were sometimes named after the saint on whose day they appeared. Less liturgical and much more clumsy was designation by latitude and longitude. For a while, alphabets were invoked—both ours and the Greek. Another suggestion was that they be named, as are constellations, after animals. But during World War II, military weathermen forced to live monastic lives began to name these storms after the girls they left behind. And for decades that pattern was official. An alphabetical roster of twenty-one feminine names was prepared each year. Queenie, Ursula, Xanthippe, Yvette, and Zenobia do represent Q, U, X, Y, and Z; but there are few others. So those letters were dropped from the list. A recent change allows a wedge of masculinity with the

appearance of an occasional John or Norman. Yet even the most ardent advocate of male chauvinism should not protest the sting of inequality should a feminine trend continue to prevail. In fact, according to one commentator, there is really no alternative. These storms are *hurricanes* and not *him*icanes.

We are directed by the commanding officer to pause for a well-earned rest: and by tradition of the sea, her word is law. She has just sung out, "Let go the port anchor." As a postscript to this chapter she explains why the port and not the starboard. We are in the northern hemisphere, where winds in the stormy half of storms tend to shift to the right. As the ship rides to her anchor, she will (the ship, not the CO!) tend to circle clockwise. Should the weather worsen so that another anchor must be dropped, the cables will lead clear of each other and there will be less fear of foul hawse. Were we in the southern hemisphere, the starboard anchor would customarily be considered first. This has gone far enough! The ship is snug and crewpersons can go off watch.

QUESTIONS

The month is August, the place is the Straits of Florida. Long swells have been sweeping by for hours and now a sinister bar of heavy, black clouds is beginning to show over the southeastern horizon. Radio warnings tell that the third tropical cyclone for the season is heading our way. A phonograph plays an old refrain of parted lovers. With slight revision the voice echoes our anxious plaint: "Chloe, I want to go where you're *not* . . ." Eat a hearty meal, lash down everything movable, and rush into the quiz!

1. In the life cycle of a tropical cyclone, the phase called
   a. *tropical disturbance* precedes that of *tropical depression.*
   b. *tropical depression* precedes that of *tropical disturbance.*

2. With reference to movement along its storm track, a tropical cyclone
   a. usually travels westward before it recurves to the east.
   b. usually moves more slowly before recurving than after.
   c. both of the above.
   d. none of the above.

3. In a tropical cyclone, maximum wind speed is to be expected
   a. in the eye.
   b. at the wall of the eye.
   c. at the bar of the storm.

4. You estimate your position to be 100 miles from the center of a tropical cyclone in the northern hemisphere. The barometer is falling rapidly and the wind is shifting to the left. You should maneuver with the wind

   a. on the port bow.
   b. on the port quarter.
   c. on the starboard bow.
   d. on the starboard quarter.

5. When the wind is steady in direction and the barometer is rising, you are
   a. on the track to the rear of the center in the northern hemisphere.
   b. on the track to the rear of the center in the southern hemisphere.
   c. either of the above.
   d. none of the above.

6. It is recommended that when maneuvering in either hemisphere,
   a. put your bow to the wind in the navigable semicircle.
   b. put your quarter to the wind in the dangerous semicircle.
   c. put your quarter to the track in either semicircle.
   d. all of the above.

7. The average width of the eye of a tropical cyclone is
   a. about 15 miles.
   b. about 50 miles.
   c. about 100 miles.

8. In the dangerous semicircle, the wind shifts
   a. to the right in the northern hemisphere.
   b. to the left in the southern hemisphere.
   c. both of the above.
   d. none of the above.

9. You are in a tropical cyclone in the southern hemisphere. The wind is due south. Buys-Ballot's Law would say the center was
   a. from east to northeast of you.
   b. from east to southeast of you.
   c. from west to northwest of you.
   d. from west to southwest of you.

10. Tropical cyclones do not occur
    a. in the South Indian Ocean.
    b. in the South Atlantic Ocean.
    c. both of the above.

ANSWERS

   A jury of 12 good ladies and true has assembled to weigh the evidence. Chloe is foreperson. With her are Candy, Carla, Carlotta, Carmen, Camille, Celeste, Celia, Clara, Claudia, Connie, and Cora. These amazons are casting thunderous looks at the answers! Oh, for the days of bare feet and pregnancy! Score, as usual, 10 points for each correct response. The verdict is to be tolled this way:

100, Not guilty by unanimous vote
90, Cora was a holdout, but finally came around
80, Acquittal by mitigating circumstances
70, A hung jury and time for a retrial
under 70, Cruel and inhuman punishment!

1. a   6. c
2. c   7. a
3. b   8. c
4. d   9. a
5. c   10. b

Chapter 10
ICE AND SO FORTH

The impact of meteorology is so pervasive that we can follow it into such related fields as polar navigation, oceanography, and the vagaries of tides. All can be important to the mariner and each facet certainly creates interest. But keep in mind as we go along that the aim is to remain within practical limits while avoiding unnecessary intrusion into the realms of specialized seafaring.

Ice is a good starting point. To many navigators the encounter is restricted to an eight-ounce glass. Yet one need not enter the Arctic Ocean to meet problems. Here are some fundamentals of ice formation. Fresh water will freeze at the expected 32°F, but sea water does so at a lower point. Salinity is a key factor and salinity varies; however, 28.6°F is a usually expected measure. Solidification starts at the top and works down. As the ice thickens, it shields the water underneath from cold air and acts to slow down the process. In shallow water where mixing can be more pronounced, the freezing can form at any depth; and if that becomes attached to the bottom the result can be *anchor ice*. When sea ice stays connected to the shore it can extend outward in an increasing layer to become *shelf ice*. As the years go by this can grow to hundreds of feet thick. Antarctica has much of it. When the outer edges of a shelf break off the result is a *tabular iceberg*, and it is huge! One was estimated to be over 200 miles long and twice the area of the state of Connecticut. During

Figure 161. USCG Icebreaker *Westwind* nudges 200 million tons of tabular iceberg in Greenland's Melville Bay. (*USCG*)

periods of drought there is the occasional suggestion that such blocks could be towed north to supplement water supplies. Apparently the loss to melting while enroute for a year or so would not be expected to make the transfer impractical.

The northern hemisphere doesn't produce such gigantic forms; but what can be spawned brings danger. Icebergs in the North Atlantic are worth discussion since, even though rarely, they penetrate south of Bermuda. A few have traveled as far as the Azores. Such icebergs usually start from glaciers on the west coast of Greenland. These frozen rivers inch across the land to meet the sea. There the buoyant water works them up and down until a chunk breaks off. That is an iceberg. Each year thousands

of them leave Greenland and move north to winter in Baffin Bay. The following summer they move south with the Labrador Current. Few travel farther than Newfoundland, but a score or two break clear to drift south of the Grand Banks.

Ice floats because it is less dense than liquid water; but the contrast is not too great. The comparison of densities reveals how much of the berg will be below the surface and how much jutting up. And an average figure is 90% down and 10% up. That, though, refers to total volume. Since the form is not a regular cube but is weathered by seas and air, a different estimate is given to depth below and height above. By that measure, depth is taken to average five times height.

Figure 162. Greenland's 200-foot-tall Pettiwick Glacier advances seaward to spawn next year's North Atlantic icebergs. (*USCG*)

As this mass floats along it will be influenced by wind and current. Coriolis is at work again to man the steering oar. In the northern hemisphere bergs are said to move, not with the wind, but about 30° to the right of its direction of flow. In the southern hemisphere the turn, of course, is to the left. As for speed, the estimate varies with roughness, size, and density. Drift is taken as a rate of from 1% to 7% of wind speed.

During its life span an iceberg undergoes much change. It can split or *calve* into smallers ones; it can fashion a hard spur or *ram* to gore the unaware. What brings special danger is the matter if visibility. On a clear day a towering berg might be seen nearly 20 miles away, but in a fog it might drift undetected until it is close aboard. On a dark, even though clear, night, it might not be seen until it is a quarter-mile off. Radar can help as a lookout, but it is by no means infallible. The above-water surfaces might slant away from the observer and not rebound a good signal. And the motion of the berg in the seaway can turn good reflecting surfaces away from the beam. Nonetheless, a careful radar conn should reveal its presence in ample time.

But smaller pieces calved off a parent berg are a different story. Some of these, about the size of a house, have been given the pet-food name of *bergy bits*. More dangerous are *growlers*, smaller yet and making a grumbling snarl as they bob in the sea. They can be overlooked, not only visually but by radar. When lost in clutter and sea return, growlers might sneak up entirely undetected. And any berg or offspring can grow rams of toughened ice ready to hole a vessel. On the lee side there might be more, but on the windward side they are more durable. Skirting any iceberg or its bits and growlers is foolish. Getting close on the windward side is more so. Should the mariner want to take a photograph of the scene, he should use a telephoto lens.

Ice fields, floes, and packs can extend for miles. And the reflection of sunlight from such masses into the sky might form a discernible pattern. *Ice blink* is a yellowish sky above a field; *snow blink* is the white reflection from a snow-covered surface. Above open water the reflection is a dark-gray *water sky*. But none of this *sky map* is much help in detecting icebergs with their smaller reflecting surfaces. No better is any sudden drop in sea or air temperature. Bergs are best detected by a keen eye on a slow-moving vessel.

Figure 163.   Dirt-streaked bergy bit in mid-Atlantic. (*USCG*)

Cold-weather navigation is not just concerned with frozen water afloat. Even more trouble arises from that which comes aboard. Extra weight can be added by the ton in a very short time. With it will come less freeboard and impaired stability. When the sea temperature hovers around freezing and the air temperature is even less, spray from waves and the ship's wake can be wind-driven to the superstructure and rigging. There it freezes on contact and forms *glaze ice*, a particularly dense and sticky sheath of solid water. If the air temperature is near 0°F, the danger is less, for the water will be solid before it strikes any top hamper aboard. At freezing temperatures, passage through a bank of fog can also bring this extra weight. How much will cling aboard depends, of course, on the surface area exposed. But it is best to assume that enough might arrive to add unwelcome tons (not pounds) in the span of a day. What are the remedies? Probably not outright cures, but at least they might serve to minimize the results. In advance, one might consider lessening the surfaces to collect glaze ice. It is not very practical to dismast the vessel or cut away the

Figure 164.   Trawler surrenders to tons of ice in the Aleutians. (*USCG*)

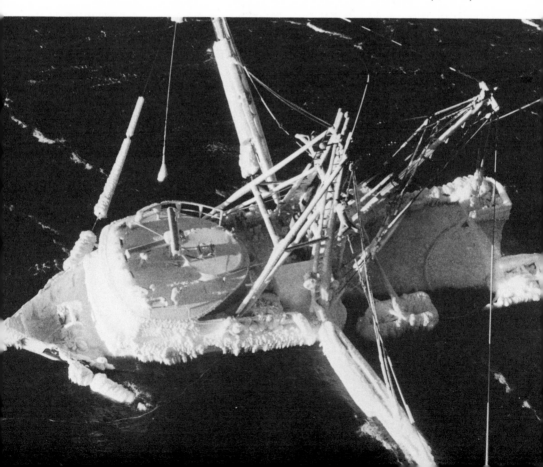

house. But what can be lowered or removed, should be. Another hint is to change course to run with the wind. That could lessen significantly the spray which comes aboard. When the buildup starts, removal of the ice is the consideration. Most of the time that means chipping, scraping, and brushing it off. This problem is one of anticipation as well as actual encounter. If the possibility might arise, then the vessel should be equipped to meet it with mallets, scrapers, and brooms. And a little forethought should be given to the ship's basic stability characteristics. It is far better to know ahead of time what tank can *safely* be filled to neutralize extra weight aloft than to experiment blindly while the glaze ice thickens. We can leave the problem, and with it the subject of ice, to this general conversation on principles. Unexpected onsets of solid water are not common. Awareness of what might be involved should now be in mind.

To describe a mariner as Jack or Jill of several trades is not inaccurate. The tailor's act is practiced in homeward-bound stitches; the role is carpenter to shore a weak bulkhead. And to an extent he is an oceanographer. This doesn't mean he must study the abysmal plains; but at least he should be familiar with influences on the skin-deep layer which is his roadbed. And there the forces of weather have great effect.

Movement of the surface is our next subject. Seismic outbursts produce long-crested swells called *tsunamis*. In deep water an observer seldom knows one has passed. Crests can be a hundred miles apart and the height be only a foot or so. The speed, though, is phenomenal. It can exceed 200 knots. Even so, there is little "at sea" risk. Near shore, on the other hand, the danger is extreme. Let such a wave climb an upslope into a bay and the water level might surge 100 feet high.

Not part of our discussion is the wave caused by the gravitational pull of moon and sun. That wave form, distorted by topography, is tide. Crests are thousands of miles apart and the height can be from a few inches in Lake Superior to 40 feet in the Bay of Fundy. But the subject is not so closely related to weather that we should give it consideration.

Ocean currents, although not wave-like, do warrant our attention. They are, in substance, masses of water flowing in streams through the oceans of the world. Movement is in different directions and at different depths. The power comes from wind and contrasts in water temperature and density. Then topography and our friend Coriolis enter to shape the final outcome. In the blaze of the equatorial sun, warm water surfaces and flows outward toward the poles. Prevailing winds shunt it to follow their courses, and then Coriolis acts to divert the flow. The result is a pattern of huge swirls as shown in Figure 165. We must expect oversimplification in such a sketch, for topography distorts what we might otherwise expect. Yet, the

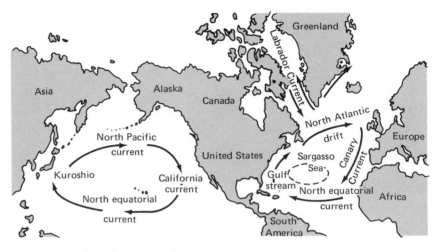

Figure 165.   Northern hemisphere ocean currents.

general principles for the northern hemisphere are still depicted. Figure 165 shows that in the northern half of both the Pacific and the Atlantic, the swirl is clockwise. The upwelling warm water meets the northeast trades and starts westward. Then Coriolis changes its course to begin a flow toward the nearest pole. Soon the prevailing westerlies are met. They join with Coriolis to alter course again. This time the direction is easterly at higher latitudes. Then Coriolis does it once more to change course toward the Equator; and the final Coriolis deviation makes it rejoin the original westerly drift.

Each leg of the pattern earns a local name. So, in the North Pacific, after the course change northward, the flow is called *Kuroshio*. This *Japan Current* is then bent to the right to create the eastward *North Pacific Current*. Near North America another turn to the right starts the *California Current*. By the time that reaches the tip of Mexico's Baja California, still another right turn brings it back where it started in the *North Equatorial Current*.

In the North Atlantic, as Figure 165 shows, the *Gulf Stream* comes after the *North Equatorial Current* turns right. Another right turn and it becomes the *North Atlantic Drift*. The pattern now becomes diverse because of flows from and toward the Arctic Ocean. But we can still detect the general scheme. Deflected by Europe's west coast, the stream now is the *Southeast Drift* which turns into the *Canary Current*. Then the turn is west again to the starting point. In the middle of the North Atlantic swirl is a somewhat currentless region called the *Sargasso Sea*. Like the stagnant center of a bowl, it collects seaweed to ready eels for the long voyage home to European palates. Laced with fancy and not fact is the story that old sailors drift aimlessly through this region on rusting derelicts.

Figure 166 sketches the cycles in the South Pacific. The *South Equatorial Current* flows westward and is turned by Coriolis to head toward the South Pole. In the South Pacific this left turn forms the *East Australia Current*. Another left turn causes it to flow easterly under the prevailing winds to move as the *West Wind Drift* toward South America. There a branch turns left again to become the *Peru* or *Humboldt Current*. Another left turn makes it rejoin the South Equatorial Current.

The South Atlantic flow, also shown in Figure 166, is about the same in in form. It moves to the westward, first, with the southeast trades as the *South Equatorial Current*. Then, by Coriolis, a change to the left to become the *Brazil Current*. Now toward the South Pole for a while until another left turn forms the *South Atlantic Current*. Near the Cape of Good Hope it makes still another left turn to become the *Benguela Current*. To the eastward of Napoleon's St. Helena Island it turns left again to merge into the South Equatorial Current.

The Indian Ocean tries to follow the same flow of clockwise in the northern half and counterclockwise in the southern part. But a combination of constriction by the subcontinent of India and the annual reversal of monsoon winds brings significant changes in form. Yet we can still discern the influence of prevailing winds and Coriolis to create clockwise and counterclockwise cycles.

Sailing Directions, Coast Pilots, and *pilot charts* depict ocean currents year-long and worldwide. They describe in detail what to expect, where, and when. Mariners intending to traverse particular regions should consider these publications as essential as food and water. We won't intrude much further on the scope of their expert coverage. It is worth noting, though, that *countercurrents* appear to flow contrary to the broad ocean rivers we have discussed. So, inshore of the California Current there appears the *Davidson Countercurrent*. It moves northward along the coast

Figure 166.   Southern hemisphere ocean currents.

from Southern California to British Columbia. And, between the two Equa-torial Currents moving westward, an *Equatorial Countercurrent* meanders eastward through the doldrums. Splits and diversions can be expected when such land masses as Greenland and Iceland interrupt the North Atlantic flow. One fork moves northwestward along Greenland's west coast to carry icebergs from glaciers through Davis Strait to hibernate in Baffin Bay. There it doubles back as the *Labrador Current* to carry icebergs south in spring and summer. This southerly flow encounters the Gulf Stream near the Grand Banks and produces, as we've read, troublesome fog. Since the meeting waters differ greatly in temperature, a *cold wall* is formed to divide their opposite tracks. Another result is a southbound countercurrent inshore to the west of the Gulf Stream.

At the southern tip of Africa a merger of large ocean currents takes place. There the *South Atlantic Current,* about ready to become the *Ben-guela*, encounters the strong *Agulhas Current* rounding the Cape of Good Hope from the Indian Ocean. Supertankers too large to negotiate the Suez Canal traverse this region bound from the Persian Gulf to western markets. Hull-wracking stress has brought grief to these ships in the area of current merger. We should, though, leave superships to cope with their problems as best they can, for our purpose has been served. Behind us is a general discussion of what overall influences came into play to create broad ocean surface movement.

Next to be discussed is the more localized effect of wind on water sur-face. The wave pattern developed is a sort of orbital form, with water moving up and forward on a crest, then down and backward in a trough. The water doesn't travel with the succession of waves at all. After each cycle it is just about back where it started from. Figure 167 sketches the idea. But the wave form has movement. It develops into a series of crests and troughs in a direction and with a speed related to wind strength. Figure 168 describes a shape and indicates some of the names given its parts.

Wavelength is the distance from one point in the train to the next point of the same kind. So, it is the distance between crests. *Wave height* is the vertical distance from top to bottom, that is, from crest to trough. *Wave period* is the time required for one form to pass by; it is the period of time from crest to crest. *Wave speed* is connected to length and period, but the relationship gets complicated. We would like to accept that if a 500-foot wavelength passes in a period of 10 seconds, then the wave is traveling at 50 feet per second. In one hour (3600 seconds) it would travel 3600×50 or 180,000 feet. Now to divide by 6076 (the feet in a nautical mile) brings us just under 30 knots. Out of this procedure has come a rule

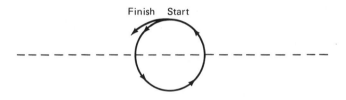

Figure 167.   Movement of water within a wave.

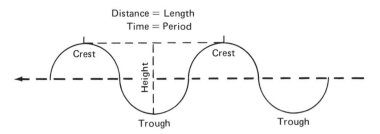

Figure 168.   The parts of a wave.

of thumb. Since 3600 seconds is about six-tenths of 6076, we could reduce things to this:

$$\text{speed in knots} = \frac{\text{wavelength in feet}}{\text{period in seconds}} \times 0.6$$

We should expect to be, like the absentminded parishioner, in the right church but not necessarily in the right pew. For wave speed is dependent on other factors than period and length. For example, it increases with wave height. Moreover, there are *two* speeds. As waves fan out they will eventually disappear. In the process there is a transfer of energy from the disappearing wave to the one behind it. The upshot is said to be that *wave systems* travel at a *group velocity* which is half the speed of individual waves. Headaches lie ahead if we pursue this much further. Let's just be satisfied that speed reckoning is devious.

What is not so devious, though, is the impact of wind to create the wave patterns. How hard it blows, for how long, and for what distance with unchanged direction over open water are the significant factors. Water depth is also important. And then these are varied by the reality that the surface to be agitated is rarely a millpond in the first place. Preexisting movement of the sea by subsiding swells or currents or whatever influences will modify the result. Yet we can still find workable generalities.

Figure 169. A tranquil North Atlantic. (*USN*)

To avoid confusion, some definitions are now important. A *wind wave* is the undulating form generated by friction between wind and the water surface. Let its crest become unstable and it is said to *break*. The general appearance of such wind waves in the area of generation is called a *sea*. And when those waves have moved beyond the region of formation they are called *swells*. By then smaller waves have disappeared and the survivors have a more regular form with longer periods, longer lengths, and flatter crests. When swells travel to shallow water they get higher and shorter. Then the name is *ground swell*. A wind wave, then, is the basic unit. While still under the influence of the forces causing the agitation, wind waves are called seas. When they radiate beyond such influence they become swells.

Wave height, period, and length all seem to increase with wind speed, duration, and fetch. We've met this last term several times before as the distance in miles over open water that the wind blows with relatively unchanged direction. Tables and graphs galore have been assembled to relate all these factors, but their value to the average mariner is not so clear. Rather than specific numbers, he should recall general trends. When wind blows for a long time over a long stretch of open sea, he can expect high waves of great length and long period. A 30-knot wind blowing for

2 days over 1000 miles of sea will produce waves more than 20 feet high, ten times as long, and needing about 8 seconds to pass.

In Chapter 2 we read of the southern hemisphere's roaring 40s. Our present discussion emphasizes why wind waves in that region are so high. By the time a mariner reaches latitudes of more than 45°S there is not much land between him and Antarctica. In fact, the only substantial land mass left is the spine of South America with Cape Horn as its stinger at 56°S. Theoretically, the fetch for the roaring 40s to roar over exceeds 12,000 miles.

Waves don't pass in review all at the same height like the Coldstream Guards. In one system there usually is a sequence of a few large ones followed by some poorly formed ones, and then another set of large. This can play havoc with statistics on wave height. Whether to average all or just to average the well-formed few is the problem. The general approach is to consider only those well formed and to disregard the runts of the litter. Taking the measure of waves, though, is not so simple. From a moving vessel bobbing in the sea, values such as direction, length, height, and period are not so easily determined. Thus, a very helpful handbook has been compiled for the use of ship's officers when preparing weather reports to be forwarded to meteorologists. It takes into account the circumstances under which observations will be made and allows for the absence of specialized apparatus. Here are some of its hints.

1. To measure wave period from a moving ship could involve errors due to relative motion, so using a stanchion, cleat, or any other object on board as the reference point is not too accurate. Instead, a distinctive patch of foam or something afloat at a distance from the vessel should be used. And as that reference moves astern, another should be chosen. When the foam is on the crest of the first well-formed wave in a series, timing in seconds is begun. Then the waves are counted and the timing continued until the foam reaches the crest of the last well-formed wave in that train. This is repeated until 15 or more waves have passed. All the times are then added together and divided by the number of waves. The result is the average period.

2. To measure wavelength, compare it with the length of the vessel. Observation is best made from a high position and with the sea dead ahead or astern. But no great degree of accuracy should be expected. Errors of perspective and those due to the ship's disturbing the wave systems are frequent.

3. To measure wave height the clues are several, and so are the sources of error. Ideally, the ship should not be rolling or pitching. Of course, if that were true, there might be no waves to measure. At least, the observer should be someplace amidships over the keel so that roll and pitch are minimized. When the ship is in a trough and the crest is in line with the

Figure 170.   Heavy gale-whipped seas. (*USN*)

horizon, then the wave height is equal to the observer's height of eye above the water. Another approach would be to move outboard and look over the side. By noting how high and low on the hull the wave reaches will give a measure. Still another way, if some vessel is nearby, is to estimate the height from trough to crest against that other's hull. If you know something about his dimensions, then you have a key to wave height. After reading this there should be no surprise why heated arguments develop about wave height. Some estimates of "the highest ever" are less than 70 feet, some others exceed 100 feet. For collectors of numbers the value might be important, but not to the average navigator.

4. To measure direction brings more vagueness. Estimates no closer than 10° are acceptable. And, like wind direction, the measure is the direction *from* which the waves are coming and not toward which they are going. The hint: sight along the wave crests and then apply 90° left or right into the wind.

Governing the speed of swells are wavelength and water depth. When the depth exceeds half the length, wavelength is controlling. A rule used is that speed in knots is about three times the period in seconds. In shallow water, when depth is half or less the wavelength, water depth controls speed. Greater depth means greater speed, but not in simple multiples.

Involved in the calculations are a square root and the acceleration of gravity. An example would show that if in water 100 feet deep a swell travels at about 56 knots, it would still be doing 40 knots in water half as deep. Time for us to change course smartly from these snags.

As wave height grows larger in relation to length, the point of breaking is approached. When the relationship is 1 : 7, the breaking point has been reached. Then the crest topples forward as a *white cap* at sea and as a *breaker* near shore. As the wave approaches shore it begins to feel bottom. Speed decreases and height increases. Should the wave system be on a course parallel to the coastline, the inshore portions will sense bottom first. Then the outerpart of the line will wheel to refract the pattern toward the beach. Except in an emergency, operation close to a line of breakers should be left to surfboards.

Much has been written about the use of storm oil to minimize wave action. The idea is that since oil has less surface tension and more viscosity than water, it will break sooner and at a lesser height. A vegetable or animal oil rather than a petroleum product is recommended. Spreading oil on

Figure 171. Hurricane Carol streaks the Gulf of Mexico. (*USN*)

troubled waters should, of course, be to windward so that the vessel can gain the benefit, but getting it up there can be a problem. A can with a petcock and fitted into a sea anchor is standard equipment for a ship's lifeboat; some large ships are equipped with storm oil tanks in the bows. Whether and how to use oil is a matter unique to each ship; for all ships it is at least worth consideration.

The effect of a train of waves on a ship can be very pronounced to the point of being downright dangerous. Let waves synchronize into neatly timed ranks against her side and even those of smaller height will produce heavy rolling. To bridge a wave with the bow on one crest and the stern on another is to bring excessive *sagging* stresses. Teetering amidships on a crest with bow and stern jutting over troughs can cause undue *hogging*. Smaller vessels gain an obvious advantage in stormy seas with long waves. But to disregard the strains when any part of any vessel is unsupported by water beneath is poor seamanship.

Danger of falling into the trough exists when a wave is twice as long as the ship. Should she find herself lengthwise in such valleys, waves will crash broadside, produce excessive rolling, and certainly threaten breaking over her entire length. Heavy-weather shiphandling is an art not now on our agenda. But in closing this discussion we can risk some final comment. One of the serious dangers is *synchronization*. Each vessel not only has a length, but also has a natural period of roll and pitch. Let all or some of those match the wave measures and severe commotion is in store. Since the mariner has no control of what the wave is doing, he should be ready to vary his course or speed or both to defeat any unfortunate rhythm. It now appears that delving into such uncertainties as wave height, length, period, and speed is not such a bad idea, after all. To know what cadence not to follow we must have some idea of the meter.

QUESTIONS

A bergy bit lies hidden in the trough of a long ocean swell racing through the Japan Current. All three subjects of this chapter demand that we demonstrate how to give it a wide berth. So, while searching for ice blink, sight along a line of wave crests and let Coriolis lead you to victory.

1. The top of an iceberg is estimated to be 60 feet above the sea. Its depth below the water should be about
   a. 500 feet.
   b. 400 feet.
   c. 300 feet.
   d. 200 feet.

2. Least detectable by radar would be
   a. a growler.
   b. a bergy bit.
   c. a tabular iceberg.

3. The danger of glaze ice from spray would be lessened by
   a. running with the wind dead ahead.
   b. running with the wind dead astern.
   c. running with the wind abeam.

4. Moving northward along the east coast of a continent is
   a. the Kuroshio.
   b. the Gulf Stream.
   c. both of the above.
   d. none of the above

5. Equatorial countercurrents generally flow
   a. westward.
   b. eastward.

6. As fetch and duration of a wind increase,
   a. the wave height increases.
   b. the wavelength increases.
   c. the wave period lengthens.
   d. all of the above.

7. The wind is from a westerly quadrant when you sight along a line of wave crests. That bearing is 315° True. You would estimate the swell or wave direction to be
   a. 225° True.
   b. 045° True.
   c. 315° True.
   d. 135° True.

8. Standing midships on your vessel you note that a wave crest is in line with the horizon. Your height of eye above the water is 11 feet. The wave height would be estimated as
   a. 5.5 feet.
   b. 11 feet.
   c. 16.5 feet.
   d. 22 feet.

9. The greatest danger of falling into the trough of a sea exists when the wavelength is
   a. half the length of the ship.
   b. the same as the length of the ship.
   c. twice the length of the ship.

10. To determine specifics on what ocean currents to expect in an area you
    would consult
    a. *Sailing Directions.*
    b. *Coast Pilot.*
    c. pilot charts.
    d. all of the above.

ANSWERS

Time and tide wait for no man, so this time we'll turn to correction with
little nonsense. Score 10 for each correct answer and measure progress this way:

        100, Sea like a mirror
         90, Small wavelets, but not breaking
         80, Scattered whitecaps
         70, She's laboring heavily; try some storm oil
    under 70, Head for the lee rail, fast!

1. c   6. d
2. a   7. a
3. b   8. b
4. c   9. c
5. b   10. d

Chapter 11

INSTRUMENTS

Through many chapters we have met such values as pressure, temperature, humidity, and wind speed; but little attention was given to their measurement. On these next pages we'll fill in the gaps by examining shipboard weather instruments. The emphasis, though, will be on "shipboard." Weathermen need an arsenal of equipment to prepare reports and bulletins, but the likelihood that we'll be shipmates with many of the tools they use is slim. Our concern is with four basic measures made aboard by four key instruments. And we can, right off, divide them into two groups. When a name ends with *-meter*, the device only measures. When, though, *-graph* is on the end, it measures and also records.

Atmospheric pressure is the first consideration, and the instrument name begins with *baro-*. There lies the whole story, for baro- refers to weight and we must measure the weight of the atmosphere on a unit of area. We've already read that *pressure* is such a statement and that atmospheric pressure at sea level amounts to 14.7 pounds per square inch or 1.033 kilograms per square centimeter. The aim of the barometer is to make a precise measure at a particular time and place.

The *mercury barometer* is used as the standard instrument, and in Chapter 3 we touched on it lightly. With a few steps backward we should review what was there said and go on to some specifics. Liquid mercury is placed in a cistern open to the atmosphere. Upended in that container is a glass

Figure 172. Aerologist stands by to release radiosonde. (*USN*)

tube, mouth down. The weight of the atmosphere pushes mercury up the
tube until a balance is reached. If the air weighs 14.7 pounds on each
square inch of mercury in the open cistern, then 14.7 pounds of mercury
will be forced up a tube of one square inch area. In metric terms we speak
of 1033.2 grams or 1.033 kilograms per square centimeter of surface. The
tube need not be so wide, for a similar relationship prevails regardless of
area. Figure 173 repeats one found in Chapter 3 to illustrate the simplicity
of this device.

But weighing the mercury standing in the tube would mean an unnecessary complication. Instead, a measure is made of how high it stands above
the cistern's surface. The result can be expressions of the standard sea level
weight of air, not as 14.7 pounds per square inch but as 29.92 inches or
760.0 millimeters of mercury. Of course, mercury is not the only liquid
available. Water has been used, as well as glycerine and sulphuric acid.
But then, because such liquids are much lighter, more would be forced
upward. Water, for example, would stand nearly 14 times as high as mercury; and it is hardly practical to consider a tube rising about 34 feet (10.4
meters) above an 8-quart (7.6-liter) pan of water. We should hardly expect

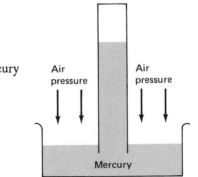

Figure 173. Principle of a mercury barometer.

to find such a structure at any weather station, for mercury is universally the fluid.

Measuring height, though, gives an indirect answer. So for weathermen the unit is the millibar, and it is kin to pounds per square inch and kilograms per square centimeter. Force is measured per unit of area, but the force is a dyne and the area is a square centimeter. One *millibar* equals 1000 dynes; it is also one-thousandth of a *bar*. This last, in turn, is a unit originally intended to describe atmospheric pressure at sea level: 1 million dynes or 1000 millibars. More precise measurements show that to miss the mark slightly, for 1.01325 bars or 1013.25 millibars is now taken as the standard value. All this we've read before; but now some new information appears.

The mercury barometer is considered the standard because of its precision. Even so, it is not adaptable to seafaring. A 3-foot pipe of fragile glass dipped in a bowl of quicksilver spells trouble on a lurching ship. We must, though, pursue its workings for a bit before veering off to meet its onboard substitute. Although the mariner might never use a mercury barometer, he should know its problems so he can relate his shipboard reading to what is reported as the standard. And the more exact measures made by the mercury involve some extra considerations. The liquid metal might move farther up the tube or, perhaps, not so far, due to influences other than the weight of air. One such factor is expansion and contraction with temperature change. Another involves differences in the pull of the earth's gravity at different latitudes. Also, such things as capillary action with the tube itself could be interfering. Determining pressure by this instrument is not so simple as just sighting the top of the mercury alongside a measuring scale.

To begin with, it is necessary to define the conditions for a standard atmosphere. Temperature is assumed to be 32°F (0°C) when the reading is made. If not, then a temperature correction is necessary. Latitude is assumed as 45°; if not, then a latitude or gravity correction must be made. This last requires some discussion. It was learned years ago that, because of the nonspherical shape of the earth, the pull of gravity is not a constant everyplace on its surface. Considering the earth to be flattened at the poles and bulging at the midriff, calculations indicated that gravity force was greater at top and bottom than near the Equator. The result would be that mercury would rise higher at low latitudes and be held lower at high ones. Thus, the average force was accepted as that at a latitude of 45° 32′ 40″, whether north or south. And if an observer is not at that level, then a correction should be made. Reprinted in "Ready Reference" are Tables 5, 6, and 7 for this and other barometer problems. Speculation could be made about the impact of more recent discoveries. During the satellite age it has been learned that the earth is not so much flattened top and bottom as it is pear-shaped, with most of its mass in the southern hemisphere. The difference is minute and should be of interest only to geophysicists. And Table 6 still seems to view the earth as having an equatorial bulge. None of this is for us to fret over. That table, reprinted from *Bowditch*, is the recommended table, and no mention is made of a needed substitute.

So now we have an icy-cold mercury barometer at a latitude of about 45°. What are its other worries? All but one of them involve motion of a liquid in a small-bore tube. Capillarity, imperfect vacuum, and the like are unique to the instrument being used; so they are gathered under the name *instrument error*. How they are found, though, is certainly outside our discussion. But the one remaining error does cross the bow. It is connected with altitude. Obviously, the higher a barometer is placed above the sea, the less air will stand above the cistern. So, an adjustment must be made for any height difference from a standard base. That base is sea level or zero feet, and the correction table is reprinted in "Ready Reference" as Table 5. Appearing there is the statement "All values positive." The presumption is that the barometer will be located above the waterline. Few would argue, for carrying a barometer in the bilges is hardly common practice.

Although the mariner will not be involved in all these complicated adjustments, he must know something of the pattern. When he compares his onboard reading with what is reported as correct for the place and time, he must recognize the various names given to a mercury reading. The first value read off the tube is called *instrument pressure*. After any instrument error is applied the result is *station pressure*. When that is adjusted for altitude, the reading is *sea level pressure*. And after allowance for temperature and latitude, the outcome is *corrected barometric reading*. It is always expected that weathermen will supply as *the* reading one already strained free of impurities. Should, though, they begin to mention a litany of possible values, the uninformed could fetch up thoroughly confused. Figure 174 pictures a mercury barometer.

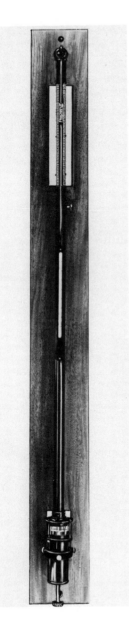

Figure 174. Mercury barometer. (*Science Associates, Inc.*)

No matter how precise the mercury barometer, it is not too useful on board. By size, fragility, and even more problems than have been mentioned, it asks for an alternative. There are mercury instruments of special design which do go to sea, but they are uncommon. It is time now for us to consider the normal barometer found aboard. Since most of the worries stem from liquid in a tube, the aim was to develop a barometer without wetness. That, in essence, is what the word *aneroid* means; no wetness or liquid. Instead of using a liquid coursing up and down a glass, it is a mechanical device containing a metal vacuum chamber with corrugated lids and sides. Atmospheric pressure would squeeze this *sylphon cell* flat were it not for a spring fitted inside. And a system of links and levers to magnify its movement is connected to the outside. On the end of the last link is a pointer which travels over a dial calibrated in any of several ways. The principle is that increased atmospheric pressure will tend to compress the cell, while under less pressure it will be expanded by the spring. The motion is not much, but the linkage system enlarges it for more precise readings. Figure 175 is a picture of such an instrument.

To defeat temperature problems, dissimilar metals are used in its construction. Such bimetallic elements, due to neutralizing characteristics of

Figure 175. Aneroid barometer reading 1026.3 mb. or 30.31 inches. (*Science Associates, Inc.*)

change with temperature, produce a *temperature-compensated* barometer. And since all the parts are connected together, there is no reason for a change in gravity force to alter the reading. So the aneroid can disregard two of the mercury barometer's problems: temperature and latitude or gravity. Not to be disregarded, though, is the problem of height. Atmospheric pressure decreases with altitude, no matter how measured. The height correction is so basic that one type of aircraft altimeter is no more than an aneroid barometer. Its dial is calibrated to show what altitude in feet or meters is considered equivalent to whatever pressure might be measured.

The three barometer correction tables in "Ready Reference" carry notations for their use. Both temperature and latitude are marked for mercury only, but height is indicated for both. About now an old-timer might be heard snorting, "All this correction business is bilgewater!" Gray hairs and a craggy face command some respect, so we'd better consider whether he is practical or just remiss. His impatience probably stems from the frequently tiny adjustments suggested. To a great extent the answer lies in the size of the ship. According to Table 5 in "Ready Reference," a barometer on a lofty bridge 50 feet above the sea would underread by 0.05 inches or more. Table 8 translates that to 2 millibars. So, 29.87 would actually be 29.92 and 1011 would mean 1013. For our crusty veteran to overlook that adjustment would be to reveal bad habits. But if the instrument were only 10 feet high, the error would shrink to about 0.01 inches, an insignificant third of a millibar. More in point for all of us is awareness that there can be a difference because of height. Then, whether the correction is used or not becomes an exercise of informed judgment.

Old Salt and new must remember that the aneroid barometer is not as good as the mercury. What justifies its use is its suitability to the maritime world. Since the mariner is more interested in *changes* of pressure rather than precise time-for-time readings, he can bear with its failure to be exact.

The aneroid dial might read in inches, millimeters, millibars, or a combination. Frequently encountered is a scale calibrated on its outside rim in inches and on its inside in millibars. To read the face, one should stand with his eye directly in front of the pointer. This avoids an error due to parallax. It is recommended that he tap the face lightly with his finger to relieve any linkage friction which might otherwise bind the pointer at a faulty reading. There are often two pointers on the dial. One is connected to the linkage and gives the reading. The other is controlled by a knob at the center of the face and serves as a memory aid. It can be placed over a reading at a previous time and then compared with a later one to show the barometric change. We need hardly say that the knob should not be turned without first checking with whoever mans the weather watch.

Mounting the aneroid barometer requires some care. It should have a permanent place free from such vibration as slamming doors or pounding bulkheads. If possible it should be at eye level. Since that might be measured by the shipmaster, it could mean inconvenience for basketball heroes sailing under jockeys. An ideal location would be near the centerline to minimize pendulous motion imparted to the pointer by roll and pitch. Reality, though, will dictate; for on many vessels the range of choice is not great.

When the aneroid barometer is mounted, it should be adjusted to *station pressure*; that is, its instrument error should be removed. Whether it is further corrected to *sea level pressure* can depend on how the draft of the vessel might be expected to change during a voyage. Incidentally, we'll ignore the mutters of the old salt out on the bridge wing. On a cargo ship, when draft can vary many feet from light to loaded, the correction may not be made. Instead, it would be applied after each reading. On other vessels with more constant draft, the altitude correction might be taken out once and for all. In any case, the determination of instrument error is made by comparing the aneroid reading to that of a mercury barometer of known fidelity. And the correction is made by manipulating an adjustment screw on the back of the instrument case to move the pointer to the proper setting. But what that screw controls is lightly built and very delicate so it is always best to have an expert meteorologist do the job. A call to a nearby office of the National Weather Service is indicated. Should, though, you do it yourself, then work carefully! The procedure should be to make adjustment for half the error first and then tap the face to free linkage friction before proceeding with the other half.

A *barograph* is a recording aneroid barometer, as shown in Figure 176. Here, the linkages control a pen fitted to ride over a special graph-lined chart. The paper, in turn, is wound around a cylinder containing a clock mechanism to rotate it slowly around a fixed gear in the base.

In Chapter 4 we discussed temperature and the various scales used to take its measure. The instruments are fairly uniform in principle. Within a glass tube having a bulb or reservoir is placed a substance which will expand and contract with changes in temperature. The face of the tube is etched in the pattern of the measuring scale. Whether the material is mercury, alcohol, or a gas depends on the use of the instrument. Mercury will freeze at $-38°F$ ($-39°C$), but alcohol remains liquid at far lower points. In a laboratory, gas might be selected when very low temperatures are expected. For shipboard use, though, such an exotic element would hardly be found unless something cryogenic like liquified natural gas (LNG) were aboard.

A *thermograph* measures and records the reading on a chart. An arc-shaped metal tube is filled with alcohol and connected by linkages to a pen.

Figure 176. Barograph showing pressure of 29.50 inches at about 0500 on Wednesday. (*Science Associates, Inc.*)

Expansion straightens the tube; contraction makes it recurve. That motion, imparted to the pen, is traced on a chart paper wrapped around a clock-driven cylinder. The outward appearance is much like a barograph. Figure 177 illustrates the types of thermometer and thermograph which might be found on board.

It is sometimes important to determine sea temperature. A sample of water is first acquired. On large ships this is usually done at the condenser intake for the engine room. A simpler method, useful on any vessel, is to scoop some up in a bucket attached to a line. A canvas container is best, and then the contents are stirred with the thermometer to get a uniform reading.

Obtaining accurate air temperature values involves some care. The reading is taken at the top of the liquid column, and not at the edge. The observer should stand downwind so that his body heat doesn't affect the measure. As for location, the instrument should not be in direct sunlight. Such heat will cause the thermometer materials to expand unduly and produce errors on the high side. In addition, there should be protection against heat from bulkheads, vents, machinery, and the like. Finally, there should

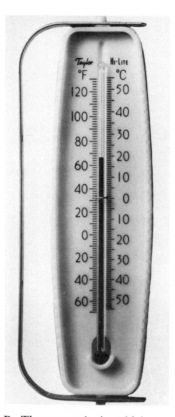

Figure 177. Thermometer and thermograph.

A. Dual-scale thermometer showing 67°F equal to 19.4°C. (*Sybron/Taylor Instruments*)

B. Thermograph, in which temperature changes detected by liquid-filled element are transferred by a linkage system to a recording pen arm. (*Science Associates, Inc.*)

be air circulating around the thermometer. Ideal placement is in a louvered box on the windward side and in the shade.

Measuring relative humidity requires a *hygrometer*. One type is called a *psychrometer* or *wet- and dry-bulb thermometer*. Its principle involves two thermometers mounted side by side. One, the wet bulb, has its reservoir wrapped in a wick of muslin. The other, called the dry bulb, is fully exposed and reads air temperature in a normal fashion. But the wick on the wet bulb is moistened with fresh water. As moisture evaporates from the muslin it takes heat from the bulb; and the more the evaporation, the more the heat loss. The result is a difference in reading between the two bulbs. By reference to a table or graph, the dry-bulb reading and the difference can be translated into the percentage of relative humidity and to the dew point temperature at which the air would be saturated. "Ready Reference" presents tables 10 and 11 for the purpose.

When the instrument is fixed in a permanent location, the wick is kept wet by being dipped in a vial of water. When the aim is more portability, the wick hangs free and must be kept wet by the user. In that case, it would be helpful to speed up the evaporating process. The *sling psychrometer* achieves that by being whirled around on a handle. A more sophisticated device has a tiny fan to do the job. But no matter how much fanning, the amount of evaporation will not alter. Attached to an aircraft propeller whirling in a steam room, it would still show that no water had vaporized. Saturated air won't take any more water vapor. What controls evaporation is not the magnitude of air currents; rather, it is the dryness of the air in which the instrument is placed.

There are some worthwhile hints to the use of the device. First of all, evaporation will not be instantaneous. The wet-bulb temperature needs time to stabilize at its lowest value. Fresh water must be used in the wick; in fact, distilled water is best. No salt water, even salt spray, should be allowed to reach the wick. If that happens the wick should be replaced. Wetting the wick should be done carefully to be sure that no water splashes on the dry bulb. If air temperature is below freezing, then the muslin should be coated with a thin sheath of ice. That can form naturally as the instrument is exposed to the air. To make certain, the wick can be touched with a piece of ice. In any case, the water used should be at air temperature. If you use hot water, expect to wait while it cools down. The location of the fixed device follows the same rules as those applying to normal thermometers: in the shade and with allowance for air circulation. Figures 178, 179, and 180 picture some of the instruments found on board.

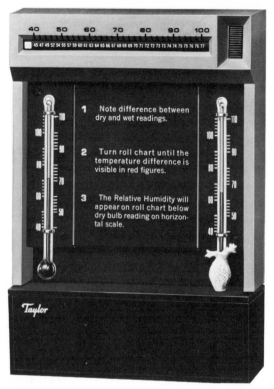

Figure 178. Wet- and dry-bulb thermometers to measure relative humidity. (*Sybron/Taylor Instruments*)

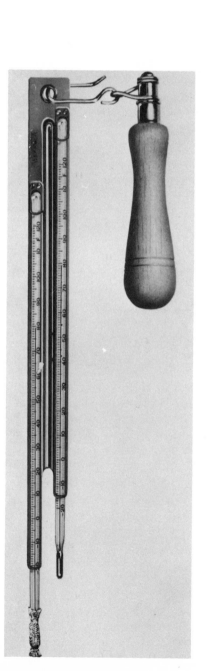

Figure 179. Twirling the sling psychrometer speeds up the reading. (*Science Associates, Inc.*)

Figure 180. Hygrothermograph, which reads and records both temperature and relative humidity. (*NOAA*)

The accuracy of wind measurement can be ranked from good to guess-timate. Available instruments are adequate, but problems arise because there are two motions to consider. *True* wind is that experienced when the observer is not moving; *apparent* wind is the combination of true and his own motion through the water. A shipboard instrument only tells the values directly when the vessel is at rest. Even so, we'll discuss the device and then clues to the procedure for conversion of *apparent* to *true*.

The *anemometer* measures wind speed and a *wind vane* shows direction, but often the first term describes both functions. We can dispose of the vane in a sentence or two. It is a horizontal pointer attached to a vertical shaft with more of its body on one side of the pivot than on the other. Its smaller end points into the wind. The anemometer itself, though, is a bit more complex. In basic principle it has a series of cups (usually 3) mounted on horizontal arms secured to a vertical shaft. Wind blowing into the cups drives them around to turn the shaft. From there the rotation passes on to an indicator which displays the motion as a speed. The number of cups and their manner of fitting can change, but the standard anemometer normally involves this approach. Another type is shaped like a miniature aircraft. Its propeller is a rotor to determine speed; fuselage and tail comprise the vane to show direction. And the state of the anemometer art is advancing to make use of other principles aimed at the same result. Figures 181 and 182 display some of the instruments in use.

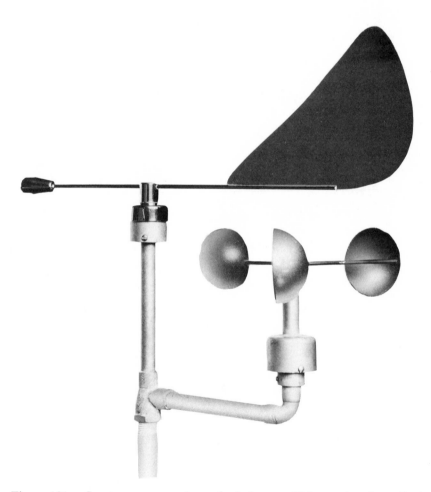

Figure 181.   Cup-type anemometer and wind vane. (*Science Associates, Inc.*)

Figure 182. Propeller-type anemometer and wind vane. (*USN*)

We can assume that an anemometer properly located will do its job; but now we must inquire into exactly what that amounts to. What is measured, as we've read, is apparent speed and direction when the ship is in motion. The result is far more accurate than a wet finger or a bucket of stew thrown to leeward, but it is still not a measure of true values. To learn such data another step might become necessary. Wind-plotting boards are available, and the National Weather Service offers a special plotting sheet to do the job. But just as effective is a simple vector diagram which can be drawn on any chart, or even a blank page, with a protractor and straightedge.

Two sets of values must be known: the vessel's true course and speed, the apparent wind's direction and speed. The first set we'll assume is in mind. The apparent wind values are supplied by a wind vane and anemometer. And the plotting procedure is described by the following example. A vessel's course is 270°at 12 knots. The apparent wind is observed as being from 45° on the port bow at 12 knots. What is the true wind speed and direction?

Figure 183, in three panels, shows the step-by-step answer. In Figure 183A, a line from 1 to 2 represents the vessel's movement in one hour:

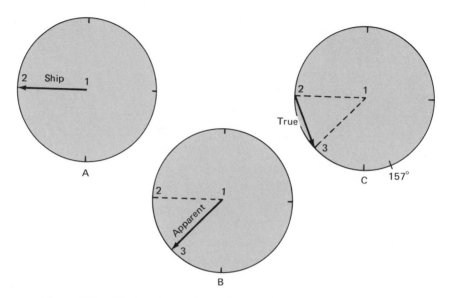

Figure 183.   Vector plot to determine true wind speed and direction.

A. From center, draw line for ship's course with length for ship's speed, or distance traveled in one hour.

B. From center, draw line for estimate of apparent wind direction with length for estimated speed. Draw line in direction *from* which apparent wind comes.

C. From the end of ship's line, draw line to end of apparent wind line. Its length is true wind speed. The direction *from* ship's line to apparent wind line is true wind direction.

270° and, from the scale provided, 12 miles. In Figure 183B a line drawn *into* the apparent wind, from 1 to 3, displays apparent values for one hour. Since the wind is from 45° on the port bow, it is from (270° − 45°) or 225°. That line is drawn into a 225° direction for 12 miles in distance. In Figure 183C we find the solution: from 2 to 3 is true wind speed and direction. The values are 157° and, says the scale, 9.2 knots. Not as simple as one, two, three, but surely not heavy with complications. To review: the first line, from 1 to 2, is the ship's true course and speed; the second, from 1 to 3, is the apparent wind direction and speed drawn *into* the wind. The third line, from 2 to 3, is the true wind direction and speed. Note that the true direction is expressed in the customary manner: the direction *from* which the wind comes.

Several valid generalities have developed from these relationships. First, the true wind always strikes the vessel on the same side as the apparent, but farther aft. Our example shows this. The apparent wind is from 45° on the port bow; the true wind works out to be from abaft the port beam. The second rule: when the apparent wind is forward of the beam, the true wind has a lesser speed. We see that in our example. The apparent wind is from forward of the beam and at 12 knots. The true wind is calculated as nearly 3 knots less. The third rule, although not shown by our example, is just as valid: when the apparent wind is from abaft the beam, the true wind has a greater speed.

In the absence of anemometer and "1–2–3 vector," the seaman's eye must be invoked. Exactness tumbles overboard, but total chaos need not be the outcome. "Ready Reference" reprints some tables (Tables 1 and 2) prepared by the National Weather Service for marine surface observers. One of them sets out the indications helpful to estimate apparent wind speed. The other deals with true wind conditions. Familiarity with them narrows the gap between fiction and fact. When, though, observations of the sea are made to surmise true wind, some additional hints are worthwhile. Sea spray and small waves run with the wind and can be an indication of direction. We've already read, with regard to swells, that sighting along crests and then applying 90° into the wind is a practical means to determine direction. The same applies to waves. When using the table of sea conditions to indicate true wind, some factors cause underestimates while others might make the appraisal too much. When rain is falling or the wind has just begun or the observer is in an offshore wind within sight of land, the estimate can be too low. When the wind is dropping or waves are encountering shoal water, the reckoning might be too high. Not every mariner will be participating with weathermen in compiling data, so many of these hints and precautions might not appear relevant. Yet every scrap of information is valuable when assessing, weather-wise, what could happen next.

Lurking below the surface in all this wind discussion has been the *Beaufort scale.* For many years, mariners have used a seemingly patternless scheme to express wind force. Admiral Francis Beaufort, a 19th-century British tar in the days of wooden ships and iron men, devised this schedule. It lists wind conditions in ascending numerical order from 0 to 17. What has brought Beaufort undeserved scorn is the apparent lack of uniform progression to the pattern. Force 2 describes winds from 4 to 6 knots, Force 3 from 7 to 10, and Force 4 from 11 to 16. Then Force 5 covers only from 17 to 21. The wind differences vary from 2 knots to 3, then 5, and back to 4. Such lack of symmetry, though, was not Beaufort's plan. In defense of his reputation, it has been revealed that the admiral was not referring to wind speed at all! What he had in mind was the number of sails which should be furled as the wind strengthened. In light airs, just one would be taken in; a gentle breeze might require three. In a moderate gale, seven would come down; in a storm, the number would be eleven. It would appear that, as with Luke Howard's cloud descriptions, Admiral Beaufort's sequence has been bent considerably in the transition to modern times. There is a tendency nowadays to ignore the Beaufort scale in favor of expressing values in knots. Yet, in the context of the seaman's world, something like the Beaufort numbers is attractive. To say "18 knots" for the wind suggests misleading exactness. "Force 5" better allows for the slack we all suspect was involved in the estimate. "Ready Reference" contains Tables 1 and 3 which correlate wind and sea.

From Canada have come some useful photographs relating to the Beaufort scale to the resulting sea state. These photos, taken from the Canadian Ocean Weather Ships *St. Catherine* and *Stonetown,* appear as Figures 184A through 184K.

Figure 184. The Beaufort Scale (*Courtesy Canadian Atmospheric Environment Service*)

A. Beaufort Force 0, wind under 1 knot. Mirror-like sea.

B. Beaufort Force 1, wind 1 to 3 knots. Ripples without foam.

C. Beaufort Force 2, wind 4 to 6 knots. Small wavelets with glassy crests.

D. Beaufort Force 3, wind 7 to 10 knots. Large wavelets with crests beginning to break.

E. Beaufort Force 4, wind 11 to 16 knots. Small waves with some foam patches.

F. Beaufort Force 5, wind 17 to 21 knots. Moderate waves with foam and spray.

G. Beaufort Force 6, wind 22 to 27 knots. Large waves with widespread foaming crests.

H. Beaufort Force 7, wind 28 to 33 knots. Heaping sea with white foam beginning to streak.

I. Beaufort Force 8, wind 34 to 40 knots. Moderately high waves with spindrift and well-marked streaks.

J. Beaufort Force 9, wind 41 to 47 knots. High waves with toppling crests, dense streaks and spray.

K. Beaufort Force 10, wind 48 to 55 knots. Very high waves with overhanging crests and sea white with spray.

QUESTIONS

A now-benevolent British admiral has overseen the preparation of this quiz. For well over a century he has borne unwelcome mockery. Should we excel in this examination, his prospects are an eternity of uninterrupted peace.

1. Standard readings by a mercury barometer are considered to be made at a temperature of
   a. 0°F.
   b. 32°F.
   c. 45°F.

2. The latitude correction made to a mercury barometer reading
   a. is due to the change of gravity influence with latitude.
   b. need not be made to a reading by an aneroid barometer.
   c. both of the above.
   d. none of the above.

3. The altitude correction made to a mercury barometer reading
   a. adjusts the reading to sea level.
   b. need not be made to a reading by an aneroid barometer.
   c. both of the above.
   d. none of the above.

4. The aneroid barometer is
   a. more precise than the mercury barometer.
   b. less precise than the mercury barometer.
   c. equal to the mercury barometer in precision.

5. A shipboard thermometer should be
   a. located in a sealed box.
   b. placed in the sunlight.
   c. both of the above.
   d. none of the above.

6. The wick of a wet- and dry-bulb thermometer
   a. is muslin cloth.
   b. should be kept moistened with salt water.
   c. both of the above.
   d. none of the above.

7. A vessel is on a course of 180° at 10 knots. The anemometer registers a wind speed of 10 knots and the wind vane shows the wind to be from dead ahead.
   a. The true wind is south at 10 knots.
   b. The true wind is north at 20 knots.
   c. There is no true wind.

8. The true wind strikes a vessel
   a. on the same side as the apparent wind.
   b. farther aft than the apparent wind.
   c. both of the above.
   d. none of the above.

9. The apparent wind is observed to strike a vessel abaft the port beam. The true wind speed would be
   a. less than the apparent wind speed.
   b. greater than the apparent wind speed.
   c. the same as the apparent wind speed.

10. When rain is falling, an observer's estimate of wind speed by viewing sea condition tends to be
    a. too low.
    b. too high.

ANSWERS

Admiral Beaufort has a long glass to his eye and is busily counting sails. No chance to hoodwink this old salt, for he knows his studs'ls and topgallants! On his scorecard, 10 points are given for each correct answer and the count is ranked this way:

      100, Everything flying, including the cook's apron
      90, Force 1: take something in, plus the apron
      80, A moderate breeze
      70, With seven sails furled, what's left?
  under 70, Bare poles!

1. b	6. a
2. c	7. c
3. a	8. c
4. b	9. b
5. d	10. a

Chapter 12

WEATHER CHARTS

In a pragmatic world any study must pass the test of usefulness. Our review of weather principles is just an enriching indulgence until put to work. And its primary job is described by two words: *weather forecast*. The mariner's need is to anticipate what the atmosphere has in store by an audit of his own observations, by interpretation of what others pass along, and by an understanding of what that all means in the region of operation.

By now we should accept that the ocean of air above has complex movement and change. Outcomes are rigidly subject to physical laws, and to that extent are predictable. But laws alone are not enough without facts to which they are applied. And weather prediction is chronically short on facts. A lone observer can, at best, measure only what transpires in his part of the ocean. Yet a weather fact taking place thousands of miles away will influence his reality within a few days. The marshalling of such data is the bane of meteorology. Adequate reports are available from busy areas, but what about the distant stretches of sea where only an occasional frigate bird travels? Satellites look down and take photographs; but they can't sample and measure the atmosphere. There is no denying that this science toils under some adversity.

To forecast what lies ahead the mariner must exploit every lead to future weather. And the starting point is a glance astern. *Weather summaries* reflect, literally, centuries of observations. By no means are they to

218

be overlooked. At any chart agent you can examine catalogues issued by such official sources as the *Defense Mapping Agency Hydrographic/Topographic Center, National Ocean Survey, National Weather Service,* and the *World Meteorological Organization,* a United Nations activity. Included will be such books and charts as *Coast Pilots, Great Lakes Pilot, Sailing Directions, atlases,* and *pilot charts.* These are priceless veins of weather treasure culled from observations made year in and out. Not to use such information is unseamanlike. Here is a sample from *Coast Pilot 4,** which treats the area from Cape Henry to Key West:

Weather.—Climatological tables for Atlantic coast localities, and meteorological tables for coastal ocean areas covered by this volume follow the appendix. The tables for ocean areas were compiled from observations made by ships in passage. Also listed in the appendix are National Weather Service offices and radio stations which transmit weather information.

General.—The coastal area from Cape Henry to Key West is low and flat. The entire shoreline is marked by inumerable indentations and irregularities, many of which cause important local climatic variations. In the area north of the Florida Peninsula there is an abrupt rise from the coastal plain which continues in an irregular terraced pattern westward, and culminates in the Blue Ridge Mountains, the Great Smokies, and other ranges of the Appalachian chain. The mountainous area, though at a considerable distance from the ocean, forms a partial barrier to the cold waves that move southeastward from the interior.

The climate of the region varies from temperate and semimarine in southern Virginia to humid and subtropical in southern Florida.

Pressure.—Over the ocean east of the southeastern seaboard there is a region of high pressure. This Azores or Atlantic High is the center of the surface circulation system in this area. During the year it migrates a limited distance to the north or south and to the east or west, but is persistent throughout the year. The circulation over the eastern seaboard is controlled largely by the proximity of the Azores High.

Winds.—In winter over the northern part of the sea area (north of latitude 30°) predominant winds are from the north through west. Southwest winds are also frequent. Along the coast north of latitude 35° wind directions are variable, though predominantly from the westerly quadrant. Along the middle coast, directions are mostly northerly to westerly. Off and along the Florida coast, south of latitude 30°, easterly winds are prominent throughout the year.

Winter storms over the entire area are modified by the Appalachian Mountain ranges. However, even the extreme southern portion occasionally experiences

---

* *United States Coast Pilot 4,* Atlantic Coast, Cape Henry to Key West (15th ed.; Washington, D.C.: National Oceanic and Atmospheric Administration, 1977), pp. 67–71.

northwesterly winds when the severest of the winter storms penetrate this far south.

In spring, over the northern part of the sea area (north of latitude 30°), winds from the southwest, south, and northeast are equal in frequency. Along the coast (north of latitude 35°) southwest winds predominate. North and south winds are also frequent. Along the middle coast south and southwest winds predominate.

In summer the persistence and dominance of the Azores High is shown in the increasing frequency of southwesterly winds over the northern part of the sea area. Along the coast (north of latitude 35°) southerly winds predominate. Along the middle coast southwest winds predominate.

In autumn the recession of the Azores High, accompanied by changing pressure systems along the coast, results in a sharp increase in the frequency of northerly winds, which are recorded about 50 percent of the time over the northern part of the sea area. Along the coast (north of latitude 35°) and the middle coast (between 30° and 35° latitude) northern winds prevail.

Along the coast a daily shift in wind direction is observed. During the warmest part of the day winds blow from the ocean toward shore (known as *sea breeze*), and during the coolest, from the land toward the sea (*land breeze*). Offshore winds, unless they are exceptionally strong, are generally considered most favorable for coastal navigation. Onshore winds have a more pronounced effect upon the surface, particularly when they have been blowing from the same direction for a long period of time. A strong sea breeze can cause heavy or choppy seas and swell, and frequently makes navigation difficult for small vessels.

Temperature.—The temperature regime of the southern Atlantic coast varies from temperate in the northern part of the area to subtropical in the southern part. The gradation from north to south is regular, decreasing with increasing latitude. Another interesting variation is the general modification process of the ocean and coastal temperatures by each other. Along the coast the sheltered land stations have warmer summers and cooler winters than do exposed points.

Temperatures along the southeastern seaboard region are conducive to a long period of small-craft operation. The southern Atlantic coast annual mean air temperatures range from 59.7°F at Norfolk. Va., to 76.8°F at Key West, Fla. January is the coldest month at most stations; July the warmest. The range in mean monthly air temperature over the area is from 41.2°F at Norfolk in January to 83.6°F at Key West in August.

Over the water area the coldest month is February and the warmest is August. Exposed coastal stations experience mean air temperatures more like those over the water than those over land, and have annual extremes in February and August.

Humidity.—Mean relative humidity is highest from July through September and lowest in April and May. Data are not summarized for water areas, but the relative humidities are known to be uniformly high. The presence of minute particles of salt in the air over the ocean together with the high moisture content in the air results in a very corrosive effect upon equipment and supplies, both on the water and at nearby shore points.

Cloudiness.—Mean cloudiness over the area is moderate to moderately high throughout the year, averaging from 35 to 65 percent sky cover. In general, however, the cloudiest month is January in the northern sections and over most of the water areas, and may be any month from June through September in the southern section. At most of the individual stations in the northern part of the area the least average cloudiness occurs in October, and in the extreme southern part least cloudiness occurs in February or March.

Since the air is usually moist, only a small decrease in temperature may cause condensation and cloud formation. At the edge of the warm northward-moving Gulf Stream and the cool southward-moving countercurrent which skirts the shore from Cape Hatteras, N.C., to Jacksonville, Fla., sharp contrasts in temperature result in the formation of heavy stratus clouds which may appear very much as a cold front. These clouds may persist for days at a time if the wind is light and may be carried inland by northeasterly winds. Such cloudiness is common during the spring when the gradient between shore water and Gulf Stream temperatures is steepest.

The fact that maximum cloudiness for the year occurs during the winter at northern coastal stations may be explained by the maximum frequency of cyclonic storms passing northward or northeastward from the central or south-central section during that season. These rarely affect the extreme southern part of the area.

Much of the cloudiness over the entire area is of the cumulus type, resulting from either the unstable conditions that accompany cyclonic activity in all seasons, or the general air mass instability during the summer. Such clouds frequently form over land during the day and drift seaward at night.

Precipitation.—Over the southeastern seaboard region precipitation is moderately heavy, averaging about 45 to 60 inches a year. Monthly departures may be large in any individual year, but over a long period of record, 50 to 75 years, a fairly uniform pattern prevails. Since the area is within both temperate and subtropical regions, the precipitation pattern shows differences in both type and amount from north to south. Irregularities from station to station in the idealized pattern are due to differences of exposure at the observing stations. Year-to-year variation is caused by overall departures from the average general circulation.

Visibility.—Visibility is generally good throughout the year over the entire area. Fog is the principal restriction to visibilty. Fog reducing visibility to 0.25 mile or less is very irregular, ranging from practically no days a year at some stations to 37 days a year at Savannah, Ga. Differences in exposure account for the considerable variation between locations. In general, however, fog decreases from north to south, and the worst fog conditions occur during the winter when air masses change frequently. Visibility is usually poorest during the night and early morning.

Along the coast radiation fog is frequent, forming shortly after sunset. These fogs generally do not extend any great distance seaward, but may seriously restrict harbor activities. Sea fogs sometimes drift onshore on hot summer days, persisting for many hours in a shallow layer along the coast. Over the land, dispersal usually begins at the surface giving the effect of lifting. Over the water, fog generally persists at the surface and restricts visibility until the last vestige of the formation disappears.

Tropical cyclones.—In the North Atlantic, tropical cyclones form over a wide range of ocean between the Cape Verde Islands and the Windward Island, over the western part of the Caribbean Sea, and the Gulf of Mexico. While some may initially move northward, especially those that form southeast of Bermuda, most take a westerly to northwesterly course. Of these, some curve gradually northward, either east of or above the larger islands of the West Indies, then turn northeastward or eastward for varying distances from the Atlantic Coast of the United States. Others pass over or to the south of the larger islands and enter the Gulf of Mexico, then curve northward or northeastward and strike some part of the east Gulf Coast. Others may continue westward and strike the west Gulf Coast.

The most common path is curved, the storms moving generally in a westward direction at first, turning later to the northwestward and finally to the northeastward. A considerable number, however, remain in low latitudes and do not turn appreciably to the northward. Freak movements are not uncommon, and there have been storms that described loops, hairpin-curved paths, and other irregular patterns. Movement toward the southeast is rare, and in any case of short duration. The entire Caribbean area, the Gulf of Mexico, the coastal regions bordering these bodies of water, and the Atlantic Coast are subject to these storms during the hurricane season.

Hurricanes develop over the southern portions of the North Atlantic, including the Gulf of Mexico and Caribbean Sea, mostly from June through October, infrequently in May and November, and rarely in other months; the hurricane season reaches its peak in September. An average of nine tropical cyclones form each year (reaching at least tropical storm intensity) and five of these reach hurricane strength. June and July storms tend to develop in the northwestern Caribbean or Gulf of Mexico while during August there is an increase in number and intensity, and the area of formation extends east of the Lesser Antilles. September storms develop between 50°W and the Lesser Antilles; in the southern Gulf of Mexico, the western Caribbean, near the Bahamas, and around the Cape Verde Islands. Formation in October shifts primarily to the western Caribbean, and off-season storms are widespread with a slight concentration in the southwestern Caribbean.

Summaries of this type outline a year-round weather story by recounting the history of regional observations. They indicate the future by telling what has happened in the past. And to the mariner who understands fundamentals, such information has great value.

Pilot charts are bonanzas of data. They appear for individual oceans at stated times of the year and also in atlas form. Principal features are prevailing winds and currents, percentages of fog, calms, and gales, isobars for pressure, and isotherms for air temperature. Also shown are ice limits, lines of equal magnetic variation, water temperature lines, and recommended routes. And often on the back side are technical discussions on a wide range of subjects from whale migration to Rules of the Road. They have limitations, of course. The scale is small. That is to be expected when the entire North Pacific Ocean appears on a sheet three feet wide and two feet high. And the information is based on averages for the time period of the chart. But used in company with *Coast Pilots* and *Sailing Directions* they serve to lay the groundwork for any forecast. Still, though, more is needed. The excerpt we've read from *Coast Pilot 4* attributes primary control of circulation over the eastern seaboard to the Azores High, but that is a generality. When it is not so high or is not located in its mean position the picture changes. A narrower focus is necessary to anticipate more timely patterns.

To present the closer views weathermen prepare bulletins and charts. And as the time span shortens, validity greatly increases. Long-range prediction leans heavily on estimates that trends noted will continue and will result in whatever such portend. But that can be like trying to anticipate the course and speed of a chipmunk. Just as he will respond unpredictably to what he hears and sees, so weather trends will be shaped by local influences. To foresee exactly what is coming far ahead is, presently, a dream. In fact, to predict specifics a month ahead is on the outskirts of practicality. Any expectation beyond a short time is a prognosis laced with "ifs." Nonetheless, *prognostic charts* and forecasts have value. They bring the application of weather history a long step closer to actuality.

When meteorologists assemble what has been recently observed they prepare a *synoptic* weather report. From it they more confidently can make short-range predictions. Such can be in the form of bulletins or charts, and are available from a range of sources. Mariners can study them at weather stations and can even receive charts on board via radiofacsimile devices. News media, whether by print, television, or radio, pass the date along. And the lay observer can even try his own hand at building one on specially prepared blank forms available from the National Weather Service.

Updates are issued throughout each day. They appear in Morse Code on continuous wave (CW) radio at 0000, 0600, 1200, and 1800 Greenwich Mean Time. Voice transmission in plain language is available during every hour. The world-wide details of weather data available by radio are found in *Worldwide Marine Weather Broadcasts*. Prepared jointly by the National Weather Service of National Oceanic and Atmospheric Administration and the Naval Weather Service Command of the Navy Department, this booklet itemizes radiotelephone, radiotelegraph, radiofacsimile, and radioteleprinter broadcast frequencies and schedules. Moreover, it includes chartlets to display what service is available where.

All this tells the observer that he is not alone with his barometer and thermometer in an uncharted atmosphere. His measures, cast against data collected by others all around, can begin to tell a logical tale. Ahead for us is a review of how these reports are presented, and an assessment of their value in the real world of the average mariner.

The information offered every six hours is twice removed from plain language. It takes special training as well as the receiver to unravel the "dot-dash" transmission by radiotelegraph. And once the Morse Code is read, then the applicable weather code must be consulted to learn what all the numbers and letters mean. Large vessels with the receivers and radio staff can pick up, decode, and plot such data, but such facility can hardly be expected of the observer on a smaller vessel. To dwell overly long on complicated weather codes is to waste time. When we are faced with these ritualistic patterns we might well have a trained meterologist nearby to act as interpreter. If not, we can consult such publications as *Weather Observing Handbook No. 1 Marine Surface Observations* or *Ship's Code Card* to gain some clues. Station observations are presented in strict adherance to a *station model.* This shows exactly where and how such details as wind temperature, cloud cover, visibility, dew point, pressure, and the like should appear. We, though, would be hard pressed to justify much more attention to such rites. That *PPP* tells sea level pressure in millibars and tenths without a decimal point and with 9 or 10 for hundreds omitted is essential to some mariners, but not to those who man less grandly outfitted vessels.

Weather charts, though, can be another matter. They share the advantages of any graphic depiction. To plot one's own position and then at a glance be told what weather is fair or foul in the neighborhood is to approach the ideal. But now we meet the problem of acquiring the weather chart. Not often will our average mariner be equipped with radiofacsimile devices to reproduce the chartwork of the experts. Yet he is not all that forlorn. When his voyage is short he can study recent weather charts at weather stations, airports, and even as reproduced in newspapers. To know the general mechanics of how they work is worthwhile.

We must begin with a shortcoming. A charted depiction of the three-dimensional atmosphere appears on a two-dimensional layout. Only length and breadth are obvious; a bit of imagination is required to grasp the missing dimension of height. We've already met cross-section sketches of warm fronts and cold fronts. But a cross-section slice is not practical. Its two dimensions show length and height, but fail to indicate width over the surface. Within an extratropical cyclone towering miles high over thousands

Figure 185.   Aerographer preparing surface weather chart. (*USN*)

of square miles, a vertical slice for each observer is impossible. The chart answer is a *plan* or downview of length and width with a symbol pattern to suggest height. Now for a close look at the devices used.

There are six basic ways to depict the works and pomps of cold and warm fronts. The approach can be by symbol alone or can invoke the aid of colors. Symbols appear on a line, and the side on which they are drawn indicates the direction of movement of the weather represented. A *cold front* is shown by ▼▼▼▼▼ . We would interpret it as moving toward the bottom of this page. If colors are used, blue is for a cold front. The selection of the form or color is so logical that most of the time there should be no question about what is being shown. But as an aid to memory we might view the cold front spikes as icicles dangling from the line on the side of movement. As for color, well, we tend to turn blue with cold. A warm front is indicated by ◗◗◗◗◗ . In color a *red* line is used. That makes sense, for when warm we do get ruddy. The symbols could be taken as icicles which have melted into mounds.

An occluded front is a merger of cold and warm, so the symbol combines both icicles and mounds alternately along one side of the line like this ▼◗▼◗▼ . The color is also a mixture: blue and red swirled together to make purple. The *stationary front* is one trying to make up its mind as to its dominant personality. Symbol-wise, that story appears as ▼◖▼◗▼ . Since the forms are on both sides of the line, no movement is suggested. The color scheme is an alternate red and blue line.

Frontal surfaces, though, are not always at ground level. They can appear at altitude. So variations are used to show their existence. When the symbol form is filled in, as with the cold icicles and warm mounds already met, the front is taken to be in contact with the earth's surface. But when the entire front is in the upper air, then the symbols have empty cores. An *upper cold front* is shown by ▽▽▽▽▽ . Its color presentation is a dashed blue line. In either case, we can look at the empty cores and the spaces between the dashes of blue as upper air. An *upper warm front* becomes ◡◡◡◡◡ . Again, the upper air shows in the cores of the mounds. Its color code is a dashed red line. And appearing in Table C is a recap of the entire pattern.

Now let's apply some of this to break the code of a weather chart. Figure 186 tells about weather observations made over a long stretch of northern hemisphere ocean. Since in the midlatitudes weather moves from west to east, we see a wave pattern spread out from left to right. The view is a synopsis of the moment, rather than like a cartoon panel telling of step-by-step developments. It is an all-at-once downview of thousands of miles east–west and probably hundreds of miles north–south. In region *A* we see a stationary front, trying to make up its mind. To the east, at *B*, is a cold

TABLE C. WEATHER CHART SYMBOLS AND COLOR CODE

Meaning	Symbol	Coloring
Cold front	▼▼▼▼▼	Blue line
Warm front	●●●●	Red line
Occluded front	▼●▼●▼	Purple line
Stationary front	▼●▼●▼	Alternate red and blue line
Upper cold front	▽▽▽▽▽	Dashed blue line
Upper warm front	◡◡◡◡	Dashed red line

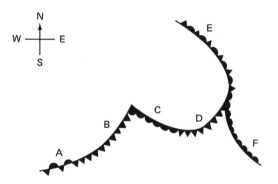

Figure 186. Symbolized view of steepening front and occlusion.

front. It is pressing on the heels of a warm front, *C*. That, in turn, chases another cold front in region *D*. It is west and south of region *E*, where an occluded front is shown. And the southeastern tail of the entire pattern shows still another warm front in region *F*.

Missing from Figure 186 is any suggestion of isobars. These lines connecting areas having the same atmospheric pressure would be present on a working synoptic weather chart, so we had better account for them. But let's do so in steps. Dissecting a weather chart is our aim. To avoid confusion by a too-early view of a busy sketch, Figure 187 shows only the isobar forms. Pressure is shown here in abbreviated form. The scale is in millibars, but the hundreds (9 or 10) are omitted. Also not shown is the

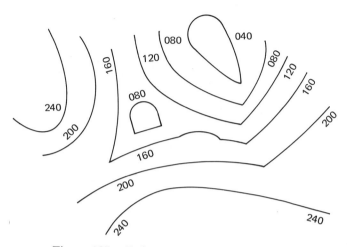

Figure 187.   Isobar patterns of frontal activity.

decimal point. Here, 240 means 1024.0 millibars and 080 means 1008.0 millibars. In other words, the left-hand and number is *tens*, the middle number is *units*, and the right-hand number is *tenths*. A high-pressure center is shown in the upper left, for there the pressure is 1024, grading eastward (to the right) down through 1020 and 1016. A ring of 080 is found near the center of the figure. This indicates a 1008 depression. To the northeast (upper right) it climbs to 1012 and then begins a descent through 1008 to 1004, another low or depression in the top right portion. At the bottom of the figure the pressure is 1024, suggesting a high. So on the entire picture we can detect two highs and two lows.

Putting the last two figures together gives us Figure 188. Now the front symbols tie in with the pressure patterns. Region C is centered on the 080 depression. To the west (left) is a cold front and to the east is a warm front. Region *E* contains the occluded front. It also has the other, even lower 040 or 1004 depression.

In Figure 188 we can also note a few new wrinkles. The words *high* and *low* are added just to confirm what the progression of isobar values indicates. Regions with high-pressure readings are piles of dense and high air; regions with low readings are sumps of less dense and low air. Particularly, though, we should examine the *wind* arrows. Two appear on either side of the stationary front in region *A*. A third is just to the left of the 080 low Another is in the upper center and a fifth is southwest of the occluded front in region *E*. Each of them reports wind direction and speed. The shafts begin from a small circle and then point *into* the wind And the feather

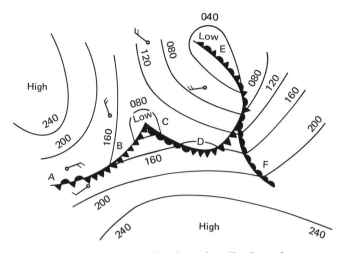

Figure 188.   Symbols and isobars describe frontal patterns.

count tells the speed. One feather is worth 10 knots, a half is worth 5 knots. So, in region *A*, at the stationary front, we see one arrow on the north side advising of a 20-knot wind from ENE. On the south side another shows a 10-knot wind from about SW. To the left of the 080 low an arrow reports a 20-knot wind from about NNW. Near the top center we see NW at 15 knots (a feather and a half). And the strongest wind, 25 knots, is shown as from nearly west. It appears below and to the left of region *E*.

Since Figure 188 is a view of northern hemisphere regions, wind direction follows our basic rule of "high to low with a right turn." But out of context, difficulty sometimes arises when deciding whether the direction is from the small circle toward the feathers or the other way around. A handy key is this: in archery, arrows have feathers on the back end. This wind arrow is no different. The small circle, like an arrowhead, is at the end toward which it flies; the feathers are at the end from which it comes. And since wind is described backward, we define it as from the small circle toward the feathers.

A series of such charts drawn for a particular area at different times can indicate the progressive movement of a disturbance. The 080 low we see in Figure 188 could be expected to move in a northeasterly direction and probably deepen. It should follow the lead of the 040 low and occlude within a few days. If the mileage from the 080 low to the 040 low were 600 and if the 080 depression were noted to be traveling at 15 knots, then in 40 hours it might reach the area where the 040 low is now located. Areas along its route would experience the weather sequences which we have seen

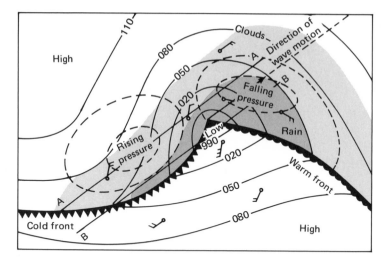

Figure 189.   Weather chart details of an extratropical cyclone.

accompany extratropical cyclones. It is quite apparent that careful weather watching requires careful analysis of recent past and present data in order to estimate the short-term future.

A few pages back we read that a little imagination is needed in order to gain a three-dimensional concept. Figure 189 shows what could be a close relative of the 080 low we met in the previous figure. This one we'll call the 990 low. Its central pressure is 999 millibars, for we've been told that weather charts show tens, units, and tenths without a decimal point and disregard the number for hundreds. The cyclonic wave is moving to the northeast, and we can recognize a quiver full of wind arrows surrounding the core. The area of falling pressure is marked in advance of the warm sector; and that of rising pressure appears behind it. Shaded regions indicate where rain could be expected within an outer fringe of cloud cover. We can apply our knowledge of basics to reason hows and whys. The low center is at the juncture of the two fronts. To the northeast, in its path, pressure will be falling; and after it passes by pressure will be rising. Before the core reaches an observer clouds will appear. Then will come rain. Behind the center more rain can be experienced within a less extensive cloud pattern. Wind will tend to blow from high to low and make a northern hemisphere right turn. Its strength will grow as the center is near, and peak power can be detected just in advance of the cold front slope. We see there a wind arrow for 30 knots.

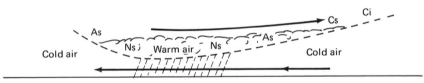

Figure 190.   Profile view when north of the low core.

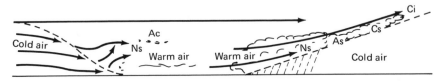

Figure 191.   Profile view of extratropical cyclone when the observer is on its track.

Suppose, though, cross-sectional slices were available to sketch in profile what several observers might experience. In Figure 189 we see two lines. One, marked *A*, describes the relative motion of Observer *A* as this disturbance passes by. The other, marked *B*, is for another more nearly in its path. Figure 190 tips the downview on edge and profiles *A*'s slice of atmosphere; Figure 191 does it for *B*. Here we gain the missing perspective of height. Observer *A* is sufficiently north of the core so that a truly cyclonic vortex is not so apparent. He is partly under the cloud umbrella and will note first a fall and then a rise in pressure. But he will not sit through the classic three-act play of warm front passing, warm sector passing, and then cold front passing. Observer *B*, though, has an aisle seat down front for the full performance. Clouds will thicken and lower as pressure drops. The wind will go to an easterly quadrant. Rain will soon begin to fall as the center draws nearer. Then, as the cold front approaches, the wind will shift and increase in strength. He will reenter a region of clouds and rain as the pressure begins to rise. Then, shortly, the disturbance will move eastward and he will be out in the clear, nippy high-pressure air.

People of different disciplines have different images of the same event. Our Jack or Jill mariner might never conjure up the likeness apparent to a weatherman. No closer to a chef's conception will be his or her view of the dinner to be cooked; and neither should expect to reproduce an astronomer's vista when celestial navigation is on deck. That, though, is the nature of seafaring. To meet astronomy, meteorology, and the culinary arts before the sun is over the yardarm schools one to define the expert seaman as a

Figure 192. Weather chart and satellite view tell a story with lines and lens. (*SMS, NOAA*)

person blessed with fundamental knowledge and a large portion of common sense. We should be satisfied with our recognition of how, in general, a weather chart works. Figures 191 and 192 show examples of patterns encountered in both hemispheres. What they relate should, by now, begin to make sense. Whether readouts from a facsimile machine or original work by a meteorologist, they tell, in very condensed form, a quite detailed story of what now prevails and what might be in store for the near future. As a wrap-up to this chapter, perhaps we should look them over to see how well our stock of information works.

QUESTIONS

Our near future is not the least in question. The line of discontinuity between this chapter and its aftermath is clearly marked by ten Qs drooping, grape-like, from the underside of a frontal surface. Whether they are colored sunny yellow or dreary black depends on how we score.

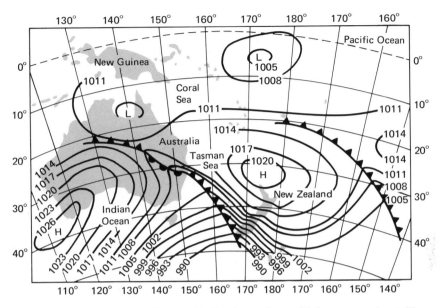

Figure 193. Australia and New Zealand weather told by pen and satellite. (*SMS, NOAA*)

1. Summaries of weather information will be found in
   a. *Coast Pilots.*
   b. *Sailing Directions.*
   c. pilot charts.
   d. all of the above.

2. On a weather chart, a surface cold front would be colored
   a. blue.
   b. red.
   c. purple.

3. When appearing on a weather chart, the symbol ▼●▼●▼ means
   a. a cold front.
   b. a warm front.
   c. an occluded front.
   d. a stationary front.

4. The side of the front line on which a symbol appears indicates
   a. the direction from which the front is moving.
   b. the direction toward which the front is moving.

5. When shown on a weather chart. 991 indicates
    a. 991 millibars.
    b. 1099.1 millibars.
    c. 999.1 millibars.
    d. none of the above.

6. The weather chart symbol   indicates a wind speed of
    a. Force 3 on the Beaufort scale.
    b. 25 knots.
    c. 12.5 knots.

7. Assuming that west is to the left and east to the right, the weather chart
   symbol ⌐─○ indicates wind direction from
    a. the west.
    b. the east.

8. At Point *A* in the area of the northern hemisphere cyclone shown, the
   wind direction would be expected to be from
    a. the northeast quadrant.
    b. the northwest quadrant.
    c. the southeast quadrant.
    d. the southwest quadrant.

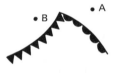

9. In the area of the northern hemisphere cyclone shown, a region of falling
   pressure would be
    a. Point A.
    b. Point B.

10. In the area of the northern hemisphere cyclone shown,
    a. occlusion is indicated in region *A*.
    b. a secondary low might develop in region *B*.
    c. a secondary low might develop in region *C*.
    d. all of the above.

ANSWERS

Reports from observers are in and plotted. All that remains is to draw some isobars, detect the fronts, and then fasten icicles or mounds. Score 10 for each correct response and evaluate your synoptic chart this way:

100, Not even a wavelet in the line
90, A minor curl, but it should flatten out
80, Some frontogenesis at work
70, Suspense along a stationary front
under 70, Adrift in an occlusion

1. d   6. b
2. a   7. a
3. c   8. d
4. b   9. a
5. c   10. d

Chapter 13

ATMOSPHERIC ODDS AND ENDS

Just one chapter away is a "shakedown cruise" during which we'll put to work the principles developed while making our voyage through weather. Beforehand, though, there remain a few things more to consider. First off, we can review some general guides for prediction based on four types of observations and a seaman's eye. The features to watch are clouds, wind, pressure, and temperature; and they are all related. Clues gained from one will usually be evident in another way. We've already studied these phases throughout the text. Listed here are broad rules based on that discussion.

CLOUDS

1. When they are of the vertically developed *cumulus* type they indicate that air is being pushed upward and reaching the dew point enroute. Such instability tells of updrafts of warm air from surface levels. In late afternoon when such a pile appears in an otherwise clear sky it might reveal approach to an island. When scattered in patchy clumps, they suggest that fair weather will continue. When towering, they could warn of thunderstorms with possible attendant squalls and wind shifts. At sea, thunderstorms occur more frequently in the early morning; over land, the time is late afternoon. Cumulus forming early in the day indicate unusual convection. They are more likely to grow into *cumulonimbus* than those making a later appearance.

Figure 194. Lenticular clouds over snow-flecked hills. (*NOAA*)

2. When clouds are sheet-like *stratus* type they tell of more stable air reaching a dew point level en masse. What weather might be on the way depends on how such forms change. If they lower and thicken, rain can be expected. If they thin and seem to evaporate, the likelihood is a change to better weather.

3. As important as cloud form is sequence of change. A steady procession gradually changing shape and altitude is a valuable hint to frontal activity. *Cirrus* congealing into *cirrocumulus* or *cirrostratus* followed by *altostratus* and *stratus* is the classic parade as a *warm front* passes.

4. Which part of the sky contains cloud cover is another clue. When in the northern hemisphere, if the concentration seems to be over the northern portion and not spreading toward you, the center of a low is to the north, but not troublesome. Should the cloud cover be breaking up, any frontal problems should be history. If, though, the cloud cover spreads from the north toward you, then you can expect to encounter more of the outfall while the low travels by. Should the clouds seem grouped over the southern

Figure 195.   Deceptive cloud formations over Antarctica's Mount Erebus warn of extremely high winds aloft and the coming of a furious blizzard. (*USCG*)

horizon, your weather will worsen if they thicken and lower toward your location. The low is probably south of you and will bring an overcast with rain, followed by clearing weather.

5. Remember perspective and that the earth is spherical. Clouds will appear to converge near the horizon and might for a while seem to be much more concentrated than when they are more nearly overhead.

6. Cloud motion reflects the strength of wind flow at altitude. Fast movement obviously results from brisk winds aloft and suggests steep pressure differences. Waves of clouds follow the direction of their short dimension. Like ocean waves, they move at right angles to the bearing along their peaks and troughs. But their course and speed differ from surface wind, particularly when the clouds are more than 2000 feet (610 meters) high. Less affected by the frictional drag of the earth's surface, they are pushed by stronger winds with greater Coriolis twist.

WIND

1. When from an easterly quadrant wind is more indicative of rain or stormy weather than when westerly. But barometric change must also be considered. Easterly wind with barometer falling probably warns of a depression to the west that is coming your way.

2. Strong winds in the early morning are exceptional. Their appearance indicates a lack of uniformity in the atmosphere and expectation of changes.

3. The characteristics of local winds in the region of operation should be determined by reference to *Coast Pilot* or *Sailing Directions*. Also to be kept in mind are periodic changes which result in regularly scheduled wind shifts. An example is the daily cycle of a morning offshore breeze and afternoon onshore breeze in a coastal region.

7. Buys-Ballot's Law states: In the northern hemisphere, face the wind and the center of a low is about abeam to your right; in the southern hemisphere, face the wind and the center of a low is about abeam to your left.

Figure 196.   Frontal cloud swirl dominates a confused skyscape. (*USN*)

8. In the northern hemisphere, when the wind shifts to the left (backs), the low will pass south of you. When the wind shifts to the right (veers), it will pass north of you.

PRESSURE

1. More important than pressure of the moment is pressure change over a period of time. A steady barometer shows no reason to expect weather changes.

2. When the barometer rises, the expectation should be for fair weather. Should it rise rapidly, the indication is that a ridge of high pressure approaches and that on the other side of the atmospheric "hill" of dense air might be some worsening weather.

3. When the barometer falls there is evidence that some degree of bad weather approaches. How much and what kind depends on rate of fall and change in wind direction. When the barometer falls and the wind shifts to an easterly quadrant, the approach of a warm front is practically assured.

TEMPERATURE

1. Temperature drop accompanied by barometer rise and wind from a westerly quadrant indicates that weather will be clearing.

2. Temperature rise accompanied by barometer fall and wind from south or from an easterly quadrant accompanies warm front conditions and the passage of a warm sector.

3. When the sea temperature is significantly different from air temperature, fog can develop.

4. As air temperature approaches the dew point, condensation is imminent. At or near the surface, that can mean fog. Readings of the wet- and dry-bulb thermometer and then reference to Tables 10 and 11 (in "Ready Reference") can indicate when the likelihood is worth noting.

Table D was prepared by weathermen to indicate generally the expectations connected with wind and barometer comparisons.

During our study so far, preferential treatment has been given to those facets bearing directly on the application of weather principles by the average mariner. Whenever a point arose which might make us deviate from our course, it was not pursued. Now, though, is the time to discuss some of those tabled topics.

What the atmosphere does to light has been exploited by wizards and writers for ages. Acting as a lens, filter, or prism it produces weird displays to stun the innocent. Even the worldly-wise can waver when air joins the laws of optics to put on a show. And we mariners often have the best seats in the house. Not trammeled by light bulbs and neon signs, our view is often as close to nature as one could find.

TABLE D. Wind–Barometer Table

Wind Direction	Barometer Reduced to Sea Level	Character of Weather
SW to NW	30.10 to 30.20 and steady	Fair, with slight temperature changes for 1 or 2 days.
SW to NW	30.10 to 30.20 and rising rapidly	Fair followed within 2 days by rain.
SW to NW	30.20 and above and stationary	Continued fair with no decided temperature change.
SW to NW	30.20 and above and falling slowly	Slowly rising temperature and fair for 2 days.
S to SE	30.10 to 30.20 and falling slowly	Rain within 24 hours.
S to SE	30.10 to 30.20 and falling rapidly	Wind increasing in force, with rain within 12 to 24 hours.
SE to NE	30.10 to 30.20 and falling slowly	Rain in 12 to 18 hours.
SE to NE	30.10 to 30.20 and falling rapidly	Increasing wind and rain within 12 hours.
E to NE	30.10 and above and falling slowly	In summer, with light winds, rain may not fall for several days. In winter, rain in 24 hours.
E to NE	30.10 and above and falling fast	In summer, rain probably in 12 hours. In winter, rain or snow with increasing winds will often set in when the barometer begins to fall and the wind set in NE.
SE to NE	30.00 or below and falling slowly	Rain will continue 1 or 2 days.
SE to NE	30.00 or below and falling rapidly	Rain with high wind, followed within 36 hours by clearing and, in winter, colder.
S to SW	30.00 or below and rising slowly	Clearing in a few hours and fair for several days.
S to E	29.80 or below and falling rapidly	Severe storm imminent, followed in 24 hours by clearing and, in winter, colder.
E to N	29.80 or below and falling rapidly	Severe NE gale and heavy rain; winter, heavy snow and cold wave.
Going to W	29.80 or below and rising rapidly	Clearing and colder.

White light, we are told, contains all colors from the long-wave red through the whole spectrum to the shortwave violet. Were it not for the atmosphere we would, every hour of the 24, view the vault of the sky as a black spacescape studded with spots of light ranging from the brilliant sun to the dimmest of stars. But the filter of the atmosphere scatters those colors with the shortest wavelengths. Violet is absorbed by the air to leave blue as the dominant remainder. When the sun is near the horizon, it passes through a greater span of atmosphere than when it is closer to overhead. The result is more absorption of blue and green to create a reddish sun. Should such materials as smoke or dust be in the air, the longer waves of red to yellow can be absorbed to show it as greenish-blue.

The major cause of optical tricks in the sky is refraction. When light passes from air of one density into another, it is bent. How much of a course change depends, among other things, on the color of the light, the contrast in density, and the angle from perpendicular at which the light encounters the dividing line. Let that angle get too large and the light will be so bent that it never enters the other medium at all. Should it travel back into the medium it left, we call the result *reflection*.

Celestial navigators measuring the altitude of sun, moon, planet, or star will observe the body as higher than reality. The light rays from the object travel from empty space and then enter the atmosphere. The outcome is a bend, as illustrated in Figure 197. The real sun is at *S*, but Navigator *A* sees it higher, at *S'*. And the amount of refraction increases as the altitude of the body decreases. So when he observes the sun perched on the horizon at sunset, it has, in fact, already gone over the edge. There is one time he will not meet refraction: when the body is directly overhead. Then the light passes from one medium to another on a line perpendicular to the "density front" without any reason for bending. In Figure 197 Navigator *B* would see the moon at *M*, exactly where it should be.

Such instances of refraction are so commonplace that they raise no eyebrows, yet the difference between them and *mirages* is not very great. Within the atmosphere itself there can exist layers of air with different densities. Cold air near the surface with a block of warm above is an example. Such would develop during a temperature inversion. Then an object actually below the horizon will be visible. Such a phenomenon is called *looming*. And what is seen can be distorted. If its upper part is raised more than the lower, the effect is called *towering*; if the image is shorter than fact because the lower part is raised more than the upper, the result is termed *stooping*. Sighting a lighthouse at night can be troubled by these effects. The navigator might "see" it before he is really within its geographic range; and then, when closer but still out of actual range, he might lose it when the rays are no longer refracted to his line of sight. For positive observations he should

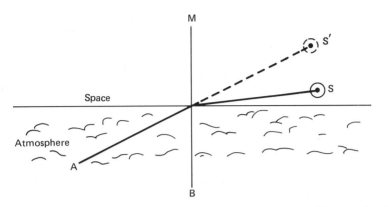

Figure 197. Light ray bends when passing into medium of different density.

keep looking to assure he actually sees that light above his horizon and is not meeting its loom, with possible distortion of characteristic and bearing.

Radar can have its refraction problems, too. Normally it can "see" about 6% farther than the naked eye, for its radio waves, longer than light, are bent down more to hug the surface. *Superrefraction* occurs when the atmospheric state allows greater downward bend; and, akin to looming, it increases the range of detection. The reverse circumstance is called *sub-refraction*. It occurs when dense air overrides that of lesser substance. Then the radar waves are either not bent down so much or are actually slanted upward. The result is less than normal detection range, and the likely locale would be where cold air overrides a shallow warm layer. Some of radar's spooky images are connected with a condition called *ducting*. A transmitted signal can be trapped within an atmospheric layer and conducted far over the edge of the horizon. During duct seasons, objects are frequently detected far beyond the working range of the equipment. Reports from some regions speak of ranges as great as 1500 miles! Of course, a radarscope cannot display a pip at any greater range than its setting. One adjusted to show objects out to 20 miles will not suddenly announce "185" when it receives an echo from that distance. Instead, it will show the pip less frequently than every sweep. And without regular reinforcement the light display will be dimmer than normal. For what it's worth, here is a rule of thumb to determine at what range such an off-beat display might show up: divide the known range to the object by the range setting of the radar. The remainder left is the range at which the object will appear; and the whole number in the answer keys at what number of antenna and sweep rotations it will appear. So, in our example of an object 185 miles off detected by a radar set to a 20-mile range, we would divide 185 by 20 to find 9 with 5 left over. The object would appear at a 5-mile range and its pip would be reinforced during the next sweep after nine swings of the antenna.

Certain areas and certain times have been noted as likely for radar ducting to occur. Extracted here from *Radar Navigation Manual*, Publication No. 1310 of the Defense Mapping Agency, are some comments on that subject:

> *U.S. Atlantic Coast:* Ducting is to be expected along the northern part of the coast in summertime and along the Florida coast in winter months.
> *U.S. Pacific Coast*: Ducting is a frequent occurrence, but no seasonal trend is clearly indicated.

Let's put aside radar anomalies for now and return to a discussion of optical specters. *Superior mirage* refers to observation of a phantom image above the actual object. It is the result of superrefraction of the light, and that is likely to happen when warm air lies over a much colder sea. There are three variations of this wraith, as shown in Figure 197. In Figure 198A the actual vessel is unseen below the horizon but an inverted image appears above. In Figure 198B the real ship appears erect beneath an inverted apparition. In Figure 198C still another ghost shows, this time right-side up, above the other two.

When air is over a much warmer surface, an *inferior mirage* might appear. This time the false image is below the real, which often seems to be floating in the sky. Figure 199 is an example. The likelihood is much greater over land, for there the surface temperature can be sufficiently warm to produce the effect. When sky is so inverted, the result can be cruel deception of the desert wanderer parched for water. Even the seafarer can encounter it, particularly when near a warm coastline. On occasion a *lateral mirage* can be detected. In principle like the inferior type, it hovers along the edge of a very warm vetrical surface.

Castles in the air can be the vision displayed by a very intricate mirage called *Fata Morgana*, and no less fanciful is the source of its label. Morgan le Fay is another name for Fata Morgana; and both refer to the sister of legendary King Arthur and the protégée of Merlin, his court magician. Apparently, an early traveler versed in myth saw illusory turrets and battlements hovering in the sky over the Mediterranean's Straits of Messina. Science explains the phantom as the result of light refracted by multistratam air of contrasting densities. Combined are superior and inferior mirages with towering, looming, and a bit of stooping added. Distortions range from wonderful to grotesque and the locale is not just between Italy and Sicily. Such fantasies are encountered along northern coasts of both the Atlantic and Pacific and have also been reported seen on the Great Lakes.

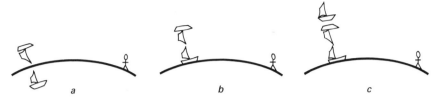

Figure 198. Types of superior mirages.

A. Vessel beyond horizon appears inverted.
B. Inverted mirage above real vessel.
C. Two images appear above the actual view.

Figure 199. Inferior mirage, with real vessel above an image.

Refraction has more to answer for. Twinkling of stars, shimmering of the sea surface, haloes, and rainbows are all its progeny. When the sun or moon appears through a veil of thin, high clouds, light will refract off ice crystals. The resulting *halo* is a more-or-less continuous ring around the body with the innermost rim tinged red. Sometimes instead of a hoop, one or two spots can appear to mock the sun or moon. Such a phantom sun is called a *parhelion, mock sun,* or *sun dog.* When the moon is mimicked, the name is *paraselene, mock moon,* or *moon dog.*

Rainbows arise from refraction, reflection, and diffraction of sunlight shining on rain clouds and their products. We've already been told of the seaman's ditty about rainbows in the morning and rainbows at night. Its validity stems from the fact that the rainbow appears in that part of the sky directly opposite the sun. And the pattern of its arc is such that red shows on the outer side with the spectrum colors ranging through orange, yellow, green, and blue to violet on the inner rim. A faint image is sometimes caused by the moon and gains the obvious name of *moonbow.*

Alert observers might note another product of refraction, the *greenflash.* When the sun sets, the first color to disappear is red. At the other end of the spectrum, blue and violet are usually so absorbed by the atmosphere that they don't show near the sun at all. But within a short second after red is gone, the only color left might be a flash of green. The atmosphere must be clear and the horizon uncluttered to observe the scene. At sunrise the order of colors is reversed. Within an instant before red makes its appearance, green might then be visible.

The indistinct outline of the sun visible through such middle clouds as altostratus might sometimes be ringed by a glow called a *corona*. The picture is halo-like, but the colors are reversed. Where the red of a halo is on the inside rim, the corona's red is on the outside, away from the body. The reason? It is connected with the fact that a halo comes from refraction while a corona arises because of diffraction. One thing worth note: the radius or thickness of the corona is inversely proportional to the size of the water droplets which are its source. So as a corona shrinks it tells of larger droplets and more likelihood of rain.

Given the ten-dollar name of *crepuscular rays* is the image which seamen describe as "the sun with its backstays down" or "the sun drawing water." When sunlight passes through openings in clouds its path seems to be a series of beams reaching down and outward from behind the clouds. Actually the beams are parallel, but because of perspective they take on a converging form. Sometimes the beams seem to focus upward, toward a point in the sky opposite the sun. Then they are called *anticrepuscular rays*.

An *aurora* is not a result of light refraction. Electronic emissions from the sun can enter the earth's magnetic field and then encounter the ionosphere. There, about 1200 miles from our magnetic poles, they can become visible as various forms of light flickering across the sky. *Aurora borealis* is the "northern lights" seen on dark, clear nights in the northern hemisphere; *aurora australis* is its counterpart in the southern.

With optical concerns behind us we can move on to another subject not in the mainstream of shipboard meteorology. The mariner's direct contact is with the lower part of the atmosphere within which he sails. But what happens above the troposphere and in its top stories can greatly influence his weather. One such circumstance is the *jet stream*. Flowing through the atmosphere can be cores of strong wind thousands of miles long, hundreds of miles wide, and thousands of feet thick. They appear at altitudes from about 25,000 feet (7620 m) to 40,000 feet (12,192 m) and contain air moving at from 100 knots (185 km/hr) to 300 knots (556 km/hr). Two general bands of these rapid atmospheric rivers have been noted. The main one seems to be related to the polar front. It shifts toward the Equator in the winter and moves poleward in the summer, as does the polar front. And it seems to have a distinct influence on how and where extratropical weather disturbances occur. Moving from the west at high speed and very near the tropopause, it can produce shearing effects to set off whirls and eddies.

Figure 200.   The sun sets her backstays with crepuscular rays. (*USN*)

Another has been noted in subtropical latitudes. It moves from the east to the west and would logically seem to have influence on what whirls and eddies develop in those climes. It is not for the practical mariner to be overly concerned with detection of such activity, for he has no means to sense what might be going on four or more miles above his head. Yet knowledge that such atmospheric turmoil is at work helps complete the scheme of causes for his surface disturbance.

Related to such upper atmosphere concerns is the matter of the *500-millibar chart*. An alarmed reaction of the mariner to such reference is understandable. Either he is being warned of the all-time champion of hurricanes, or he has a gaping hole in his skein of knowledge. Well, the weatherman doesn't speak of Terrible Tanya. On the other hand, the rent in the mariner's learning is easily mended. As we have seen, surface weather patterns are closely related to happenings aloft. Airflow about three miles high provides valuable clues to what might take place on the surface. So

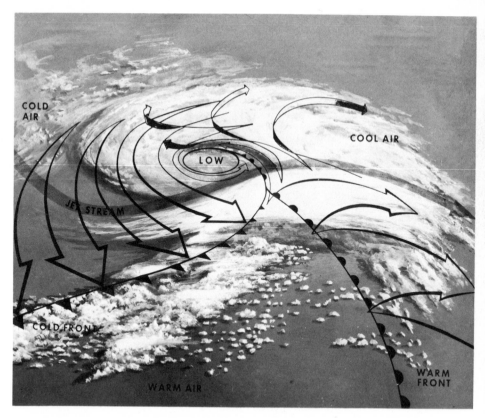

Figure 201. Jet stream flow curving through a frontal system. (*NOAA*)

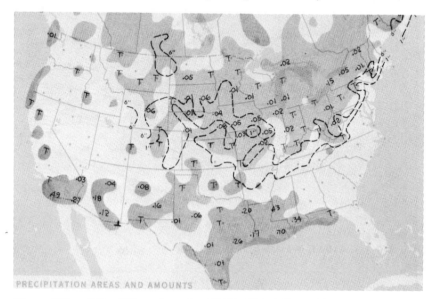

PRECIPITATION AREAS AND AMOUNTS

Figure 202. 500-millibar chart for GMT 1200 (*EDS, NOAA*)

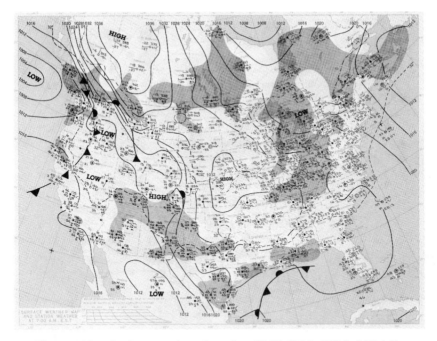

Figure 203. Surface weather chart for GMT 1200 (*EDS, NOAA*)

meteorologists prepare a 500-millibar chart based on data collected by instrument packages carried to that lofty low-pressure level. It has been found that surface weather seems steered by winds at such troposphere heights of 18,000 feet or about 5500 meters. So, with the equipment to take the measures, weather experts can estimate what might be the course and speed of a surface low or high. From our vantage point a few meters above the surface, we'll take them at their word. How they reached their conclusions with radiosondes and other high-flying atmospheric probes is not our concern. What they then predict is much more in point.

Also in point about now is some relief from this barrage of jet streams flowing beneath the northern lights. We'll set a sun dog to guard a 500-millibar chart while we assess what this chapter is all about.

QUESTIONS

Our quizmasters this time sit at a round table in a place called Camelot. Prince Valiant makes sure that full goblets of mead sit before Sirs Gawain,

Lancelot, and that shifty-eyed one, Modred. The Lady Guinevere discreetly signals King Arthur and he raps for order with Excalibur. About to begin is trial by ordeal!

1. At sea, the time of day when thunderstorms are most likely is
   a. morning.
   b. afternoon.

2. More indicative of rain or stormy weather is
   a. wind from the west.
   b. wind from the east.

3. When the wind shifts to a westerly quadrant and the barometer is rising rapidly, the weather expected will be
   a. rain within a matter of hours.
   b. a severe storm.
   c. clearing and probably colder.

4. When an object actually below the horizon is seen,
   a. the atmospheric condition is called looming.
   b. a temperature inversion might exist.
   c. both of the above.
   d. none of the above.

5. Radar range is usually
   a. more than visual with the naked eye.
   b. less than visual with the naked eye.

6. When warm air lies over a much colder sea, the result could be
   a. a superior mirage.
   b. an inferior mirage.

7. When the sun is in the east, a rainbow would be expected
   a. in the west.
   b. in the east.

8. A halo appears through _____ clouds with red on the _____ rim of the ring.
   a. high clouds / inside
   b. middle clouds / outside

9. Jet streams flow
   a. from west to east around the earth.
   b. from east to west around the earth.
   c. both of the above.

10. A 500-millibar weather chart describes observations taken at
    a. sea level.
    b. about 18,000 feet or 5500 meters.

ANSWERS

Morgan le Fay, alias Fata Morgana, has been detailed by the Knights of the Round Table to score our progress. A pinch of mandrake is ground by pestle in a mortar as she and Merlin make incantations to a full moon. The measure is 10 points, as usual, for each correct answer. And here is how she weights the outcome:

100, Merlin is impressed!
90, Card-carrying wizard or witch
80, Sorcerer's apprentice
70, A somewhat inverted image
under 70, Castles in the Straits of Messina?

1. a   6. a
2. b   7. a
3. c   8. a
4. c   9. c
5. a   10. b

Chapter 14

A CRUISE WITH WEATHER

There is only one way to measure how a ship behaves, and that is by a shakedown cruise. What would be helpful now is an onboard experience putting our shipload of basics to practical use. All we need do is invoke the gods of wind, and with a mighty puff they whisk us to a sturdy yacht pushing westward before a moderate breeze. It is September 15 when we join, and she is bound from Bermuda to Jacksonville, Florida.

This is not the best season to be traveling such waters, for busy in the Intertropical Convergence Zone can be easterly waves prone to combine with other aberrations into hurricanes. But the master is in a hurry to finish his summer cruise. The kids are already late for the beginning of school, and his business sorely needs attention. Before leaving Hamilton he made a careful check of weather data and learned that no troublesome tropical cyclone activity had been reported. To cover 880 miles according to his reckoning of expected speed would take five or six days. There was a risk that a hurricane could move from its spawning grounds to intersect his track, but urgency won out. At first light on September 12 departure was made and so far they have bustled along at a shade over 7 knots.

We join at dawn of the third day when the position is 31°N and 75°W. The weather tools aboard are a barometer, thermometer, anemometer, and hygrometer. Radio equipment includes a direction finder, telephone, and a multiband receiver. Perched about ten feet above the deck is a radar antenna, and the maximum range setting on the receiver is 20 miles. In the bookrack is a *Coast Pilot*; on the chart table is a North Atlantic pilot chart for the time of the year. We also possess ideas on how wind and cloud observations relate to weather, and that all-important seaman's ration of common sense.

The course, we're told, is 264° True, the present speed seems to be a brisk 8 knots, and almost exactly 350 miles remain to be traveled. If we maintain speed we can project arrival as in the early hours of September 17. Time now, though, to look at what the pilot chart has to offer. Figure 204 reproduces an excerpt from what we see.

Much background information is presented. Starting at Charleston is a dotted line marked 80°. Another, labeled 82°, passes through Miami. These are isotherms indicating air temperature in Fahrenheit units. The translation to Celsius is made by Table 9 (in "Ready Reference") and emerges as 26.7°C and 27.8°C. Our position is between the two lines and closer to 80°F (26.7°C). If averages prevail, a warm day lies ahead. Short, solid lines, sometimes curling and always marked with numbers such as 2.5 or 0.5, tell of ocean currents to be expected. Between us and Jacksonville our course will intersect some northbound ones. There lies the Gulf Stream. Very near our location is one bending toward the southwest and indicating 0.8 knots. That might account for at least part of the dozen-or-so miles we seem to be south of our intended track. No reason, though, to make any

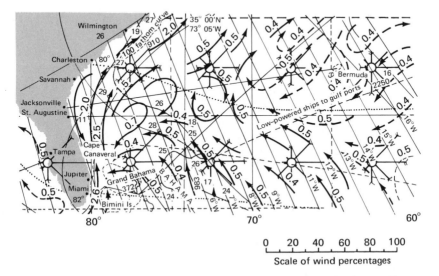

Figure 204. Excerpt from "Pilot Chart of the North Atlantic Ocean, September." (*DMAHTC*)

course correction. By tomorrow evening we will be meeting the Gulf Stream. Its northward set at up to 2.5 knots will more than be a cure to stay with us until we are some 60 miles off the coast. Then will come another, but weaker current, setting to the south.

We also note some finer lines marked at intervals with numbers within small circles. These are tracks of severe storms which have raged through in the past. The number is for the day of the month and the circle is the storm position at noon GMT on that day. Although the lines need not always refer to tropical cyclones, we must remember September. It is the peak month for hurricanes, and the curves of those fine lines are probably echoes of tropical cyclones. Four of them cross the ship's track, and three of those show movement that intersected our remaining passage to Jacksonville. We'd better take a closer look. One of those storm lines is shown to have passed over the tip of Florida on the tenth of a September and reached offshore from St. Augustine on the eleventh. That computes to a speed of over 12 knots for a 300-mile movement. Another is shown to have crossed our track on a prior September 29. Following its line backward we see that it had moved less than 200 miles from its September 28 position. But by backtracking even more we see that it was an unusual hurricane. Between September 26 and 27 it negotiated a loop to start northwestward again after earlier recurving between September 24 and 25. Such lines are history, of course, but they warn us how erratic such ogres can be Someone aboard had better monitor radio reception to pick up any mention of a storm that might be surging northward from the Bahamas. There's probably little risk that one will sneak up on us in the next 48 hours; yet, should one be on the move it might already have been detected with broadcasts out on its progress.

The pilot chart has some other information to offer. A heavy dotted line bends southeasterly from Cape Canaveral. It marks the average northern limits of the northeast trades this month, and is so identified on the portions of the chart not reproduced. Several *wind roses* also are shown. These appear as circles from which arrow shafts of varying lengths are drawn. At the tips are feathers to indicate speed. Admiral Beaufort would be pleased to learn that the feather count is not in the more modern pattern of "one feather for 10 knots and half a feather for 5." Rather, pilot charts still follow his scheme of forces. So, three feathers tells of Force 3; and our "Ready Reference" informs us (Table 3) that that means a wind speed of from 7 to 10 knots.

The shaft flies with the wind, so direction is named by looking from the center out toward the feathers. And shaft length is the key to frequency of wind from that direction. A scale is printed on a full chart; we have moved it to appear on our excerpt below the longitude scale between 60° and 70°. The idea is to measure with dividers the shaft from the rim of the circle to its tip. That length is then checked against the scale to find the percent of the total number of observations in which the wind has blown from that direction. Here's an example. Between our position and Charleston we find such a wind rose, and its longest shaft is from the northeast. The length, cast against the scale, relates that about 25% of the time in that area the wind is northeast at Force 4. Sometimes the arrow is broken and a small number inserted between the circle and its end. None such appear in Figure 203; but when they might we are to interpret the number as telling us the percentage directly. That procedure is used when winds prevail much of the time from a particular direction. Since the shaft would then be so long it would extend beyond the region covered, the number procedure is used instead. Within the wind rose circle we note a number. Between us and Charleston the rose shows *4*. This tells us the percentage of calms, light airs, and variable winds. Just 4% of the observations were in that category.

A full pilot chart is not to be scanned by speed readers. Insets will be found telling of pressure patterns, gales, fogs, and sea temperature. Well-packed paragraphs describe all sorts of other valuable data for the place and time. Even *isogonic lines* are depicted, to tell of magnetic variation throughout the area. By now, though, we've squeezed this chart dry. Time to pursue some other sources of weather data.

We tap the barometer face lightly and note its reading as 1015 after minor correction for instrument error. Despite what the old salt might say, we also check for height above the sea. We estimate that as being 5 to 10 feet. Table 5 (in "Ready Reference") reports the correction as 0.01 inches. Table 8 advises that the millibar equivalent is barely 0.3. Since we've gone this far, we might as well complete the task. The barometer, we report, reads 1015.3 corrected. The air temperature registers as 72°F or, says Table 9, 22.2°. The hygrometer shows the wet bulb to read 65°F or 18.3°C. Consulting our tables for relative humidity and dew point (found in "Ready Reference" as Tables 10 and 11) we learn that when dry is 72°F and the wet-dry difference is 7°, the relative humidity is 69% and the dew point is 61°F. We are shrouded by a maritime air mass being fed from the Azores High far over the eastern horizon and there seems little reason to expect significant changes.

While we're at it we might as well check the sea temperature. No canvas bucket is found aboard so we decide to use one made of plastic. A tagline is fastened and over the side it goes. We haul a sample aboard and then use the thermometer as a swizzle stick. In a few minutes we read the sea temperature as 77°F or 25°C. These are warm waters, and in September we can expect the reading to equal or even exceed that of the air. At the moment our air mass might warrant the abbreviation *m T k* since it is maritime tropical air colder than the sea surface. Later in the day it will approach *m T w.* But such fine distinctions are not important since there is no great contrast between sea and air. No startling mirages are due today unless some freak layer of cold air should move in over the warm sea.

Next comes our determination of wind. It seems to be directly on the starboard beam; but we sight along crests of whitecaps and find it is really from abaft the beam. A check with the anemometer reveals its apparent speed as 12 knots. And the windvane retells that it is at right angles to course. Since our true heading is 264°, abeam to starboard means we add 90° and find the apparent wind as 354°. Out of the drawer come straightedges, dividers, and a plotting sheet to handle our "1-2-3" routine converting apparent to true values. Figure 205 shows the result. Actual wind measures as 028° True at 14.4 knots. That squares with what we've read: the true wind is on the same side as the apparent wind, but farther aft. We find it, not abeam, but three points abaft. Admiral Beaufort can be faintly heard describing it as NNE½ E and Force 4. A less salty compromise is NNE at 15 knots.

Incidentally, Table 4 in "Ready Reference" is a tabular means of converting from apparent to true. As a double-check we put it to work by these steps:

1. *Divide apparent wind speed by ship's speed.* This converts apparent speed into multiples or decimal parts of ship's speed. We do it here by dividing apparent 12 knots by ship 8 knots and find 1.5.

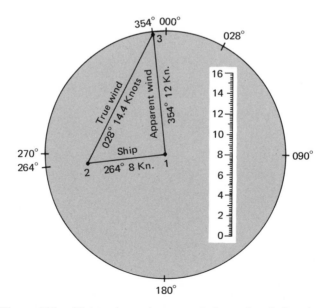

Figure 205.　Plot to determine true wind speed and direction.

2. *Determine the angular difference between the ship's course and the apparent wind direction.* Here it is 90°, for the wind is apparently directly on the starboard beam. What we have found is a relative measure from the bow, and it is measured left or right. So, if the wind had appeared abeam to port we would still use 90°.

3. *Enter Table 4 with the speed factor from Step #1 and the angle factor from Step #2; then read out the angle from the bow to the true wind and also a multiplier. True course plus or minus the angle on the bow equals true wind direction. Ship's speed times the multiplier equals true wind speed.* The readout for our values is 124° and 1.8. The true wind is at an angle of 124° from the ship's course. Since the wind is on the starboard side, we add 124° to our course of 264°. The result is 388° or 028° True. Then we multiply the ship's speed by the other factor (1.8) to find true wind speed. The result here of 8 knots times 1.8 is 14.4 knots.

Since the accuracy of measuring entry values can be low, interpolation when using the table is not recommended. The steps are slightly tricky and the lack of a graphic picture can impede a real image. We should know about Table 4, and some of us might prefer it to the "1-2-3" sketch. In any case, the option is now ours.

Here, then, is a summary of the weather data we've so far observed:

Atmospheric pressure: 1015.3 mb
Atmospheric temperature: Dry, 72°F or 22.2°C
Wet, 65°F or 18.3°C
Relative humidity: 69%
Dew point: 61°F or 16.1°C
Sea state: moderate with small waves and numerous whitecaps
Wind: NNE at 15 knots (actually 028° at 14.4 knots) or Force 4
Current: southwesterly at less than 1 knot
Sea state: moderate with small waves and numerous whitecaps
Visibility: more than 12 miles (unrestricted)
Clouds: none

We check the barometer again at 10 A.M. and find it reads 1018. This is not surprising, for there is a daily pattern of an increase at about 10 A.M. and 10 P.M., with two low points at 4 A.M. and 4 P.M. Noting the entries made for yesterday's weather we see there has been little change in any values. The barometer was somewhat higher; but the ship was then almost 200 miles closer to the Azores High. Temperatures, wind, sea, and sky were reported in almost identical terms. In the afternoon's heat scattered cumulus clouds were seen. That was probably due to unstable air rising from lower levels and condensing into a few clumps.

After lunch, schedules are consulted to determine what radio weather broadcasts are available. Station WWV emits an hourly stream of data

Figure 206.   Satellite shows all clear from Bermuda to Jacksonville. (*EDS,
NOAA*)

from a Fort Collins, Colorado, installation. Its scope is the western North
Atlantic, Gulf of Mexico, and the Caribbean Sea. A companion station,
WWVH in Hawaii, handles the North Pacific and much of the South
Pacific. Both are operated by the National Bureau of Standards and broad-
cast bulletins prepared by the National Weather Service.

To gain a full list of what else can be heard, we consult a Marine Weather
Services Chart prepared by the National Weather Service. Our attention is
to MSC–5, which covers the region from Savannah, Georgia, to Apalachicola, Florida. Figure 207 reproduces its front side and Figure 208 shows
the back. Our attention quickly moves to the back, for there are listed
scores of possibilities on a wide range of voice radio frequencies and from
many sources. We disregard VHF-FM schedules from Florida or Georgia,
for we are far beyond the range of such broadcasts. We also must determine
whether bulletins from stations within range handle just coastal waters or
tell of weather at sea. After a few minutes' study we discover quite a selection of sources. Among those available are marine forecasts direct from
National Weather Service offices, recaps on news programs from a host of
entertainment stations, and Coast Guard bulletins on radiotelephone frequencies. Another short time with *Worldwide Marine Weather Broadcasts,*
published jointly by National Weather Service and the Naval Weather
Service Command, could add more. And a session with *Radio Weather*

Aids, Publication 118 of the Defense Mapping Agency, would complete the spectrum.

The selection is made, and within a surprisingly short time two bulletins are received. Our first reaction is delight. Conditions for our region are described much the same as we have measured. Here on the west flank of the Bermuda Triangle, many observations can be pooled to compile the official word. Such confirmation does much to build confidence. The situation, though, can be different for the lonesome mariner in the empty reaches of the southern Indian Ocean. When by radio he hears recounted, chapter and verse, what he might earlier have transmitted as his report, suspicions of having heard the song before are not unfounded. But that unavoidable problem is not our concern. The teeming maritime world around reinforces our conclusions.

What we do note, though, are two potential worries. A tropical disturbance has been discovered at about 15°N and 45°W, some 1900 miles to the southeast. It will have to mature in a hurry and travel an average of 40 knots to catch us before we reach Jacksonville; but we'll keep a weather eye over the port quarter all the same. The other item concerns a vagrant core of low pressure which seems to be deepening west of the Appalachians. Any disturbance to the westward bears a particular watch, for although cyclones move westward in tropical regions, weather tends to move from west to east in middle latitudes. Whatever that low might be, we seem well south of its probable path and should meet no inconvenience. But now another eye must be kept over the starboard bow. Should that low mature into an early-season extratropical cyclone, we might feel its influence. And our location on the southeast fringe of its possible track is no basis for complacency. We've read that a secondary low can develop as a spin-off from a larger storm. Such a fallout often arises when the parent storm reaches occlusion, and the likelihood is greater to the southeast along a warm front and to the southwest along a cold front. Should a new vortex form, it might either follow the course of its parent or head out on its own. In any case, it tends to build up rapidly and bring quick weather changes. Our present location might be an uncomfortable place to suffer an engine breakdown. Should the tropical depression grow into a hurricane and a secondary low develop to the southeast of the parent—well, we could be in the middle when Godzilla meets up with Wolf Boy.

Now approaching is midnight of September 15. We hear more weather broadcasts and learn that the Appalachian low previously reported has advanced and is occluding near Chesapeake Bay. If a secondary is to be spawned, the time is at hand. The good news, though, was that the tropical depression seems to be stalled about 900 miles due east of Martinique. Let's hope such dalliance leads to a short and dissipated life.

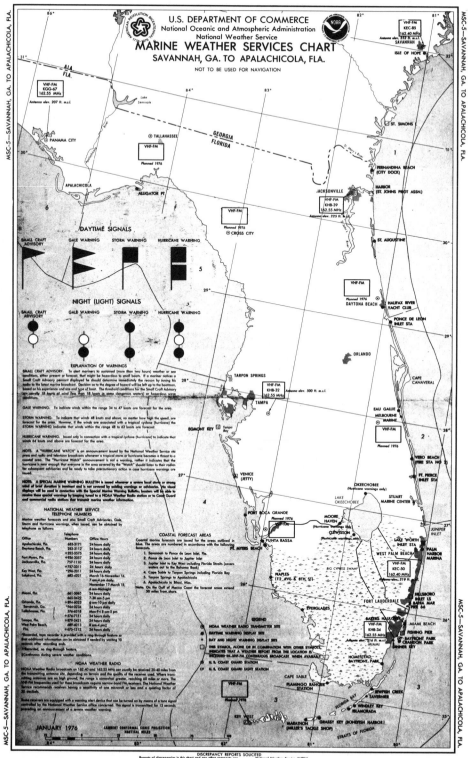

Figure 207. (*Above*). Front of "Marine Weather Services Chart 5" Savannah, Ga., to Apalachicola, Fla. (*NWS, NOAA*). Figure 208 (*Facing Page*), Back of the same chart.

CONTINUOUS WEATHER BROADCASTS

City	Station	Frequency (kHz/MHz)	Broadcast times
Jacksonville, Fla.	KHB-39	162.55 MHz	Continuously 24 hrs a day
Miami, Fla.	KHB-34	162.55 MHz	Continuously 24 hrs a day
Panama City, Fla.	KEC-67	162.55 MHz	Continuously 24 hrs a day
Savannah, Ga.	KEC-85	162.55 MHz	Continuously 24 hrs a day
Tampa, Fla.	KHB-32	162.55 MHz	Continuously 24 hrs a day
West Palm Beach, Fla.	KEC-50	162.40 MHz	Continuously 24 hrs a day

These VHF-FM radio stations are managed by the National Weather Service. Forecasts are issued every 6 hours, broadcast tapes are updated frequently and amended as required. Continuous broadcasts vary, but in general contain the following types of information:

1. Special bulletins and statements concerning hurricanes or other severe weather.
2. Forecasts and warnings for nearby coastal waters.
3. Forecasts for the local areas.
4. Description of weather patterns affecting the southeastern part of the country.
5. Radar summaries.
6. Selected marine observations.

MARINE FORECASTS AND WARNINGS BROADCAST
DIRECT FROM NATIONAL WEATHER SERVICE OFFICES

City	Station	Freq AM/FM (kHz/MHz)	Antenna Coordinates	Broadcast times (EST unless noted)
Ft. Myers, Fla.	WCAI	1350	26°37'31"N 81°52'29"W	Mon. Sat 8:01 am
Ft. Myers, Fla.		+1240	26°39'03"N 81°51'20"W	12:03 pm, Sun. 12:11 pm Mon. Sat 8:20 am
Ft. Myers, Fla.	WINK-FM	96.9	81°51'20"W	12:03 pm Mon.-Fri. (Nov.-Mar.) 3:40 pm Sun 12:11 pm
Ft. Myers, Fla.	WMYR	+1410	26°37'23"N 81°51'10"W	Mon.-Sat 8:14 am 12:30 pm Sun. 12:11 pm
Key West, Fla.	WKWF	1600	24°34'30"N 81°48'49"W	Daily 5:25, 7:15, 11:15 am
Key West, Fla.			24°34'01"N 81°48'54"W	Daily 5:25, 7:15, 11:15 am
Key West, Fla.	WKIZ	‡1500		Daily 5:25, 5:15, 6:15 am

OTHER AM AND FM RADIO STATIONS BROADCASTING
MARINE WEATHER FORECASTS AND WARNINGS

The following standard broadcast stations (AM and FM) broadcast marine weather forecasts as part of their news programs.

City	Station	Freq AM/FM (kHz/MHz)	AM Antenna Location
		FLORIDA	
Arlington	WKTZ	1180	30°19'30"N 81°34'15"W
Atlantic Beach	WJNJ	1600	30°19'30"N 81°25'42"W
Belle Glade	WSWN-FM	900	26°42'24"N 80°40'38"W
Boca Raton	WSBR	1740	26°20'46"N 80°12'32"W
Bradenton	WBRD	1490	27°30'05"N 82°33'12"W
Bradenton	WTEL	1490	27°30'00"N 82°34'25"W
Brooksville	WWJB	1450	28°33'20"N 82°22'34"W
Clearwater	WTAN	1340	27°57'50"N 82°48'15"W
Coral Gables	WVCG	1080	25°43'42"N 80°18'20"W(Day)
			25°44'48"N 80°32'47"W(Night)
Cypress Gardens	WGTO	+540	28°00'26"N 81°43'08"W
Dade City	WDCF	1350	28°20'10"N 82°11'23"W
Daytona Beach	WROD	1340	29°11'13"N 81°00'28"W
Deland	WOOO	1420	29°00'58"N 81°17'10"W
Delray Beach	WDBF	1420	26°27'27"N 80°05'58"W
Englewood	WENG	1530	26°57'55"N 82°19'15"W
Ft. Lauderdale	WEXY	1520	26°10'30"N 80°09'22"W

OTHER AM AND FM RADIO STATIONS BROADCASTING
MARINE WEATHER FORECASTS AND WARNINGS

City	Station	(kHz/MHz)	Location
Jacksonville	WAPE	+690	30°32'29"N 81°45'55"W(Day)
			30°18'27"N 81°56'38"W(Night)
Jacksonville (Orange Park)	WAYR	550	30°08'50"N 81°45'14"W
Jacksonville	WJAX	+930	30°17'00"N 81°44'52"W
Jacksonville	WMBR	+1460	30°19'40"N 81°44'50"W
Jacksonville	WPDQ	1320	30°16'40"N 81°39'11"W
Jacksonville	WPPG	+600	30°18'00"N 81°43'34"W
Jacksonville	WVOJ	+1320	30°17'50"N 81°44'35"W
Jacksonville	WZNZ	+1010	30°20'42"N 81°40'36"W
Lake Worth	WLIZ	1380	26°37'27"N 80°04'20"W
Marathon	WFFG	‡1300	24°41'28"N 81°08'30"W
Marianna	WTYS	1340	30°45'49"N 85°13'52"W
Marianna	WTOT-FM	980	30°45'00"N 85°23'00"W
Marianna	WWAB	100.9	
Melbourne	WMMB	1240	28°04'40"N 80°35'15"W
Miami	WEDR-FM	99.1	25°47'33"N 80°22'12"W
Miami	WFUN	790	25°43'28"N 80°24'02"W
Miami	WGBS	710	25°59'03"N 80°09'08"W
Miami	WINZ	940	25°57'36"N 80°16'20"W
Miami	WIOD	‡610	25°50'58"N 80°09'18"W
Miami	WQAM	560	25°47'19"N 80°11'20"W
Miami	WQBA	‡1140	25°43'09"N 80°22'30"W
Miami	WVCG	‡1260	25°43'44"N 80°25'22"W
Miami Beach	WKAT	1360	28°15'32"N 82°43'54"W
Miami Beach	WMBM	1490	25°50'58"N 80°11'51"W
Naples	WNOG	1270	26°09'08"N 81°45'07"W
New Port Richey	WGUL	1500	28°15'32"N 82°43'54"W
New Smyrna Beach	WSBB	1230	29°00'48"N 80°54'00"W
New Smyrna Beach	WOCQ	92.1	
Orlando	WABR	1440	28°34'50"N 81°27'00"W
Orlando	WBJW	+580	28°37'17"N 81°21'34"W
Orlando	WDBO	+580	
Orlando	WHOO	+990	28°32'53"N 81°25'37"W
Orlando	WHOO-FM	96.5	
Orlando	WKIS	+740	28°32'55"N 81°32'20"W
Orlando	WLOF	+950	28°34'41"N 80°50'21"W
Palm Beach	WDBF	+590	28°34'30"N 83°36'49"W
Panama City	WDLP	590	30°10'20"N 85°35'44"W
Panama City	WGNE	+1480	30°10'33"N 85°48'03"W
Panama City	WPCF	+1290	30°08'54"N 85°40'15"W
Panama City Beach	WPCM	1290	30°11'54"N 85°45'55"W
Panama City Beach	WPFM	107.9	30°13'46"N 85°49'29"W
Pensacola	WPLA	910	28°00'01"N 82°47'20"W
Plant City	WYFE	+980	28°01'25"N 82°07'06"W
Pompano Beach	WLOD	1470	26°14'25"N 80°13'14"W
Pompano Beach	WRBD	+1470	26°13'47"N 80°08'33"W
Port St. Joe	WJOE	1580	29°49'28"N 85°22'42"W
Punta Gorda	WCCF	1580	26°55'33"N 82°03'02"W
Quincy	WCNH	1230	30°34'35"N 80°04'35"W

City	Station	(kHz/MHz)	Location
Rivera Beach	WPOM	+1600	26°45'43"N 80°06'20"W
St. Augustine	WAOC	1420	29°51'00"N 81°19'45"W
St. Augustine	WFOY	1240	29°53'58"N 81°18'56"W
St. Petersburg	WLIZ	+1590	27°44'03"N 82°41'08"W
St. Petersburg	WLCY	+1380	27°53'15"N 82°37'03"W
St. Petersburg	WSUN	+620	27°45'34"N 82°37'38"W
St. Petersburg	WYBA	680	27°49'45"N 82°29'52"W
Stuart	WSTU	1450	27°12'58"N 80°15'19"W
Tallahassee	WBGM-FM	98.9	
Tallahassee	WFSU-FM	91.5	
Tallahassee	WGLF-FM	104.1	
Tallahassee	WOWD	1330	30°29'00"N 84°17'13"W
Tallahassee	WTAL	1450	30°29'35"N 84°15'30"W
Tallahassee	WTNT	+1450	30°22'58"N 84°20'30"W
Tampa	WDAE	+1250	28°00'42"N 82°29'52"W
Tampa	WFLA	+970	27°57'56"N 82°33'07"W
Tampa	WQYK	+1110	27°52'36"N 82°37'53"W
Tampa	WYOU	1550	27°55'16"N 82°21'41"W
Treasure	WFTL	1400	28°33'13"N 84°33'11"W
Venice	WAMR	1320	27°06'20"N 82°27'01"W

*National Weather Service VHF-FM continuous weather is rebroadcast daily at 12:35, 3:32, 6:10 am, 6:35, 9:35 pm.

WEATHER BROADCASTS BY AIR NAVIGATION
RADIO STATIONS

Airways and pilot weather reports, including terminal and area weather and forecasts are broadcast by aviation radio stations (local time) and frequencies as follows:

City	Station		kHz	Schedules
Jacksonville, Fla.	JA	344	365	Continuous broadcast
Miami, Fla.	MI	344		Continuous broadcast
Tallahassee	TL	379		Continuous broadcast
Tampa, Fla.	AM	388		Continuous broadcast

OTHER AM AND FM RADIO STATIONS BROADCASTING
MARINE WEATHER FORECASTS AND WARNINGS

City	Station	(kHz/MHz)	Location
		GEORGIA	
Brunswick	WMOG	+1490	31°09'55"N 81°28'28"W
Brunswick	WGIG	+1380	31°08'40"N 81°34'56"W
Garden City	WGST-FM		
Savannah	WBMQ	630	32°05'52"N 81°08'36"W
Savannah	WEAS-FM	93.1	
Savannah	WSGA	1400	32°04'17"N 81°06'41"W
Savannah	WSAV	630	32°03'51"N 81°00'52"W
Savannah	WSGC	1400	
Savannah	WTOC	1290	32°04'08"N 81°04'47"W
Savannah	WTOC-FM	97.3	
Savannah	WZAT-FM	102.1	

NOTES

1. Antenna locations for AM stations are list-ed for use in direction finding or in "homing" on the radio signal.
2. | preceding the radio frequency indicates directional antenna during daytime hours.
   ‡ preceding the radio frequency indicates directional antenna during nighttime hours.
   | preceding the radio frequency indicates directional antenna day and night.

The absence of a symbol indicates the antenna is omnidirectional.

The locations, obtained from Federal Communications Commission, are current as of December 1974.

Bearings on standard broadcast stations should be used with caution because of coastal refraction of the radio beam and infrequent calibration of the radio frequency.

BROADCASTS OF MARINE WEATHER FORECASTS
AND WARNINGS BY MARINE RADIOTELEPHONE STATIONS

City	Station		Frequency kHz/MHz	Broadcast Time (Local)
Nassau, Bahama Is	VPN-2		2558	
Mayport, Fla	VPN-2			1:20 am, 8:20 am, 10:20 am,
				1:20 pm(Warnings on receipt)
Jacksonville, Fla	NMA-10 (USCG)		+2670 A3H	6:10 am, 12:10 pm, 5:10 pm (Warnings on receipt)
	WNI (Tel Co)		1157.1 MHz (ch 22)	7:00 am, 7:00 pm (Warnings on receipt and odd hours)
Miami, Beach, Fla	NCT (USCG)		2566	4:00 am, 6:00 am, 8:00 pm, 10:50 am, 4:00 pm, 1:00 pm, 7:00 pm
Miami, Fla	WDR (Tel Co)		1157.1 MHz (ch 22)	10:50 pm(Warnings on receipt) 6:30 am, 12:30 am, 5:30 pm (Warnings on receipt)
Miami, Fla	WOM (A.T.&T)		+2442	7:20 am, 9:20 am, 11:20 am (Warnings on odd hours)
			2490	2:20 pm(Warnings on receipt)
Key West, Fla	NOK (USCG)		+2670 A3H	6:50 am, 12:50 pm, 5:10 pm (Warnings on receipt)
St. Petersburg, Fla	NCF (USCG)		+2670 A3H	7:00 am, 7:00 pm (Warnings on receipt and even hours)
Tampa, Fla	WFA (Tel Co)		1157.1 MHz (ch 22)	
Washington, D.C.	NMH (USCG)		2670 A3H 2550 A3H 157.2 MHz	3:00 am, 11:00 am — Forecasts for western North Atlantic Waters, West Central North Atlantic, including Gulf of Mexico and Caribbean Sea

OTHER AM AND FM RADIO STATIONS BROADCASTING
MARINE WEATHER FORECASTS AND WARNINGS

City	Station	(kHz/MHz)	Location
Vero Beach	WAXE	+690	
Vero Beach	WTTB	1490	
West Palm Beach	WEAT	850	
West Palm Beach	WIRK	+1290	
West Palm Beach	WJNO	+1290	

WEATHER RULES FOR SAFE BOATING

Before setting out:

Obtain the latest available weather forecast for the boating area. Where they can be received, the NOAA Weather Radio continuous broadcasts (VHF-FM) are the best way to keep informed of expected weather conditions. If there is any indication that the weather warnings are in effect, or any fog or lights or warning display stations, don't venture out on the water unless you are confident your boat can be navigated safely under forecast conditions of wind and sea.

While afloat:

1. Keep a weather eye out for:
   - the approach of dark, threatening clouds, which may foretell a squall or thunderstorm;
   - any steady increase in wind or sea; any increase in wind velocity opposite in direction to a strong tidal current. A dangerous rip tide condition may form steep waves capable of broaching a boat.

2. Check radio weather broadcasts for latest forecasts and warnings.

3. Heavy static on your AM radio may be an indication of nearby thunderstorm activity.

4. If a thunderstorm catches you while afloat, you should remember that not only gusty winds but also lightning poses a threat to safety.
   - stay below deck if possible
   - keep away from metal objects that are not grounded to the boat's protection system
   - don't touch more than one grounded object at the same time (or you may become a shortcut for electrical surges passing through the protection system)

OTHER MARINE WEATHER SERVICES CHARTS
AVAILABLE

MSC-1	Eastport, Me. to Montauk Point, N.Y.
MSC-2	Montauk Point, N.Y. to Manasquan, N.J.
MSC-3	Manasquan, N.J. to Cape Hatteras, N.C.
MSC-4	Cape Hatteras, N.C. to Savannah, Ga.
MSC-5	Savannah, Ga. to Apalachicola, Fla.
MSC-6	Apalachicola, Fla. to Morgan City, La.
MSC-7	Morgan City, La. to Brownsville, Tex.
MSC-8	Mexican Border to Point Conception, Calif.
MSC-9	Point Conception, Calif. to Point St. George, Calif.
MSC-10	Point St. George, Calif. to Canadian Border
MSC-11	Great Lakes, Michigan and Superior
MSC-12	Great Lakes, Huron, Erie and Ontario
MSC-13	Hawaiian Waters
MSC-14	Puerto Rico and Virgin Islands
MSC-15	Alaskan Waters

Copies of these charts are available from:

National Ocean Survey
Distribution Division (C44)
Riverdale, MD 20840, at 25 cents each.
Telephone 301-344-2613

Nautical charts for navigation purposes for these coastal zones are available from local marinas, marine supply stores and above address.

RADIO WWV/WWVH STORM INFORMATION
BROADCASTS

HIGH SEAS STORM INFORMATION for the North Atlantic and North Pacific is provided mariners through a cooperative program of two Department of Commerce agencies, the National Weather Service (National Oceanic and Atmospheric Administration) and the National Bureau of Standards. Bulletins are compiled by the National Weather Service and broadcast every hour by the National Bureau of Standards' Radio Stations WWV (Ft. Collins, Colorado, and WWVH, Kauai, Hawaii.

WWV (FT. COLLINS, COLO.)

Frequencies	Times of Broadcast
2.5, 5, 10, 15, 20, and 25 MHz	8 minutes past the hour Atlantic, including Gulf of Mexico and Caribbean Sea

The weather broadcast is in 45-second segments separated by a 15-second interval.

Figure 209. A frontal system moving eastward with a possible secondary low on its southern fringe. (*EDS, NOAA*)

Meanwhile, we are much closer to the Gulf Stream. Tomorrow the ocean should begin turning deep, deep blue. The radar shows an occasional pip moving off the screen and we account for each as a ship passing in the night. No telltale blotches appear to suggest any buildup of clouds. Radar can be a weather aid, for echoes will return from some atmospheric conditions. Thunderstorms rebound good signals and show up as fuzzy-edged concentrations. A series of them can warn of a cold front. Widespread and dimmer fuzz might be return from the stratus-type clouds connected with a warm front. But our antenna is not very high and the maximum range setting of 20 miles is a limitation. Theoretically, when more than 125 miles away we could detect clouds at 10,000 feet (3048 meters). But even if the signal had enough energy to survive the round trip, it would show a pip at about 5 miles only on every seventh swing of the antenna. We could hardly detect it in the sprinkle of light following the wake of the radarscope's sweep. Should we pick up any clouds, they will not be far over the horizon when they appear.

Just before dawn of September 16 we note a wind change. It seems to be veering from NNE around to east. And the barometer is down. We expect it to take a dip at 0400, for that is the time of one of its daily troughs. But at 0600 it reads 1012. Perhaps that secondary low is ready to put in an appearance. By midmorning the reading is 1010 and thereafter it continues a gradual descent. To the northwest the procession of stratified clouds seems to lower and thicken. The wind is now SE and we have firm evidence that a low is not too far away over the western horizon.

First we see the wisps of mare's tails. Following along is cirrostratus and then altostratus. It won't be long before we are beneath the southern edge of rain clouds. Our estimate is that the wind will continue to veer while the effects of this low core are passing by. When the cold front vestiges are felt, the wind will move into a westerly quadrant. Then, after all is cleared away, our previous situation of wind from the east should be restored. In a matter of a few short hours the secondary low promises to run us through the gamut of warm front to cold front and then back where we started.

As the hours pass our weather scene develops according to the script. And by radio we are reassured that no possibility of a tropical cyclone threatens us. The earlier depression is deepening toward a tropical storm and might well reach hurricane status in a few days. Should that develop, then Jacksonville might still be bruised in about a week. We had better check *Coast Pilot 4* to learn what is recommended as the best procedure when a hurricane visits the region. Meanwhile, though, we should be able to complete our passage without too much alarm.

The estimated time of arrival (ETA) at Jacksonville is now about 0400 on September 17, for we have lost a few hours while jousting with that secondary low. Now, though, we decide to delay our arrival even more. Approaching the coast in daylight is better, and a reading of *Coast Pilot 4* (excerpted in Chapter 12) adds further weight to the argument. Offshore winds during the coolest part of the day are considered better for an approach. The seas are less choppy and navigation is easier for small vessels. We'll adjust speed to arrive about 0800. By the time breakfast is over we will be in St. Johns River ready to wash down and secure from a successful voyage.

Our trip has been fictional, but it is not that much removed from what might take place. Throughout the performance we were alert to receive any evidence of tropical cyclone activity. Yet diagnosing such ailments was not for us. We just took our measurements and listened to the radio as we progressed along our track. The difference, though, was that we did so with some comprehension of what the indications meant.

More than a voyage from Bermuda is ended. We have also completed our travel through the tortuous channels of weather. As with any long journey, the point of departure and what took place early in the cruise might seem wrapped in mist. But what we have assembled is a structure of basics resting on a sturdy foundation. To be weather-wise involves more than just the experience gained from having withstood a host of gales. And it certainly sums more than a facility to distinguish the ITCZ from an adiabat. Knowledgeable observation is closer to the mark, and to achieve that has been our aim. Skill increases many-fold with application. Words in print must now step aside to make room for the final test. We encounter no quiz at the end of this, our last chapter. Instead, Luke Howard, Buys-Ballot, and Admiral Beaufort join all the other quizmasters met along the way to urge us toward a new awareness of the atmospheric ocean within which we sail.

READY REFERENCE

The metric system is sufficiently new to us that a review of its basics is in order. The starting point is with prefixes:

giga- means one billion times a standard unit
mega- means one million times a standard unit
myria- means ten thousand times a standard unit
kilo- means one thousand times a standard unit
hecto- means one hundred times a standard unit
deca- means ten times a standard unit

deci- means one-tenth of a standard unit
centi- means one-hundredth of a standard unit
milli- means one-thousandth of a standard unit
micro- means one-millionth of a standard unit
nano- means one-billionth of a standard unit

In our fast-fading older system this pattern doesn't appear. Even so, we can recognize some of the new regime in such words as *giga*ntic, *mega*phone *myria*d and *micro*meter.

Weather by no means deals with the full metric scale; but we find regular use of a few of its elements. Here are some highlights of metric weights and measures:

Linear

Kilometer = 1000 meters = 3280 feet = 0.54 naut. mile = 0.62 stat. mile
Meter   =   3.28 feet = 39.37 inches
Centimeter = 0.01 meter =   .39 inch
Millimeter = 0.001 meter =   .004 inch

Volume

cubic meter (m³) = 35.286 cubic feet = 1.307 cubic yards
cubic centimeter (cm³) = 0.01 cubic meter = 0.061 cubic inch

Weight

metric ton = 1000 kilo-
                  grams = 2204 pounds   = 1.1 short tons = 0.984 long ton
kilogram   = 1000
                  grams =   2.204 pounds = 35.264 ounces
gram   =   0.0352 ounces
centigram = 0.01 gram
milligram = 0.001 gram

Capacity

liter   = 1.06   quarts = 0.265 U.S. gallons = 61.02 cubic inches
centiliter = 0.01   liter   = 0.34 ounce
millileter = 0.001 liter   = 0.034 ounce

Pressure and temperature are already within the metric fold. Following along will be some tables to convert Fahrenheit degrees to Celsius and Kelvin and to switch from inches to millimeters and millibars. By way of introduction, set out below are fundamental equations which might be useful when a table runs out of scope but the batteries in a hand calculator are still charged:

Temperature:

Celsius = $\frac{5}{9}$ (Fahrenheit − 32)
                              or Celsius   = $\frac{5}{9}$ (Fahrenheit + 40) − 40
Fahrenheit = $\frac{9}{5}$ Celsius + 32
                              or Fahrenheit = $\frac{9}{5}$ (Celsius + 40)   − 40

Pressure

Millibars = Inches × 33.865
Inches = $\dfrac{\text{Millibars}}{33.865}$

TABLES

Next appearing are three tables dealing with the estimation of wind and sea conditions. The first two are reprinted from *Weather Bureau Observing Handbook No. 1, Marine Surface Observations* prepared by the Weather Bureau (now National Weather Service) for the guidance of ships' officers in taking weather observations on the high seas. Table 1 deals with determination of wind speed by sea condition and would have value in both receiving and reporting weather conditions. It is also found in some editions of *Coast Pilot*. Table 2 will assist in selecting what speed range to assign to apparent wind measurement. Table 3 is Appendix R from *American Practical Navigator (Bowditch)*, Publication No. 9 of the Defense Mapping Agency Hydrographic/Topographic Center. It sets out in parallel columns the codes and terms used to describe true wind and sea observations. Included is the Beaufort scale as well as the terms and numbers used by systems of the World Meteorological Organization.

TABLE 1. DETERMINATION OF WIND SPEED BY SEA CONDITION

Knots	Descriptive	Sea Conditions	Wind force (Beaufort)	Probable wave height in ft.
0–1	Calm	Sea smooth and mirror-like	0	—
1–3	Light air	Scale-like ripples without foam crests.	1	¼
4–6	Light breeze	Small, short wavelets; crests have a glassy appearance and do not break.	2	½
7–10	Gentle breeze	Large wavelets; some crests begin to break; foam of glassy appearance. Occasional white foam crests.	3	2
11–16	Moderate breeze	Small waves, becoming longer; fairly frequent white foam crests.	4	4
17–21	Fresh breeze	Moderate waves, taking a more pronounced long form; many white foam crests; there may be some spray.	5	6
22–27	Strong breeze	Large waves begin to form; white foam crests are more extensive everywhere; there may be some spray.	6	10
28–33	Near gale	Sea heaps up and white foam from breaking waves begins to be blown in streaks along the direction of the wind; spindrift begins.	7	14
34–40	Gale	Moderately high waves of greater length; edges of crests break into spindrift; foam is blown in well-marked streaks along the direction of the wind.	8	18
41–47	Strong gale	High waves; dense streaks of foam along the direction of the wind; crests of waves begin to topple, tumble, and roll over; spray may reduce visibility.	9	23
48–55	Storm	Very high waves with long overhanging crests. The resulting foam in great patches is blown in dense white streaks along the direction of the wind. On the whole, the surface of the sea is white in appearance. The tumbling of the sea becomes heavy and shocklike. Visibility is reduced.	10	29

| 56–63 | Violent storm | Exceptionally high waves that may obscure small and medium-sized ships. The sea is completely covered with long white patches of foam lying along the direction of the wind. Everywhere the edges of the wave crests are blown into froth. Visibility reduced. | 11 | 37 |
| 64–71 | Hurricane | The air is filled with foam and spray. Sea completely white with driving spray; visibility very much reduced. | 12 | 45 |

SOURCE: Table 3–1 from *Weather Bureau Observing Handbook No. 1, Marine Surface Observations* (Washington, D.C.: National Weather Service, 1969).

TABLE 2. APPARENT WIND SPEED

Speed (knots)	Indication
Less than 1	Calm; smoke rises vertically.
1–3	Smoke drifts from funnel.
4–6	Wind felt on face.
7–10	Wind extends light flag.
11–16	Wind raises dust and loose paper on deck.
17–21	Wind waves and snaps flag briskly.
22–27	Whistling in rigging.
28–33	Inconvenience felt walking against wind.
34–40	Walking becomes difficult.

SOURCE: Table 3–2 from *Weather Bureau Observing Handbook No. 1, Marine Surface Observations* (Washington, D.C.: National Weather Service, 1969).

TABLE 3. BEAUFORT SCALE

WITH CORRESPONDING SEA STATE CODES

Beaufort number	Wind Speed				Seaman's term	World Meteorological Organization (1964)	Effects observed at sea	Effects observed on hand (Estimating Wind Speed)	Hydrographic Office		World Meteorological Organization	
	knots	mph	meters per second	km per hour					Term and height of waves, in feet	Code	Term and height of waves, in feet	Code
0	under 1	under 1	0.0–0.2	under 1	Calm	Calm	Sea like mirror.	Calm; smoke rises vertically.	Calm, 0	0	Calm, glassy, 0	0
1	1–3	1–3	0.3–1.5	1–5	Light air	Light air	Ripples with appearance of scales; no foam crests.	Smoke drift indicates wind direction; vanes do not move.	Smooth, less than 1	1	Calm rippled, 0–⅓	1
2	4–6	4–7	1.6–3.3	6–11	Light breeze	Light breeze	Small wavelets; crests of glassy appearance, not breaking.	Wind felt on face; leaves rustle; vanes begin to move.	Slight, 1–3	2	Smooth, wavelets, ⅓–1⅔	2
3	7–10	8–12	3.4–5.4	12–19	Gentle breeze	Gentle breeze	Large wavelets; crests begin to break; scattered whitecaps.	Leaves, small twigs in constant motion; light flags extended.			Slight, 2–4	3
4	11–16	13–18	5.5–7.9	20–28	Moderate breeze	Moderate breeze	Small waves, becoming longer; numerous whitecaps.	Dust, leaves, and loose paper raised up; small branches move.	Moderate, 3–5	3	Moderate, 4–8	4
5	17–21	19–24	8.0–10.7	29–38	Fresh breeze	Fresh breeze	Moderate waves, taking longer form; many whitecaps; some spray.	Small trees in leaf begin to sway.			Rough, 8–13	5
6	22–27	25–31	10.8–13.8	39–49	Strong breeze	Strong breeze	Larger waves forming; whitecaps everywhere; more spray.	Larger branches of trees in motion; whistling heard in wires.	Rough, 5–8	4		
7	28–33	32–38	13.9–17.1	50–61	Moderate gale	Near gale	Sea heaps up; white foam from breaking waves begins to be blown in streaks.	Whole trees in motion; resistance felt in walking against wind.				
8	34–40	39–46	17.2–20.7	62–74	Fresh gale	Gale	Moderately high waves of greater length; edges of crests begin to break into spindrift; foam is blown in well-marked streaks.	Twigs and small branches broken off trees; progress generally impeded.	Very rough, 8–12	5		
9	41–47	47–54	20.8–24.4	75–88	Strong gale	Strong gale	High waves; sea begins to roll; dense streaks of foam; spray may reduce visibility.	Slight structural damage occurs; slate blown from roofs.	High, 12–20	6	Very rough, 13–20	6
10	48–55	55–63	24.5–28.4	89–102	Whole gale	Storm	Very high waves with overhanging crests; sea takes white appearance as foam is blown in very dense streaks; rolling is heavy and visibility reduced.	Seldom experienced on land; trees broken or uprooted; considerable structural damage occurs.	Very high, 20–40	7	High, 20–30	7
11	56–63	64–72	28.5–32.6	103–117	Storm	Violent storm	Exceptionally high waves; sea covered with white foam patches; visibility still more reduced.	Very rarely experienced on land; usually accompanied by widespread damage.	Mountainous, 40 and higher	8	Very high, 30–45	8
12	64–71	73–82	32.7–36.9	118–133	Hurricane	Hurricane	Air filled with foam; sea completely white with driving spray; visibility greatly reduced.		Confused	9	Phenomenal, over 45	9
13	72–80	83–92	37.0–41.4	134–149								
14	81–89	93–103	41.5–46.1	150–166								
15	90–99	104–114	46.2–50.9	167–183								
16	100–108	115–125	51.0–56.0	184–201								
17	109–118	126–136	56.1–61.2	202–220								

NOTE: Since January 1, 1955, weather map symbols have been based upon wind speed in knots, at five-knot intervals, rather than upon Beaufort number.
SOURCE: Appendix R from *American Practical Navigator (Bowditch)*, vol. 1 (Washington, D.C.: Defense Mapping Agency, Publication 9, 1966).

TABLE 4.
Direction and Speed of True Wind in Units of Ship's Speed

Apparent wind speed	Difference between the heading and apparent wind direction										Apparent wind speed
	0°		10°		20°		30°		40°		
0.0	180	1.00	180	1.00	180	1.00	180	1.00	180	1.00	0.0
0.1	180	0.90	179	0.90	178	0.91	177	0.91	176	0.93	0.1
0.2	180	0.80	178	0.80	175	0.81	173	0.83	171	0.86	0.2
0.3	180	0.70	176	0.71	172	0.73	169	0.76	166	0.79	0.3
0.4	180	0.60	173	0.61	168	0.64	163	0.68	160	0.74	0.4
0.5	180	0.50	170	0.51	162	0.56	156	0.62	152	0.70	0.5
0.6	180	0.40	166	0.42	155	0.48	148	0.57	144	0.66	0.6
0.7	180	0.30	159	0.33	145	0.42	138	0.53	136	0.65	0.7
0.8	180	0.20	147	0.25	132	0.37	127	0.50	127	0.64	0.8
0.9	180	0.10	126	0.19	117	0.34	116	0.50	118	0.66	0.9
1.0	calm	0.00	95	0.17	100	0.35	105	0.52	110	0.68	1.0
1.1	0	0.10	66	0.21	85	0.38	95	0.55	103	0.72	1.1
1.2	0	0.20	49	0.28	73	0.43	86	0.60	96	0.78	1.2
1.3	0	0.30	39	0.36	64	0.50	79	0.66	90	0.84	1.3
1.4	0	0.40	33	0.45	57	0.57	73	0.73	85	0.90	1.4
1.5	0	0.50	29	0.54	51	0.66	68	0.81	81	0.98	1.5
1.6	0	0.60	26	0.64	47	0.74	64	0.89	78	1.05	1.6
1.7	0	0.70	24	0.74	44	0.83	61	0.97	75	1.13	1.7
1.8	0	0.80	22	0.83	42	0.93	58	1.06	72	1.22	1.8
1.9	0	0.90	21	0.93	40	1.02	56	1.15	70	1.30	1.9
2.0	0	1.00	20	1.03	38	1.11	54	1.24	68	1.39	2.0
2.5	0	1.50	17	1.52	32	1.60	47	1.71	60	1.85	2.5
3.0	0	2.00	15	2.02	29	2.09	43	2.19	56	2.32	3.0
3.5	0	2.50	14	2.52	28	2.58	41	2.68	53	2.81	3.5
4.0	0	3.00	13	3.02	26	3.08	39	3.17	51	3.30	4.0
4.5	0	3.50	13	3.52	25	3.58	38	3.67	50	3.79	4.5
5.0	0	4.00	12	4.02	25	4.08	37	4.16	49	4.28	5.0
6.0	0	5.00	12	5.02	24	5.07	36	5.16	47	5.27	6.0
7.0	0	6.00	12	6.02	23	6.07	35	6.15	46	6.27	7.0
8.0	0	7.00	11	7.02	23	7.07	34	7.15	45	7.26	8.0
9.0	0	8.00	11	8.02	22	8.07	34	8.15	44	8.26	9.0
10.0	0	9.00	11	9.02	22	9.06	33	9.15	44	9.26	10.0

Apparent wind speed	50°		60°		70°		80°		90°		Apparent wind speed
0.0	180	1.00	180	1.00	180	1.00	180	1.00	180	1.00	0.0
0.1	175	0.94	175	0.95	174	0.97	174	0.99	174	1.00	0.1
0.2	170	0.88	169	0.92	169	0.95	168	0.99	169	1.02	0.2
0.3	164	0.84	163	0.89	163	0.94	163	0.99	163	1.04	0.3
0.4	158	0.80	157	0.87	156	0.94	157	1.01	158	1.08	0.4
0.5	151	0.78	150	0.87	150	0.95	152	1.04	153	1.12	0.5
0.6	143	0.77	143	0.87	145	0.97	147	1.07	149	1.17	0.6
0.7	136	0.77	137	0.89	139	1.01	142	1.12	145	1.22	0.7
0.8	128	0.78	131	0.92	134	1.05	138	1.17	141	1.28	0.8
0.9	121	0.81	125	0.95	129	1.09	134	1.22	138	1.35	0.9
1.0	115	0.85	120	1.00	125	1.15	130	1.29	135	1.41	1.0
1.1	109	0.89	115	1.05	121	1.21	127	1.35	132	1.49	1.1
1.2	104	0.95	111	1.11	118	1.27	124	1.42	130	1.56	1.2
1.3	99	1.01	107	1.18	114	1.34	121	1.50	128	1.64	1.3
1.4	95	1.08	104	1.25	112	1.42	119	1.57	126	1.72	1.4
1.5	92	1.15	101	1.32	109	1.49	117	1.65	124	1.80	1.5
1.6	89	1.23	98	1.40	107	1.57	115	1.73	122	1.89	1.6
1.7	86	1.31	96	1.48	105	1.65	113	1.82	120	1.97	1.7
1.8	84	1.39	94	1.56	103	1.73	111	1.90	119	2.06	1.8
1.9	81	1.47	92	1.65	101	1.82	110	1.99	118	2.15	1.9
2.0	79	1.56	90	1.73	100	1.91	108	2.07	117	2.24	2.0
2.5	72	2.01	83	2.18	94	2.35	103	2.53	112	2.69	2.5
3.0	68	2.48	79	2.65	89	2.82	99	2.99	108	3.16	3.0
3.5	65	2.96	76	3.12	87	3.29	96	3.47	106	3.64	3.5
4.0	63	3.44	74	3.61	84	3.78	94	3.95	104	4.12	4.0
4.5	61	3.93	72	4.09	83	4.26	93	4.44	103	4.61	4.5
5.0	60	4.42	71	4.58	81	4.75	92	4.93	101	5.10	5.0
6.0	58	5.41	69	5.57	79	5.74	90	5.91	99	6.08	6.0
7.0	57	6.40	68	6.56	78	6.72	88	6.90	98	7.07	7.0
8.0	56	7.40	67	7.55	77	7.72	87	7.89	97	8.06	8.0
9.0	55	8.39	66	8.54	76	8.71	86	8.88	96	9.06	9.0
10.0	55	9.39	65	9.54	76	9.70	86	9.88	96	10.01	10.0

TABLE 4.
Direction and Speed of True Wind in Units of Ship's Speed

Apparent wind speed	Difference between the heading and apparent wind direction										Apparent wind speed
	90°		100°		110°		120°		130°		
0.0	180	1.00	180	1.00	180	1.00	180	1.00	180	1.00	0.0
0.1	174	1.00	174	1.02	175	1.04	175	1.05	176	1.07	0.1
0.2	169	1.02	169	1.05	170	1.08	171	1.11	172	1.14	0.2
0.3	163	1.04	164	1.09	166	1.14	167	1.18	169	1.21	0.3
0.4	158	1.08	160	1.14	162	1.20	164	1.25	166	1.29	0.4
0.5	153	1.12	156	1.19	158	1.26	161	1.32	164	1.38	0.5
0.6	149	1.17	152	1.25	155	1.33	158	1.40	162	1.46	0.6
0.7	145	1.22	148	1.32	152	1.40	156	1.48	160	1.55	0.7
0.8	141	1.28	145	1.38	149	1.48	154	1.56	158	1.63	0.8
0.9	138	1.35	143	1.46	147	1.56	152	1.65	156	1.72	0.9
1.0	135	1.41	140	1.53	145	1.64	150	1.73	155	1.81	1.0
1.1	132	1.49	138	1.61	143	1.72	148	1.82	154	1.90	1.1
1.2	130	1.56	136	1.69	141	1.81	147	1.91	153	2.00	1.2
1.3	128	1.64	134	1.77	140	1.89	146	2.00	152	2.09	1.3
1.4	126	1.72	132	1.86	138	1.98	145	2.09	151	2.18	1.4
1.5	124	1.80	130	1.94	137	2.07	143	2.18	150	2.28	1.5
1.6	122	1.89	129	2.03	136	2.16	142	2.27	149	2.37	1.6
1.7	120	1.97	128	2.12	135	2.25	141	2.36	148	2.46	1.7
1.8	119	2.06	127	2.21	134	2.34	141	2.46	147	2.56	1.8
1.9	118	2.15	125	2.30	133	2.43	140	2.55	147	2.66	1.9
2.0	117	2.24	124	2.39	132	2.52	139	2.65	146	2.75	2.0
2.5	112	2.69	120	2.85	128	2.99	136	3.12	144	3.23	2.5
3.0	108	3.16	117	3.32	126	3.47	134	3.61	142	3.72	3.0
3.5	106	3.64	115	3.80	124	3.96	132	4.09	140	4.21	3.5
4.0	104	4.12	113	4.29	122	4.44	131	4.58	139	4.71	4.0
4.5	103	4.61	112	4.78	121	4.93	130	5.07	138	5.20	4.5
5.0	101	5.10	111	5.27	120	5.42	129	5.57	138	5.69	5.0
6.0	99	6.08	109	6.25	118	6.41	128	6.56	137	6.69	6.0
7.0	98	7.07	108	7.24	117	7.40	127	7.55	136	7.68	7.0
8.0	97	8.06	107	8.23	116	8.39	126	8.54	135	8.68	8.0
9.0	96	9.06	106	9.23	116	9.39	125	9.54	135	9.67	9.0
10.0	96	10.01	106	10.22	115	10.39	125	10.54	134	10.67	10.0
	140°		150°		160°		170°		180°		
0.0	180	1.00	180	1.00	180	1.00	180	1.00	180	1.00	0.0
0.1	177	1.08	177	1.09	178	1.09	179	1.10	180	1.10	0.1
0.2	174	1.16	175	1.18	177	1.19	178	1.20	180	1.20	0.2
0.3	171	1.24	173	1.27	175	1.29	178	1.30	180	1.30	0.3
0.4	169	1.33	172	1.36	174	1.38	177	1.40	180	1.40	0.4
0.5	167	1.42	170	1.45	173	1.48	177	1.50	180	1.50	0.5
0.6	165	1.51	169	1.55	173	1.58	176	1.60	180	1.60	0.6
0.7	164	1.60	168	1.64	172	1.68	176	1.69	180	1.70	0.7
0.8	162	1.69	167	1.74	171	1.77	176	1.79	180	1.80	0.8
0.9	161	1.79	166	1.84	171	1.87	175	1.89	180	1.90	0.9
1.0	160	1.88	165	1.93	170	1.97	175	1.99	180	2.00	1.0
1.1	159	1.97	164	2.03	170	2.07	175	2.09	180	2.10	1.1
1.2	158	2.07	164	2.13	169	2.17	175	2.19	180	2.20	1.2
1.3	157	2.16	163	2.22	169	2.27	174	2.29	180	2.30	1.3
1.4	157	2.26	162	2.32	168	2.36	174	2.39	180	2.40	1.4
1.5	156	2.36	162	2.42	168	2.46	174	2.49	180	2.50	1.5
1.6	155	2.45	161	2.52	168	2.56	174	2.59	180	2.60	1.6
1.7	155	2.55	161	2.61	167	2.66	174	2.69	180	2.70	1.7
1.8	154	2.65	161	2.71	167	2.76	174	2.79	180	2.80	1.8
1.9	154	2.74	160	2.81	167	2.86	173	2.89	180	2.90	1.9
2.0	153	2.84	160	2.91	167	2.96	173	2.99	180	3.00	2.0
2.5	151	3.33	158	3.40	166	3.46	173	3.49	180	3.50	2.5
3.0	150	3.82	157	3.90	165	3.95	172	3.99	180	4.00	3.0
3.5	149	4.31	157	4.39	164	4.45	172	4.49	180	4.50	3.5
4.0	148	4.81	156	4.89	164	4.95	172	4.99	180	5.00	4.0
4.5	147	5.31	155	5.39	164	5.45	172	5.49	180	5.50	4.5
5.0	146	5.80	155	5.89	163	5.95	172	5.99	180	6.00	5.0
6.0	145	6.80	154	6.88	163	6.95	171	6.99	180	7.00	6.0
7.0	145	7.79	154	7.88	162	7.95	171	7.99	180	8.00	7.0
8.0	144	8.79	153	8.88	162	8.95	171	8.99	180	9.00	8.0
9.0	144	9.79	153	9.88	162	9.95	171	9.99	180	10.00	9.0
10.0	143	10.78	153	10.88	162	10.95	171	10.98	180	11.00	10.0

SOURCE: Table 10 from *American Practical Navigator (Bowditch)*, vol. 2 (Washington, D.C.: Defense Mapping Agency Hydrographic/Topographic Center, Publication 9, 1975).

TABLE 5.

Correction of Barometer Reading for Height Above Sea Level

All barometers.   All values positive.

Height in feet	Outside temperature in degrees Fahrenheit													Height in feet
	−20°	−10°	0°	10°	20°	30°	40°	50°	60°	70°	80°	90°	100°	
	Inches	*Inches*	*Inches*	*Inches*	*Inches*	*Inches*	*Inches*	*Inches*	*Inches*	*Inches*	*Inches*	*Inches*	*Inches*	
5	0.01	0.01	0.01	0.01	0.01	0.01	0.01	0.01	0.01	0.01	0.01	0.01	0.01	5
10	0.01	0.01	0.01	0.01	0.01	0.01	0.02	0.02	0.02	0.02	0.02	0.02	0.02	10
15	0.02	0.02	0.02	0.02	0.02	0.02	0.02	0.02	0.02	0.02	0.02	0.02	0.02	15
20	0.03	0.02	0.02	0.02	0.02	0.02	0.02	0.02	0.02	0.02	0.02	0.03	0.03	20
25	0.03	0.03	0.03	0.03	0.03	0.03	0.03	0.03	0.03	0.03	0.03	0.03	0.03	25
30	0.04	0.04	0.04	0.04	0.04	0.04	0.03	0.03	0.03	0.03	0.03	0.03	0.03	30
35	0.04	0.04	0.04	0.04	0.04	0.04	0.04	0.04	0.04	0.04	0.04	0.04	0.04	35
40	0.05	0.05	0.05	0.05	0.05	0.05	0.04	0.04	0.04	0.04	0.04	0.04	0.04	40
45	0.06	0.06	0.05	0.05	0.05	0.05	0.05	0.05	0.05	0.05	0.05	0.05	0.05	45
50	0.06	0.06	0.06	0.06	0.06	0.06	0.06	0.06	0.05	0.05	0.05	0.05	0.05	50
55	0.07	0.07	0.07	0.07	0.06	0.07	0.06	0.06	0.06	0.06	0.06	0.06	0.06	55
60	0.08	0.07	0.07	0.07	0.07	0.07	0.07	0.07	0.06	0.06	0.06	0.06	0.06	60
65	0.08	0.08	0.08	0.08	0.08	0.07	0.07	0.07	0.07	0.07	0.07	0.07	0.07	65
70	0.09	0.09	0.09	0.08	0.08	0.08	0.08	0.08	0.08	0.07	0.07	0.07	0.07	70
75	0.10	0.09	0.09	0.09	0.09	0.09	0.08	0.08	0.08	0.08	0.08	0.08	0.08	75
80	0.10	0.10	0.10	0.10	0.09	0.09	0.09	0.09	0.09	0.08	0.08	0.08	0.08	80
85	0.11	0.10	0.10	0.10	0.10	0.10	0.10	0.09	0.09	0.09	0.09	0.09	0.09	85
90	0.11	0.11	0.11	0.11	0.11	0.10	0.10	0.10	0.10	0.10	0.10	0.09	0.09	90
95	0.12	0.12	0.12	0.11	0.11	0.11	0.11	0.10	0.10	0.10	0.10	0.10	0.10	95
100	0.13	0.12	0.12	0.12	0.12	0.11	0.11	0.11	0.11	0.11	0.10	0.10	0.10	100
105	0.13	0.13	0.13	0.13	0.12	0.12	0.12	0.12	0.11	0.11	0.11	0.11	0.11	105
110	0.14	0.14	0.13	0.13	0.13	0.13	0.12	0.12	0.12	0.12	0.12	0.12	0.11	110
115	0.15	0.14	0.14	0.14	0.13	0.13	0.13	0.13	0.13	0.12	0.12	0.12	0.12	115
120	0.15	0.15	0.15	0.14	0.14	0.14	0.13	0.13	0.13	0.13	0.12	0.12	0.12	120
125	0.16	0.16	0.15	0.15	0.15	0.14	0.14	0.14	0.13	0.13	0.13	0.13	0.12	125

SOURCE: Table 11 from *American Practical Navigator (Bowditch)*, vol. 2 (Washington, D.C.: Defense Mapping Agency Hydrographic/Topographic Center, Publication 9, 1975).

TABLE 6.

Correction of Barometer Reading for Gravity

Mercurial barometers only.

Latitude	Correction	Latitude	Correction	Latitude	Correction	Latitude	Correction
°	*Inches*	°	*Inches*	°	*Inches*	°	*Inches*
0	−0.08	25	−0.05	50	+0.01	75	+0.07
5	−0.08	30	−0.04	55	+0.03	80	+0.07
10	−0.08	35	−0.03	60	+0.04	85	+0.08
15	−0.07	40	−0.02	65	+0.05	90	+0.08
20	−0.06	45	0.00	70	+0.06		

SOURCE: Table 12 from *American Practical Navigator (Bowditch)*, vol. 2 (Washington, D.C.: Defense Mapping Agency Hydrographic/Topographic Center, Publication 9, 1975).

TABLE 7.

Correction of Barometer Reading for Temperature

Mercurial barometers only.

Temp. F	Height of barometer in inches								Temp. F
	27.5	28.0	28.5	29.0	29.5	30.0	30.5	31.0	
°	Inches	Inches	Inches	Inches	Inches	Inches	Inches	Inches	°
−20	+0.12	+0.12	+0.13	+0.13	+0.13	+0.13	+0.14	+0.14	−20
18	0.12	0.12	0.12	0.12	0.13	0.13	0.13	0.13	18
16	0.11	0.11	0.12	0.12	0.12	0.12	0.12	0.13	16
14	0.11	0.11	0.11	0.11	0.11	0.12	0.12	0.12	14
12	0.10	0.10	0.11	0.11	0.11	0.11	0.11	0.11	12
−10	+0.10	+0.10	+0.10	+0.10	+0.10	+0.11	+0.11	+0.11	−10
8	0.09	0.09	0.10	0.10	0.10	0.10	0.10	0.10	8
6	0.09	0.09	0.09	0.09	0.09	0.09	0.10	0.10	6
4	0.08	0.08	0.08	0.09	0.09	0.09	0.09	0.09	4
−2	0.08	0.08	0.08	0.08	0.08	0.08	0.09	0.09	−2
0	+0.07	+0.07	+0.07	+0.08	+0.08	+0.08	+0.08	+0.08	0
+2	0.07	0.07	0.07	0.07	0.07	0.07	0.07	0.08	+2
4	0.06	0.06	0.06	0.07	0.07	0.07	0.07	0.07	4
6	0.06	0.06	0.06	0.06	0.06	0.06	0.06	0.06	6
8	0.05	0.05	0.05	0.05	0.06	0.06	0.06	0.06	8
+10	+0.05	+0.05	+0.05	+0.05	+0.05	+0.05	+0.05	+0.05	+10
12	0.04	0.04	0.04	0.04	0.04	0.05	0.05	0.05	12
14	0.04	0.04	0.04	0.04	0.04	0.04	0.04	0.04	14
16	0.03	0.03	0.03	0.03	0.03	0.03	0.03	0.04	16
18	0.03	0.03	0.03	0.03	0.03	0.03	0.03	0.03	18
+20	+0.02	+0.02	+0.02	+0.02	+0.02	+0.02	+0.02	+0.02	+20
22	0.02	0.02	0.02	0.02	0.02	0.02	0.02	0.02	22
24	0.01	0.01	0.01	0.01	0.01	0.01	0.01	0.01	24
26	+0.01	+0.01	+0.01	+0.01	+0.01	+0.01	+0.01	+0.01	26
28	0.00	+0.00	0.00	0.00	0.00	0.00	0.00	0.00	28
+30	0.00	0.00	0.00	0.00	0.00	0.00	0.00	0.00	+30
32	−0.01	−0.01	−0.01	−0.01	−0.01	−0.01	−0.01	−0.01	32
34	0.01	0.01	0.01	0.01	0.01	0.01	0.01	0.02	34
36	0.02	0.02	0.02	0.02	0.02	0.02	0.02	0.02	36
38	0.02	0.02	0.02	0.02	0.03	0.03	0.03	0.03	38
+40	−0.03	−0.03	−0.03	−0.03	−0.03	−0.03	−0.03	−0.03	+40
42	0.03	0.03	0.03	0.04	0.04	0.04	0.04	0.04	42
44	0.04	0.04	0.04	0.04	0.04	0.04	0.04	0.04	44
46	0.04	0.04	0.04	0.05	0.05	0.05	0.05	0.05	46
48	0.05	0.05	0.05	0.05	0.05	0.05	0.05	0.05	48
+50	−0.05	−0.05	−0.06	−0.06	−0.06	−0.06	−0.06	−0.06	+50
52	0.06	0.06	0.06	0.06	0.06	0.06	0.06	0.07	52
54	0.06	0.06	0.07	0.07	0.07	0.07	0.07	0.07	54
56	0.07	0.07	0.07	0.07	0.07	0.07	0.08	0.08	56
58	0.07	0.07	0.08	0.08	0.08	0.08	0.08	0.08	58
+60	−0.08	−0.08	−0.08	−0.08	−0.08	−0.09	−0.09	−0.09	+60
62	0.08	0.08	0.09	0.09	0.09	0.09	0.09	0.09	62
64	0.09	0.09	0.09	0.09	0.09	0.10	0.10	0.10	64
66	0.09	0.09	0.10	0.10	0.10	0.10	0.10	0.10	66
68	0.10	0.10	0.10	0.10	0.11	0.11	0.11	0.11	68
+70	−0.10	−0.10	−0.11	−0.11	−0.11	−0.11	−0.11	−0.12	+70
72	0.11	0.11	0.11	0.11	0.12	0.12	0.12	0.12	72
74	0.11	0.11	0.12	0.12	0.12	0.12	0.13	0.13	74
76	0.12	0.12	0.12	0.12	0.13	0.13	0.13	0.13	76
78	0.12	0.12	0.13	0.13	0.13	0.13	0.13	0.14	78
+80	−0.13	−0.13	−0.13	−0.13	−0.14	−0.14	−0.14	−0.14	+80
82	0.13	0.14	0.14	0.14	0.14	0.14	0.15	0.15	82
84	0.14	0.14	0.14	0.15	0.15	0.15	0.15	0.16	84
86	0.14	0.15	0.15	0.15	0.15	0.16	0.16	0.16	86
88	0.15	0.15	0.15	0.16	0.16	0.16	0.16	0.17	88
+90	−0.15	−0.16	−0.16	−0.16	−0.16	−0.17	−0.17	−0.17	+90
92	0.16	0.16	0.16	0.17	0.17	0.17	0.17	0.18	92
94	0.16	0.17	0.17	0.17	0.17	0.18	0.18	0.18	94
96	0.17	0.17	0.17	0.18	0.18	0.18	0.18	0.19	96
98	0.17	0.18	0.18	0.18	0.18	0.19	0.19	0.19	98
100	0.18	0.18	0.18	0.19	0.19	0.19	0.20	0.20	100

SOURCE: Table 13 from *American Practical Navigator (Bowditch)*, vol. 2 (Washington, D.C.: Defense Mapping Agency Hydrographic/Typographic Center, Publication 9, 1975).

TABLE 8.

Conversion Table for Millibars, Inches of Mercury, and Millimeters of Mercury

Millibars	Inches	Millimeters	Millibars	Inches	Millimeters	Millibars	Inches	Millimeters
900	26.58	675.1	960	28.35	720.1	1020	30.12	765.1
901	26.61	675.8	961	28.38	720.8	1021	30.15	765.8
902	26.64	676.6	962	28.41	721.6	1022	30.18	766.6
903	26.67	677.3	963	28.44	722.3	1023	30.21	767.3
904	26.70	678.1	964	28.47	723.1	1024	30.24	768.1
905	26.72	678.8	965	28.50	723.8	1025	30.27	768.8
906	26.75	679.6	966	28.53	724.6	1026	30.30	769.6
907	26.78	680.3	967	28.56	725.3	1027	30.33	770.3
908	26.81	681.1	968	28.58	726.1	1028	30.36	771.1
909	26.84	681.8	969	28.61	726.8	1029	30.39	771.8
910	26.87	682.6	970	28.64	727.6	1030	30.42	772.6
911	26.90	683.3	971	28.67	728.3	1031	30.45	773.3
912	26.93	684.1	972	28.70	729.1	1032	30.47	774.1
913	26.96	684.8	973	28.73	729.8	1033	30.50	774.8
914	26.99	685.6	974	28.76	730.6	1034	30.53	775.6
915	27.02	686.3	975	28.79	731.3	1035	30.56	776.3
916	27.05	687.1	976	28.82	732.1	1036	30.59	777.1
917	27.08	687.8	977	28.85	732.8	1037	30.62	777.8
918	27.11	688.6	978	28.88	733.6	1038	30.65	778.6
919	27.14	689.3	979	28.91	734.3	1039	30.68	779.3
920	27.17	690.1	980	28.94	735.1	1040	30.71	780.1
921	27.20	690.8	981	28.97	735.8	1041	30.74	780.8
922	27.23	691.6	982	29.00	736.6	1042	30.77	781.6
923	27.26	692.3	983	29.03	737.3	1043	30.80	782.3
924	27.29	693.1	984	29.06	738.1	1044	30.83	783.1
925	27.32	693.8	985	29.09	738.8	1045	30.86	783.8
926	27.34	694.6	986	29.12	739.6	1046	30.89	784.6
927	27.37	695.3	987	29.15	740.3	1047	30.92	785.3
928	27.40	696.1	988	29.18	741.1	1048	30.95	786.1
929	27.43	696.8	989	29.21	741.8	1049	30.98	786.8
930	27.46	697.6	990	29.23	742.6	1050	31.01	787.6
931	27.49	698.3	991	29.26	743.3	1051	31.04	788.3
932	27.52	699.1	992	29.29	744.1	1052	31.07	789.1
933	27.55	699.8	993	29.32	744.8	1053	31.10	789.8
934	27.58	700.6	994	29.35	745.6	1054	31.12	790.6
935	27.61	701.3	995	29.38	746.3	1055	31.15	791.3
936	27.64	702.1	996	29.41	747.1	1056	31.18	792.1
937	27.67	702.8	997	29.44	747.8	1057	31.21	792.8
938	27.70	703.6	998	29.47	748.6	1058	31.24	793.6
939	27.73	704.3	999	29.50	749.3	1059	31.27	794.3
940	27.76	705.1	1000	29.53	750.1	1060	31.30	795.1
941	27.79	705.8	1001	29.56	750.8	1061	31.33	795.8
942	27.82	706.6	1002	29.59	751.6	1062	31.36	796.6
943	27.85	707.3	1003	29.62	752.3	1063	31.39	797.3
944	27.88	708.1	1004	29.65	753.1	1064	31.42	798.1
945	27.91	708.8	1005	29.68	753.8	1065	31.45	798.8
946	27.94	709.6	1006	29.71	754.6	1066	31.48	799.6
947	27.96	710.3	1007	29.74	755.3	1067	31.51	800.3
948	27.99	711.1	1008	29.77	756.1	1068	31.54	801.1
949	28.02	711.8	1009	29.80	756.8	1069	31.57	801.8
950	28.05	712.6	1010	29.83	757.6	1070	31.60	802.6
951	28.08	713.3	1011	29.85	758.3	1071	31.63	803.3
952	28.11	714.1	1012	29.88	759.1	1072	31.66	804.1
953	28.14	714.8	1013	29.91	759.8	1073	31.69	804.8
954	28.17	715.6	1014	29.94	760.6	1074	31.72	805.6
955	28.20	716.3	1015	29.97	761.3	1075	31.74	806.3
956	28.23	717.1	1016	30.00	762.1	1076	31.77	807.1
957	28.26	717.8	1017	30.03	762.8	1077	31.80	807.8
958	28.29	718.6	1018	30.06	763.6	1078	31.83	808.6
959	28.32	719.3	1019	30.09	764.3	1079	31.86	809.3
960	28.35	720.1	1020	30.12	765.1	1080	31.89	810.1

SOURCE: Table 14 from *American Practical Navigator (Bowditch)*, vol. 2 (Washington, D.C.: Defense Mapping Agency Hydrographic/Typographic Center, Publication 9, 1975).

TABLE 9.

Conversion Tables for Thermometer Scales

F = Fahrenheit, C = Celsius (centigrade), K = Kelvin

F	C	K	F	C	K	C	F	K	K	F	C
−20	−28.9	244.3	+40	+4.4	277.6	−25	−13.0	248.2	250	−9.7	−23.2
19	28.3	244.8	41	5.0	278.2	24	11.2	249.2	251	7.9	22.2
18	27.8	245.4	42	5.6	278.7	23	9.4	250.2	252	6.1	21.2
17	27.2	245.9	43	6.1	279.3	22	7.6	251.2	253	4.3	20.2
16	26.7	246.5	44	6.7	279.8	21	5.8	252.2	254	2.5	19.2
−15	−26.1	247.0	+45	+7.2	280.4	−20	−4.0	253.2	255	−0.7	−18.2
14	25.6	247.6	46	7.8	280.9	19	2.2	254.2	256	+1.1	17.2
13	25.0	248.2	47	8.3	281.5	18	−0.4	255.2	257	2.9	16.2
12	24.4	248.7	48	8.9	282.0	17	+1.4	256.2	258	4.7	15.2
11	23.9	249.3	49	9.4	282.6	16	3.2	257.2	259	6.5	14.2
−10	−23.3	249.8	+50	+10.0	283.2	−15	+5.0	258.2	260	+8.3	−13.2
9	22.8	250.4	51	10.6	283.7	14	6.8	259.2	261	10.1	12.2
8	22.2	250.9	52	11.1	284.3	13	8.6	260.2	262	11.9	11.2
7	21.7	251.5	53	11.7	284.8	12	10.4	261.2	263	13.7	10.2
6	21.1	252.0	54	12.2	285.4	11	12.2	262.2	264	15.5	9.2
−5	−20.6	252.6	+55	+12.8	285.9	−10	+14.0	263.2	265	+17.3	−8.2
4	20.0	253.2	56	13.3	286.5	9	15.8	264.2	266	19.1	7.2
3	19.4	253.7	57	13.9	287.0	8	17.6	265.2	267	20.9	6.2
2	18.9	254.3	58	14.4	287.6	7	19.4	266.2	268	22.7	5.2
−1	18.3	254.8	59	15.0	288.2	6	21.2	267.2	269	24.5	4.2
0	−17.8	255.4	+60	+15.6	288.7	−5	+23.0	268.2	270	+26.3	−3.2
+1	17.2	255.9	61	16.1	289.3	4	24.8	269.2	271	28.1	2.2
2	16.7	256.5	62	16.7	289.8	3	26.6	270.2	272	29.9	1.2
3	16.1	257.0	63	17.2	290.4	2	28.4	271.2	273	31.7	−0.2
4	15.6	257.6	64	17.8	290.9	−1	30.2	272.2	274	33.5	+0.8
+5	−15.0	258.2	+65	+18.3	291.5	0	+32.0	273.2	275	+35.3	+1.8
6	14.4	258.7	66	18.9	292.0	+1	33.8	274.2	276	37.1	2.8
7	13.9	259.3	67	19.4	292.6	2	35.6	275.2	277	38.9	3.8
8	13.3	259.8	68	20.0	293.2	3	37.4	276.2	278	40.7	4.8
9	12.8	260.4	69	20.6	293.7	4	39.2	277.2	279	42.5	5.8
+10	−12.2	260.9	+70	+21.1	294.3	+5	+41.0	278.2	280	+44.3	+6.8
11	11.7	261.5	71	21.7	294.8	6	42.8	279.2	281	46.1	7.8
12	11.1	262.0	72	22.2	295.4	7	44.6	280.2	282	47.9	8.8
13	10.6	262.6	73	22.8	295.9	8	46.4	281.2	283	49.7	9.8
14	10.0	263.2	74	23.3	296.5	9	48.2	282.2	284	51.5	10.8
+15	−9.4	263.7	+75	+23.9	297.0	+10	+50.0	283.2	285	+53.3	+11.8
16	8.9	264.3	76	24.4	297.6	11	51.8	284.2	286	55.1	12.8
17	8.3	264.8	77	25.0	298.2	12	53.6	285.2	287	56.9	13.8
18	7.8	265.4	78	25.6	298.7	13	55.4	286.2	288	58.7	14.8
19	7.2	265.9	79	26.1	299.3	14	57.2	287.2	289	60.5	15.8
+20	−6.7	266.5	+80	+26.7	299.8	+15	+59.0	288.2	290	+62.3	+16.8
21	6.1	267.0	81	27.2	300.4	16	60.8	289.2	291	64.1	17.8
22	5.6	267.6	82	27.8	300.9	17	62.6	290.2	292	65.9	18.8
23	5.0	268.2	83	28.3	301.5	18	64.4	291.2	293	67.7	19.8
24	4.4	268.7	84	28.9	302.0	19	66.2	292.2	294	69.5	20.8
+25	−3.9	269.3	+85	+29.4	302.6	+20	+68.0	293.2	295	+71.3	+21.8
26	3.3	269.8	86	30.0	303.2	21	69.8	294.2	296	73.1	22.8
27	2.8	270.4	87	30.6	303.7	22	71.6	295.2	297	74.9	23.8
28	2.2	270.9	88	31.1	304.3	23	73.4	296.2	298	76.7	24.8
29	1.7	271.5	89	31.7	304.8	24	75.2	297.2	299	78.5	25.8
+30	−1.1	272.0	+90	+32.2	305.4	+25	+77.0	298.2	300	+80.3	+26.8
31	0.6	272.6	91	32.8	305.9	26	78.8	299.2	301	82.1	27.8
32	0.0	273.2	92	33.3	306.5	27	80.6	300.2	302	83.9	28.8
33	+0.6	273.7	93	33.9	307.0	28	82.4	301.2	303	85.7	29.8
34	1.1	274.3	94	34.4	307.6	29	84.2	302.2	304	87.5	30.8
+35	+1.7	274.8	+95	+35.0	308.2	+30	+86.0	303.2	305	+89.3	+31.8
36	2.2	275.4	96	35.6	308.7	31	87.8	304.2	306	91.1	32.8
37	2.8	275.9	97	36.1	309.3	32	89.6	305.2	307	92.9	33.8
38	3.3	276.5	98	36.7	309.8	33	91.4	306.2	308	94.7	34.8
39	3.9	277.0	99	37.2	310.4	34	93.2	307.2	309	96.5	35.8
+40	+4.4	277.6	+100	+37.8	310.9	+35	+95.0	308.2	310	+98.3	+36.8

SOURCE:　Table 15 from *American Practical Navigator (Bowditch)*, vol. 2 (Washington, D.C.: Defense Mapping Agency Hydrographic/Typographic Center, Publication 9, 1975).

TABLE 10.

Relative Humidity

Dry-bulb temp. F	Difference between dry-bulb and wet-bulb temperatures														Dry-bulb temp. F
	1°	2°	3°	4°	5°	6°	7°	8°	9°	10°	11°	12°	13°	14°	
°	%	%	%	%	%	%	%	%	%	%	%	%	%	%	°
−20	7														−20
18	14														18
16	21														16
14	27														14
12	32														12
−10	37														−10
8	41	2													8
6	45	9													6
4	49	16													4
−2	52	22													−2
0	56	28													0
+2	59	33	7												+2
4	62	37	14												4
6	64	42	20												6
8	67	46	25	5											8
+10	69	50	30	11											+10
12	71	53	35	17											12
14	73	56	40	23	7										14
16	76	60	44	28	13										16
18	77	62	48	33	19	4									18
+20	79	65	51	37	24	10									+20
22	81	68	55	42	29	16	4								22
24	83	70	58	45	33	21	10								24
26	85	73	61	49	38	26	15	4							26
28	86	75	64	53	42	31	20	10							28
+30	88	77	66	56	45	35	25	15	6						+30
32	89	79	69	59	49	39	30	20	11	2					32
34	90	81	71	62	52	43	34	25	16	8					34
36	91	82	73	64	55	47	38	29	21	13	5				36
38	91	83	74	66	58	50	42	33	25	18	10	2			38
+40	92	84	76	68	60	52	45	37	30	22	15	7			+40
42	92	84	77	69	62	54	47	40	33	26	19	12	5		42
44	92	85	78	70	63	56	49	43	36	29	23	17	10	4	44
46	93	86	79	72	65	58	52	45	39	32	26	20	14	8	46
48	93	86	79	73	66	60	54	47	41	35	29	24	18	12	48
+50	93	87	80	74	68	61	55	49	44	38	32	27	21	16	+50
52	94	87	81	75	69	63	57	51	46	40	35	29	24	19	52
54	94	88	82	76	70	64	59	53	48	42	37	32	27	22	54
56	94	88	82	77	71	65	60	55	50	44	39	35	30	25	56
58	94	88	83	77	72	67	61	56	51	46	42	37	32	28	58
+60	94	89	83	78	73	68	63	58	53	48	43	39	34	30	+60
62	95	89	84	79	74	69	64	59	54	50	45	41	37	32	62
64	95	89	84	79	74	70	65	60	56	51	47	43	38	34	64
66	95	90	85	80	75	71	66	61	57	53	49	44	40	36	66
68	95	90	85	81	76	71	67	63	58	54	50	46	42	38	68
+70	95	90	86	81	77	72	68	64	59	55	51	48	44	40	+70
72	95	91	86	82	77	73	69	65	61	57	53	49	45	42	72
74	95	91	86	82	78	74	69	65	62	58	54	50	47	43	74
76	95	91	87	82	78	74	70	66	63	59	55	51	48	45	76
78	96	91	87	83	79	75	71	67	63	60	56	53	49	46	78
+80	96	91	87	83	79	75	72	68	64	61	57	54	50	47	+80
82	96	92	88	84	80	76	72	69	65	62	58	55	52	48	82
84	96	92	88	84	80	76	73	69	66	62	59	56	53	49	84
86	96	92	88	84	81	77	73	70	67	63	60	57	54	51	86
88	96	92	88	85	81	77	74	71	67	64	61	58	55	52	88
+90	96	92	89	85	81	78	74	71	68	65	61	58	55	52	+90
92	96	92	89	85	82	78	75	72	68	65	62	59	56	53	92
94	96	93	89	85	82	79	75	72	69	66	63	60	57	54	94
96	96	93	89	86	82	79	76	73	70	67	64	61	58	55	96
98	96	93	89	86	83	79	76	73	70	67	64	61	59	56	98
+100	96	93	90	86	83	80	77	74	71	68	65	62	59	57	+100

TABLE 10.
Relative Humidity

Dry-bulb temp. F	Difference between dry-bulb and wet-bulb temperatures														Dry-bulb temp. F
	15°	16°	17°	18°	19°	20°	21°	22°	23°	24°	25°	26°	27°	28°	
°	%	%	%	%	%	%	%	%	%	%	%	%	%	%	°
+46	2														+46
48	7	1													48
+50	10	5													+50
52	14	9	4												52
54	17	12	7	3											54
56	20	16	11	7	2										56
58	23	19	14	10	6	2									58
+60	26	21	17	13	9	5	1								+60
62	28	24	20	16	12	8	4	1							62
64	30	26	22	19	15	11	8	4							64
66	32	29	25	21	17	14	10	7	4						66
68	34	31	27	23	20	16	13	10	7	3					68
+70	36	33	29	26	22	19	16	12	9	6	3				+70
72	38	34	31	28	24	21	18	15	12	9	6	3			72
74	40	36	33	30	26	23	20	17	14	11	8	6	3		74
76	41	38	35	31	28	25	22	19	16	14	11	8	5	3	76
78	43	39	36	33	30	27	24	21	18	16	13	10	8	5	78
+80	44	41	38	35	32	29	26	23	20	18	15	13	10	8	+80
82	45	42	39	36	33	30	28	25	22	20	17	15	12	10	82
84	46	43	40	38	35	32	29	27	24	21	19	17	14	12	84
86	48	45	42	39	36	33	31	28	26	23	21	18	16	14	86
88	49	46	43	40	37	35	32	30	27	25	22	20	18	16	88
+90	50	47	44	41	39	36	34	31	29	26	24	22	19	17	+90
92	51	48	45	42	40	37	35	32	30	28	25	23	21	19	92
94	51	49	46	44	41	39	36	34	31	29	27	25	23	20	94
96	52	50	47	45	42	40	37	35	33	30	28	26	24	22	96
98	53	51	48	45	43	41	38	36	34	32	29	27	25	23	98
+100	54	51	49	46	44	42	39	37	35	33	31	29	27	25	+100

Dry-bulb temp. F	Difference between dry-bulb and wet-bulb temperatures														Dry-bulb temp. F
	29°	30°	31°	32°	33°	34°	35°	36°	37°	38°	39°	40°	41°	42°	
°	%	%	%	%	%	%	%	%	%	%	%	%	%	%	°
+78	3														+78
+80	5	3													+80
82	7	5	3	1											82
84	10	7	5	3	1										84
86	11	9	7	5	3	1									86
88	13	11	9	7	5	3	1								88
+90	15	13	11	9	7	5	3	1							+90
92	17	15	13	11	9	7	5	3	1						92
94	18	16	14	12	11	9	7	5	3	2					94
96	20	18	16	14	12	10	9	7	5	4	2				96
98	21	19	17	16	14	12	10	9	7	5	4	2	1		98
+100	23	21	19	17	15	14	12	10	9	7	5	4	2	1	+100

SOURCE: Table 16 from *American Practical Navigator (Bowditch)*, vol. 2 (Washington, D.C.: Defense Mapping Agency Hydrographic/Topographic Center, Publication 9, 1975).

TABLE 11.
Dew Point

Dry-bulb temp. F	Difference between dry-bulb and wet-bulb temperatures														Dry-bulb temp. F
	1°	2°	3°	4°	5°	6°	7°	8°	9°	10°	11°	12°	13°	14°	
−20															−20
18	−52														18
16	45														16
14	39														14
12	34														12
−10	−29	−75													−10
8	25	50													8
6	22	39													6
4	18	39													4
−2	15	32													−2
0	−12	−26													0
+2	9	21	−49												+2
4	6	16	35												4
6	3	12	27												6
8	−1	9	20	−50											8
+10	+2	−5	−15	−34											+10
12	5	−2	10	24											12
14	7	+1	6	17											14
16	10	4	−2	11											16
18	12	7	+1	6											18
+20	+15	+10	+5	−2											+20
22	17	13	8	+2											22
24	20	16	11	6											24
26	22	18	14	10	+4	−4									26
28	24	21	17	13	8	+1	−8	−22							28
+30	+27	+24	+20	+16	+11	+6	−1	−12	−31						+30
32	29	26	23	19	15	10	+4	−4	16	−47					32
34	32	29	26	22	18	14	9	+2	−7	22					34
36	34	31	28	25	22	18	13	7	0	11	−30				36
38	36	33	31	28	25	21	17	12	+6	−2	14	−42			38
+40	+38	+35	+33	+30	+27	+24	+20	+16	+11	+4	−4	−18	−79		+40
42	40	38	35	33	30	27	23	19	15	10	+3	−7	23		42
44	42	40	37	35	32	29	26	23	19	14	9	+2	−9	−29	44
46	44	42	40	37	35	32	29	26	22	18	13	7	0	11	46
48	46	44	42	40	37	35	32	29	26	22	18	13	+6	−2	48
+50	+48	+46	+44	+42	+40	+37	+35	+32	+29	+25	+21	+17	+12	+5	+50
52	50	48	46	44	42	40	37	35	32	29	25	21	17	11	52
54	52	50	49	47	44	42	40	37	35	32	28	25	21	16	54
56	54	53	51	49	47	45	42	40	37	35	32	28	25	21	56
58	56	55	53	51	49	47	45	43	40	38	35	32	28	25	58
+60	+58	+57	+55	+53	+51	+49	+47	+45	+43	+40	+38	+35	+32	+28	+60
62	60	59	57	55	54	52	50	48	45	43	41	38	35	32	62
64	62	61	59	57	56	54	52	50	48	46	43	41	38	35	64
66	64	63	61	60	58	56	54	52	50	48	46	44	41	39	66
68	67	65	63	62	60	58	57	55	53	51	49	46	44	42	68
+70	+69	+67	+66	+64	+62	+61	+59	+57	+55	+53	+51	+49	+47	+45	+70
72	71	69	68	66	64	63	61	59	58	56	54	52	50	47	72
74	73	71	70	68	67	65	63	62	60	58	56	54	52	50	74
76	75	73	72	70	69	67	66	64	62	61	59	57	55	53	76
78	77	75	74	72	71	69	68	66	65	63	61	59	57	55	78
+80	+79	+77	+76	+74	+73	+72	+70	+68	+67	+65	+64	+62	+60	+58	+80
82	81	79	78	77	75	74	72	71	69	67	66	64	62	61	82
84	83	81	80	79	77	76	74	73	71	70	68	67	65	63	84
86	85	83	82	81	79	78	76	75	74	72	70	69	67	66	86
88	87	85	84	83	81	80	79	77	76	74	73	71	70	68	88
+90	+89	+87	+86	+85	+84	+82	+81	+79	+78	+76	+75	+73	+72	+70	+90
92	91	89	88	87	86	84	83	82	80	79	77	76	74	73	92
94	93	92	90	89	88	86	85	84	82	81	79	78	76	75	94
96	95	94	92	91	90	88	87	86	84	83	82	80	79	77	96
98	97	96	94	93	92	91	89	88	87	85	84	83	81	80	98
+100	+99	+98	+96	+95	+94	+93	+91	+90	+89	+87	+86	+85	+83	+82	+100

TABLE 11.
Dew Point

Dry-bulb temp. F	Difference between dry-bulb and wet-bulb temperatures														Dry-bulb temp. F
	15°	16°	17°	18°	19°	20°	21°	22°	23°	24°	25°	26°	27°	28°	
+46	−36														+46
48	14	−45													48
+50	−3	−17	−78												+50
52	+4	−5	21												52
54	10	+3	−7	−25											54
56	16	10	+2	−8	−29										56
58	20	16	10	+2	−10	−34									58
+60	+25	+20	+15	+9	+1	−11	−39								+60
62	29	25	20	15	9	+1	−12	−45							62
64	32	29	25	20	15	9	0	−13	−52						64
66	36	33	29	25	21	15	+9	0	−14	−59					66
68	39	36	33	29	25	21	16	+9	0	−14	−68				68
+70	+42	+39	+36	+33	+30	+26	+21	+16	+9	0	−14	−76			+70
72	45	43	40	37	34	30	26	22	16	+10	+1	−14	−77		72
74	48	46	43	40	37	34	31	27	22	17	10	+1	−13	−70	74
76	51	48	46	44	41	38	35	31	27	23	17	11	+2	−12	76
78	53	51	49	47	44	41	38	35	32	28	23	18	11	+3	78
+80	+56	+54	+52	+50	+47	+45	+42	+39	+36	+32	+28	+24	+19	+12	+80
82	59	57	55	53	50	48	45	43	40	37	33	29	25	20	82
84	61	59	57	55	53	51	49	46	43	41	37	34	30	26	84
86	64	62	60	58	56	54	52	49	47	44	41	38	35	31	86
88	66	64	63	61	59	57	55	52	50	48	45	42	39	36	88
+90	+69	+67	+65	+63	+62	+60	+58	+55	+53	+51	+48	+46	+43	+40	+90
92	71	69	68	66	64	62	60	58	56	54	52	49	47	44	92
94	73	72	70	68	67	65	63	61	59	57	55	52	50	47	94
96	76	74	73	71	69	67	66	64	62	60	58	56	53	51	96
98	78	77	75	73	72	70	68	67	65	63	61	59	57	54	98
+100	+80	+79	+77	+76	+74	+73	+71	+69	+67	+66	+64	+62	+60	+57	+100

Dry-bulb temp. F	Difference between dry-bulb and wet-bulb temperatures														Dry-bulb temp. F
	29°	30°	31°	32°	33°	34°	35°	36°	37°	38°	39°	40°	41°	42°	
+76	−61														+76
78	−11	−53													78
+80	+4	−10	−45												+80
82	13	+5	−8	−39											82
84	20	14	+6	−6	−33										84
86	27	21	15	+7	−4	−28									86
88	32	27	22	16	+9	−2	−23								88
+90	+36	+33	+28	+24	+18	+10	0	−18							+90
92	41	37	34	30	25	19	+12	+2	−14						92
94	45	42	38	35	31	26	20	13	+4	−10					94
96	48	46	43	39	36	32	27	22	15	+6	−7	−43			96
98	52	49	47	44	40	37	33	28	23	17	+9	−4	−30		98
+100	+55	+53	+50	+47	+45	+41	+38	+34	+30	+25	+19	+11	0	−21	+100

SOURCE: Table 17 from *American Practical Navigator (Bowditch)*, Vol. 2 (Washington, D.C.: Defense Mapping Agency Hydrographic/Typographic Center, Publication 9, 1975).

GLOSSARY OF WEATHER TERMS

Listed here are definitions which either do not appear in the text or have been chosen as warranting repetition. The sources are *Navigation Dictionary*, Publication No. 220 of the Defense Mapping Agency, and *Glossary of Oceanographic terms*, Special Publication No. 35.

adiabatic process: a heat change without transfer across the boundaries of the system. Compression results in warming, expansion in cooling.

advection: horizontal movement of part of the atmosphere.

aerology: the study of the atmosphere throughout its vertical extent rather than its surface layer.

afterglow: arch of radiance in western sky above high clouds at twilight and caused by scattering of light by dust in upper atmosphere.

air current: air moving any way but horizontally; particularly, air moving vertically.

airglow: luminescence at night in low and middle latitudes probably caused by release of energy absorbed from sun during daytime.

air mass: widespread body of air about homogeneous in horizontal extent.

alto-: cloud prefix meaning middle level (6500–20,000 feet).

ambient temperature: temperature of surroundings.

anemograph: recording anemometer.

antitrades: westerly winds above surface trade winds; on equatorward side of midlatitude westerlies at upper levels rather than at surface.

antitwilight: pink or purplish light opposite sun after sunset or before sunrise.

backing: 1. international usage: wind change counterclockwise in either hemisphere. 2. U.S. usage: wind change counterclockwise in northern hemisphere and clockwise in southern hemisphere.

banner cloud: bannerlike cloud streaming off mountain peak in strong wind.

bar: unit of pressure equal to 1,000,000 dynes per square centimeter or 1,000 millibars.

barometric tendency: pressure change in a specified time, including direction of change and characteristics of rise or fall.

bathymetry: study of sea floor topography by depth measurements.

blizzard: violent cold wind laden with fine snow picked up from ground.

brave west winds: prevailing westerly winds in midlatitudes; often used as alternative name for roaring 40s in southern hemisphere.

breaker: wave breaking on shore or in shallow water when it becomes unstable; classified as *spilling* when breaks gradually, *plunging* when breaks with a crash, and *surging* when does neither but surges up on beach.

British Thermal Unit (BTU): unit of heat required to raise temperature of one pound of water one degree Fahrenheit; equal to 252.1 calories.

calm belt: latitude region with winds light and variable. Principal ones are *doldrums* and *horse latitudes* (also called calms of Cancer and Capricorn).

calorie: unit of heat required to raise temperature of one gram of water one degree Celsius; equal to 0.00397 BTU.

calving: breaking off of ice mass from parent glacier, iceberg, or shelf.

cap cloud: cloud on isolated mountain peak being formed to windward and dissipated to leeward.

cat's paw: puff of wind; light breeze in small area causing patches of ripples.

ceiling: altitude of base of clouds which are obscuring and not thin.

ceilometer: instrument for measuring cloud height by shining light on base, detecting reflection, and measuring angle.

Celsius temperature: international designation for measure formerly known as *centigrade*.

centrifugal force: that on a body constrained to follow a curved path and tending to move it at a tangent from center of rotation.

centripetal force: that on a body which directs it toward center of rotation.

cirro-: cloud prefix meaning high level (above 20,000 feet).

climate: prevalent or characteristic meteorological conditions of a region, in contrast with *weather* which is the state of atmosphere at any given time.

cloud base: lower surface of a cloud.

cloud deck: upper surface of a cloud.

cloud height: altitude of cloud base.

comber: 1. deepwater wave larger than a whitecap. 2. long-period spilling breaker.

condensation: formation of liquid or solid from a vapor; when water vapor is condensed, heat is released and surrounding temperature is raised.

convergence: inflow of winds resulting in vertical movement upward.

Coriolis force: apparent deflection caused by the earth's rotation, to the right in northern hemisphere and to the left in southern.

countercurrent: one adjacent to main current but flowing in opposite direction and usually slower with less volume.

current speed: rate at which current moves, expressed in knots or miles per day; sometimes called *drift*.

deepening: decrease in atmospheric pressure within a system, usually a low.

density: the mass of a substance per unit of volume it occupies.

depression: an area of low atmospheric pressure compared to surroundings.

dew point: temperature at which air reaches saturation and below which dew or frost will usually form.

diffraction: bending of light rays around an obstacle.

diffusion: spreading or scattering of light rays.

direction, of current: direction toward which current flows; set.

　of swell or waves: direction from which they are moving.

　of wind: direction from which it is blowing.

discontinuity: atmospheric zone within which there is a transition of a meteorological element, as pressure or temperature or both.

disturbance: extreme local departure from normal or average wind conditions.

divergence: outflow of winds resulting in vertical movement downward.

drift: speed of current in knots or nautical miles per day.

drift current: broad, shallow, and slow-moving ocean current.

dropsonde: instrument package dropped from aircraft to measure temperature, pressure, and relative humidity, and then to radio readings to a base.

duct: atmospheric layer within which sound or electromagnetic waves are trapped by refraction and reflection.

eddy: circular water movement where counterflowing currents are adjacent, or at edge of permanent current, or where current passes obstruction.

English system: measurement of length, mass, and time in units of foot, pound, and second.

equilibrium: balance of forces within system so that no change occurs if system were to be isolated.

evaporation: change of liquid or solid to a vapor; involves loss of heat by material.

fall wind: cold wind blowing down a slope; a type of katabatic wind.

false cirrus: debris of upper frozen parts of cumulonimbus cloud.

Ferrel's Law: expression of Coriolis effect on wind.

filling: increase in atmospheric pressure within a system, usually a low.

foehn: warm, dry wind blowing down a slope; a type of katabatic wind.

fogbow: white or yellowish arc in fog like a rainbow but without colors of spectrum.

fracto-: cloud prefix indicating torn, ragged, and scattered appearance due to strong winds.

freezing: change from liquid to solid, usually by removal of heat.

front: intersection of frontal surface and horizontal plane where contrasting air masses meet.

frontal surface: zone of discontinuity between contrasting air masses.

geostrophic wind: hypothetical wind blowing parallel to isobars without tendency to curve.

glaze: smooth, transparent or translucent ice coating from heavy fall of freezing rain.

gradient wind: hypothetical wind blowing tangent to isobar curve.

gravity wind: one blowing down an incline; a katabatic wind.

greenhouse effect: heating of the earth and lower atmosphere by radiation trapped between the earth and atmosphere layer such as clouds.

ground swell: long, deep swell caused by long-lasting gale or seismic disturbance and rising to prominent height in shallow water.

gust: sudden brief wind increase followed by lull or slackening.

heap clouds: British terminology for clouds with vertical development.

high: area of high atmospheric pressure; anticyclone.

hoarfrost: frost; light, feathery deposit of ice caused by condensation of water vapor directly in crystalline form on terrestrial objects.

hurricane wave: sudden rise in sea level along a shore due to hurricane; in low latitudes appears in region of eye; at higher latitudes appears more in dangerous semicircle.

hydrometeor: any product of condensation of atmospheric water vapor whether formed in atmosphere or at the earth's surface.

hygrograph: recording hygrometer.

hygrometer: instrument to measure humidity; psychrometer; wet- and dry-bulb thermometer.

ice blink: yellowish-white glare on underside of cloud cover over ice surfaces.

insolation: solar radiation received by the earth's surface; acronym from *inc*oming *sol*ar radi*ation*.

instability: atmospheric state when vertical temperature distribution tends to make air particle move up or down from original level.

inversion: atmospheric condition in which temperature increases with height.

iridescent cloud: cirrostratus or cirrocumulus with brilliant spots, usually red or green, when within 30° of sun.

isallobar: line connecting points with same rate of pressure change.

isallotherm: line connecting points with same rate of temperature change.

isobar: line connecting points having same pressure.

isodrosotherm: line connecting points having same dew point.

isohyet: line connecting points having same precipitation rate.

isoneph: line connecting points having same amount of cloudiness.

isopectic: line connecting points where ice begins to form at same time in winter.

isotac: line connecting points where ice begins to melt at same time in spring.

isotach: line connecting points of equal wind speed.

isotherm: line connecting points of equal temperature.

katabatic wind: one blowing down an incline; also called gravity wind.

kymatology: science of waves and wave motion.

land sky: dark appearance of cloud cover in polar regions over land not covered with snow or ice.

lapse rate: rate of temperature decrease with height.

latent heat: that released or absorbed in a change of state without change of temperature.

lenticular: describing an apparently stationary cloud, broad in middle and tapering at ends and smooth in appearance. Cloud actually is forming to windward and dissipating to leeward.

line blow: strong wind on Equator side of anticyclone and with little change in direction.

line squall: one occurring on a squall line.

lipper: slight ruffling on water surface; light spray from small waves.

lithometeor: solid matter suspended in atmosphere.

little brother: secondary tropical cyclone following one more severe.

low: area of low atmospheric pressure; cyclone.

maelstrom: whirlpool similar to Maelstrom off west coast of Norway.

mistbow: same as fogbow.

monsoon: seasonal wind blowing from large land mass to ocean in winter and opposite in summer; derived from Arabic "mausim" meaning season, was first applied to such winds over Arabian Sea.

narceous cloud: cirrostratus-like cloud at about 15 miles seen at twilight when observer is in the earth's shadow. Appearance is luminous due to reflected sunlight and iridescent due to diffracted light, and is said to be composed of extremely small water droplets.

nephology: study of clouds

névé: compacted snow in transition from soft snow to ice. Upper portions of glaciers and ice shelves are usually composed of such.

noctilucent cloud: luminous cirrus-type cloud faintly visible when sun is just below horizon. Appears at about 50-mile altitude.

occlusion: process by which air is forced aloft when overtaken by contrasting air mass.

offshore wind: one blowing from land toward sea; land breeze.

onshore wind: one blowing from sea toward land; sea breeze.

overcast: a cloud cover. Pertaining to cover of 95% or more.

permafrost: permanently frozen subsoil. That which has been below freezing for two years or more is considered such.

pibal: derived from *pi*lot *bal*loon and refers to wind observation by theodolite tracking of a pilot balloon ascending at an assumed standard rate.

pocky cloud: a mammatus cloud with pouches hanging from underside.

polynya: an oblong water area enclosed by ice.

precipitation: all types of condensed water vapor, whether liquid, freezing, or frozen, which falls to the earth's surface.

pressure gradient: change in atmospheric pressure per unit of horizontal distance.

pressure jump line: fast-moving line of sudden atmospheric pressure increase followed by continued higher pressure; region conducive to thunderstorm development.

pressure tendency: amount and nature of pressure change between observations.

pseudo front: area of normal front characteristics without definite air mass discontinuity.

psychrometer: wet- and dry-bulb thermometer; type of hygrometer; instrument to measure humidity.

pumping: unsteadiness of mercury barometer resulting from either pressure difference caused by gusting wind or from motion of ship.

rabal: derived from *ra*dio *bal*loon and refers to wind observation by theodolite tracking of a radiosonde balloon which is transmitting back its height.

radiosonde: instrument package carried by unmanned balloon and containing devices to measure and transmit temperature, pressure, and relative humidity.

rain shadow: description of diminished rainfall on lee side of mountain.

raob: derived from *ra*diosonde *ob*servation and refers to values of temperature, pressure, and relative humidity measured aloft and transmitted by radio from radiosonde.

rawin: derived from *ra*dio *win*ds aloft and refers to wind observation by tracking radiosonde by radio direction finder or by tracking radar-reflective balloon.

rawinsonde: combination of raob and rawin.

reflection: return of light which encounters but does not enter a substance.

refraction: direction change of light obliquely moving from one substance to another of different density.

revolving storm: cyclonic storm; one revolving around a low core.

ridge: narrow extension of a high-pressure area; extension connecting two high-pressure areas.

roller: massive wave retaining form without breaking until it reaches shoal region.

saturation: atmospheric condition when no water vapor can be added at existing temperature without producing condensation or supersaturation.

scarf cloud: cirrus-like and thin cloud above a developing cumulus.

scintillation: rapid change in position, brightness, or color of object viewed through atmosphere; twinkling; shimmering.

scud: shreds of cloud moving before wind.

sea: height, length, and direction of waves generated in local region.

secondary: smaller low-pressure area accompanying a larger one.

sinking: abnormal lowering of distant objects by refraction; opposite of looming.

skyhook balloon: large balloon used for determining high-altitude atmospheric measurements.

sky map: light reflection on cloud areas from the earth's surface in polar regions.

sleet: 1. U.S. meteorological terminology: raindrop-sized grains of ice rebounding from hard surface. 2. U.S. popular terminology: glaze, or smooth ice coating from freezing rain. 3. British terminology: snow and rain falling together.

slush: partly melted wet snow.

snow: translucent or white ice crystals falling separately or in loose clusters.

snow blink: bright white reflection from clouds over snow-covered surface.

source region: extensive earth surface area with uniform conditions over which air mass may remain long enough to acquire its characteristics.

specific gravity: ratio of density of a substance to that of a standard (which is usually distilled water at 4°C).

specific heat: amount of heat required (in calories or BTUs) to change one unit of weight one degree in temperature without change in state.

stability: atmospheric state resisting change or tending to return to original conditions after disturbance.

strato-: cloud prefix referring to low level (under 6500 feet).

sublimation: transition directly from solid to vapor or vapor to solid without passing through liquid state.

subsidence: sinking of air mass, usually followed by divergence.

swell: ocean waves which have traveled beyond generating area and have flatter crests, are more regular, and have longer periods than seas or the waves still within the generating area.

temperature: degree of hotness or coldness measured on a definite scale.

temperature inversion: increase in temperature with increase in altitude; inverted lapse rate.

theodolite: optical instrument for measuring horizontal and vertical angles.

trough: elongated area of low pressure extending from center of cyclone.

udometer: rain gauge; instrument for measuring amount of rainfall.

upwelling: rise of water from greater to lesser depth, usually because of divergence and offshore currents. On a coastline, likely to occur when persistent wind blows parallel to land so wind-driven current sets away from shore. Over open sea, occurs where wind is more or less permanently cyclonic and where southern trade winds cross the Equator.

veering: 1. international usage: wind change to right. 2. U.S. usage: wind change to right in northern hemisphere and to left in southern.

visibility: extreme horizontal distance at which prominent objects can be identified by naked eye; radius of circle of such range from observer at center.

warm sector: surface area bounded by warm and cold fronts of cyclone.

water sky: dark reflection on clouds from open water in polar region.

waterspout: small whirling vortex usually in tropical region and having funnel cloud extending into cumulus cloud; tornado at sea.

wave crest: highest part of wave.

wave height: distance from trough to crest measured perpendicular to direction of travel.

wavelength: horizontal distance between points on two successive waves and measured perpendicular to wave crest.

wave period: time for passage of successive wave crests.

wave trough: lowest part of a wave form between successive crests.

weather: atmospheric state defined by temperature, pressure, wind, humidity, cloudiness, precipitation, and other meteorological elements.

wedge: narrow extension of high-pressure area.

whitecap: breaking crest of wave in deep water; white wind-driven froth on crest of a wave.

white squall: sudden gust of wind without warning other than whitecaps or broken water. Its actual existence is considered doubtful.

whiteout: polar region phenomenon in which observer is in white glow with neither shadows, horizon, nor clouds discernible.

wind shear: wind change in short distance producing turbulence.

yellow snow: snow with golden or yellow appearance when containing pollen.

zephyr: warm, gentle breeze, usually from west.

BIBLIOGRAPHY

Official agencies compile much valuable data related to weather. Named here are some of those sources and their publications. Many of the titles are available from the Government Printing Office and nautical chart dealers as well as directly from the issuing offices. Not listed are scores of booklets and pamphlets dealing with a wide range of weather topics. A study of catalogs prepared by these organizations is well worth the time.

U.S. DEPARTMENT OF COMMERCE, WASHINGTON, D.C.

Federal Aviation Administration
Aviation Weather
Realm of Flight

National Oceanic and Atmospheric Administration
Environmental Data Service
Climatic Summaries
Daily Weather Maps Weekly Series
Mariners Weather Log (bimonthly)

National Ocean Survey
Coast Pilots
Great Lakes Pilot

National Weather Service
Marine Weather Services Charts
Worldwide Marine Weather Broadcasts

U.S. DEPARTMENT OF DEFENSE, WASHINGTON, D.C.

Defense Mapping Agency Hydrographic/Topographic Center
  American Practical Navigator (Bowditch) Vol. 1, Pub. No. 9
  Pilot Charts . . .
    North Atlantic Ocean (quarterly)
    North Pacific Ocean (quarterly)
    Central American Waters and South Atlantic (atlas)
    Northern North Atlantic (atlas)
    South Pacific and Indian Oceans (atlas)
  Sailing Directions (Foreign areas)

U.S. Navy Oceanographic Office
  Environmental Atlases and Guides (various areas)
  Major Currents of North and South Atlantic Oceans
  Major Currents off the West Coast of North and South America
  Oceanographic Atlas of North Atlantic Ocean

BRITISH MINISTRY OF DEFENCE

The Hydrographic Department, Taunton, Somerset, England
  Admiralty Pilots
  Meteorology for Mariners
  Ocean Passages of the World
  The Mariner's Handbook
  World Climatic Atlases

CANADIAN DEPARTMENT OF FISHERIES AND ENVIRONMENT, OTTAWA, CANADA

Canadian Hydrographic Service
  Great Lakes Pilot
  Ice Navigation in Canadian Waters
  Sailing Directions
  Small Craft Guides

UNITED NATIONS

World Meteorological Organization, Geneva, Switzerland
  WMO Bulletin (quarterly)

INDEX